Catherine Spalding, SCN

Catherine Spalding, SCN

A Life in Letters

MARY ELLEN DOYLE, SCN

Scholarly publisher for the Commonwealth,
serving Bellarmine University, Berea College, Centre College of Kentucky, Eastern Kentucky University, The Filson Historical Society, Georgetown College, Kentucky Historical Society, Kentucky State University, Morehead State University, Murray State University, Northern Kentucky University, Transylvania University, University of Kentucky, University of Louisville, and Western Kentucky University.

Editorial and Sales Offices: The University Press of Kentucky
663 South Limestone Street, Lexington, Kentucky 40508-4008
www.kentuckypress.com

Library of Congress Cataloging-in-Publication Data

Names: Doyle, Mary Ellen, 1932- author.
Title: Catherine Spalding, SCN : a life in letters / Mary Ellen Doyle, SCN.
Description: Lexington, Kentucky : University Press of Kentucky, 2016. | Includes bibliographical references and index.
Identifiers: LCCN 2016041684| ISBN 9780813168845 (hardcover : alk. paper) | ISBN 9780813168975 (pdf) | ISBN 9780813168968 (epub)
Subjects: LCSH: Spalding, Catherine, 1793-1858. | Sisters of Charity of Nazareth (Nazareth, Ky.)--Biography. | Sisters of Charity of Nazareth (Nazareth, Ky.)--Correspondence.
Classification: LCC BX4456.Z8 D69 2016 | DDC 271/.9102 [B] --dc23
LC record available at https://lccn.loc.gov/2016041684

This book is printed on acid-free paper meeting the requirements of the American National Standard for Permanence in Paper for Printed Library Materials.

Manufactured in the United States of America.

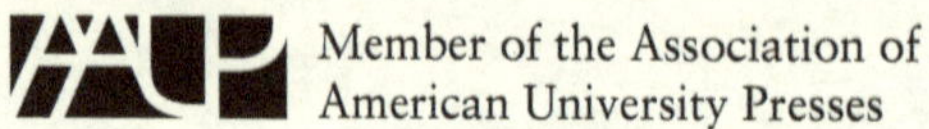

In honor of the Sisters, friends, and colleagues
of Mother Catherine,
who preserved her legacy in letters and passed it on to us

Contents

Preface

When a woman has done much but written little about it—or little that was preserved—why is it important to study and publish that little? And why create a new edition of Mother Catherine Spalding's correspondence now?

The Sisters of Charity of Nazareth (SCN), the congregation Catherine led in its earliest years, was, like her, a doer of good deeds and a developer of mission to children and young women, the sick, the poor, and the orphan, but not a chronicler of its own history and accomplishments. Only in 1870 was Sister Marie Menard commissioned by Mother Frances Gardiner to interview the remaining pioneers and to compile their memories before the SCN's beginnings were lost in the mist of time. Sister Marie's document remained for nearly a hundred years the main source for knowledge of Catherine Spalding and her companions, friends, and colleagues in the development of community and mission. Knowledge of her character depended on the views of those interviewed and on glimpses to be found in other scattered church and civic documents. What writings by Catherine herself existed, what letters from and to her, were known only to those who had the respect and foresight to preserve them. Several Sisters, chiefly Sister Claudia Elliott, became the congregation's benefactors in this regard. But when, and by whom, Catherine's correspondence was first collected remains a historian's wish to know.

At some point, possibly about the time of the SCN's centennial in 1912, some letters were gathered and stored in an archive at Nazareth. In 1968, when Sister James Maria Spillane wrote *Kentucky Spring*, a story of Catherine Spalding for her students, she created verisimilitude by constructing dialogue from Mother Catherine's own writing in her letters. Later, when researching for the biography *Pioneer Spirit,* I found in the Nazareth Archives all her letters that had been discovered by a series of archivists, transcribed and compiled in a spiral-bound book with helpful annotations. I have also been given access to the numerous extant letters written to Mother Catherine, which reveal much about her circumstances and challenges, as well as the personality and spirit with which she met them.

Kentucky Spring caught the attention of many Sisters as well as students, bringing a new awareness of Mother Catherine to those who knew little of her beyond the main facts of her life as founder of community and missions. Interest grew into keen devotion and activism to make her accomplishments better known and more widely appreciated. Over the years, recognition grew and found expression in a series of events: the Kentucky Commission on Women placed Catherine Spalding in the Kentucky Women Remembered exhibit in the State Capitol in Frankfort in 1997; and the *Louisville Courier-Journal* on January 6, 2003, named her as the only woman among the sixteen "most influential persons" in the city's history. The felt need of a full biography was met by publication in 2006 of *Pioneer Spirit: Catherine Spalding, Sister of Charity of Nazareth* by the University Press of Kentucky. And a group of Louisville women obtained approval, raised funds, and selected an artist to create a statue of Catherine Spalding, which was erected in front of the Cathedral of the Assumption in 2015. It is the first public statue honoring a woman anywhere in Kentucky.

As the 2012 bicentennial of the congregation approached, it became evident that completion of Catherine's public record by a new and complete edition of her correspondence was imperative—one that contained all the original letters in the archives and that would provide all available information and sources about the writers, recipients, and context of the letters and the persons mentioned in them. Such a volume would reveal to all interested persons the true character and personality of Catherine Spalding, as letter writer and as the woman responsible for the foundation of the Sisters of Charity of Nazareth and, by her lasting influence, the continuance of the SCN and its mission.

Process

To assure authenticity, the current Director of the Nazareth Archives scanned the original letters in Mother Catherine's own hand and carefully compared them with the typed compilation then in circulation. She discovered that the latest transcriber had indeed respected her source; the contents were essentially what Catherine wrote. Only some spelling and punctuation had been normalized for readers' ease. However, to reach back to Catherine as authentically as possible, she restored in transcription the original form of each letter.

The nineteenth century was quite flexible about spelling, sentence structure, and even grammar. Catherine, taught in a frontier home school and tutored by an educated Sister, can be rated a good writer; yet she did often write under pressure, sometimes with less accuracy of detail than she may have known. Through the letters as they came from Catherine's hand—and handwriting—a reader can assess the education and style, the mood and intent, the speed or deliberation that she brought at various times to her communication. In this volume, in order to aid the reader, obvious significant errors and "handwritten typos" in the letters have been corrected and the spelling of proper nouns has been made more consistent. Any who wish copies of the exact transcripts or to read originals on site may consult the archives at Nazareth, Kentucky.

A particularly original "error" was the nineteenth century's casual attitude to spelling, even of proper names. Catherine herself signed her name with an *e* (Cath*e*rine) until the 1840s; after 1846, she began almost consistently to use an *a* (Cath*a*rine), except to some clergy and alumnae accustomed to her *e*. One enduring supposition about this odd switch is that she adopted the French spelling used by Bishop John Baptist David, then after his death reverted to the spelling of her English ancestry and girlhood. In this volume, her variations are honored and retained.

With much assistance from the archivists and even more from an assistant, I researched the recipients and writers of all the letters, the persons mentioned in them, and the situations they addressed. The letter to Bishop Benedict Joseph Flaget concerning a possible merger of the Nazareth community into that of Emmitsburg, Maryland, is of central importance in SCN history. It was cosigned by multiple Sisters; each was traced and identified so as to achieve an understanding of the diverse Sisters with whom Catherine was collaborating, whose collective identity she was defending (see Appendix B).

For the most part, research on individual Sisters of Charity of Nazareth began with the permanent record and biographical cards of Sisters and followed all cross-references to other sources in the archives. In addition, of course, letters, both by and to Catherine, name many persons outside the congregation. Information on each of these individuals was sought in news clippings, census and marriage records, books of all sorts, and the modern tool of the Internet. Fortunate happenstance uncovered significant connections of names, dates, and activities. But when all sources (and the searchers) were exhausted, it was clear that many persons connected with Catherine and the community, school, and ministries of her time simply could not be found or described in this text. They had attended to their crops, businesses, and families, sent their daughters to Nazareth, perhaps paid their bills, and then disappeared from historic record.

Research has offered abundant knowledge not gleaned earlier. Yet anyone dealing with the letters of Catherine Spalding must confront their minimal number, especially when compared with letters of other founders of religious orders, which often number in the hundreds and are collected in several volumes. Catherine's harvest numbers only about sixty texts, and some of these are short notes or memoranda. A similarly puzzling scarcity pertains to letters written to her. The first letter by Catherine is dated 1821, nearly ten years after the foundation of the community; the first one to her is over a decade later, in 1832. Letters to her from Sisters and friends are sparse indeed. Mostly she heard from parents or guardians of students concerning matters of finance, or from her agents for purchases, payments, and collection for the school and convent. Yet she must have both received and written many more letters over her forty-five years as a Sister of Charity of Nazareth, twenty-five of them as leader.

Efforts to account for this scarcity come inevitably to vague traditions and speculations. One is that a trunk of papers was destroyed when the orphanage where Catherine lived and died was moved to another location. Perhaps. The more probable cause is the movements of the Sisters themselves over the years and their disinclination to carry papers with them, or their unawareness of the lasting value of what they were discarding. Many letters, of course, were likely destroyed deliberately to keep them forever private.

Of all the letters we do not have, the most puzzling gap is any correspondence with the order's cofounder, Bishop John Baptist David. In the early years, that is readily explained: the two were both on St. Thomas Farm and in constant contact. But after 1819, he was in Bardstown. He had to be involved in deciding the community's necessary move to Nazareth; were no messages exchanged in writing? And during the crisis of the 1830s, while Catherine was in Louisville and Flaget in France, David was lonely and ill in a Bardstown residence he named "The Solitude." Did he never write to Catherine such outpourings as he sent to Sister Elizabeth Suttle in western Kentucky, and did Catherine never reply? Any answer is speculation, but it is not a wild one to suppose that both were intensely private about such correspondence and consigned their letters to the flames.

Bishop David's replacement as ecclesiastical superior at Nazareth was the Reverend Ignatius Reynolds; his tenure was only two years. He was followed by the Reverend Joseph Haseltine, who remained for years a wise counselor and good friend to both Mothers Catherine Spalding and Frances Gardiner, collaborating in the management of community, school, and farm. He collected debts and gave spiritual direction to the Sisters; he conducted the liturgy and compiled a registry of Nazareth students. And he left some letters behind him, now in the archives. But if Catherine ever wrote him any letters concerning their relationship and joint activities, they were either too personal or too confidential for him to preserve.

The same mystery surrounds the lack of correspondence with Mother Frances Gardiner, Catherine's consistent alternate in office after the resignation of Mother Angela Spink. Did she never inform Catherine in writing of the troubles of the 1830s, of the cholera at Nazareth and Bardstown, of the condition of school or farm? Were there no personal communiqués about the Council's decisions relating to the orphanage or infirmary in the 1840s? And when Frances was sent in the early 1850s to try to save the mission and community in Nashville, were letters never written, or were they prudently destroyed? If Frances did write, did Catherine never reply? No letters have been found, not at Nazareth or Louisville, and not at Leavenworth, Kansas, where the Nashville Sisters eventually settled (and where the modern archivist generously shared with me all remaining materials). Aside from reasons of confidentiality and burned-up letters, the likeliest explanation is that when Catherine left office, she prudently and firmly stepped out of her successor's way, leaving her to lead by her own lights and judgment.

While many letters of Catherine Spalding are doubtless, regrettably, lost, there remain many letters or memos written to her. These exceed greatly the number of extant letters by her, yet they seem never to relate directly to any letter of hers. Some are very long, even tedious, tales (and details) of family news and effusions of feeling for Catherine and Nazareth. Business letters are especially numerous in her years as Mother and headmistress of Nazareth Academy; they are also highly repetitive—a succession of shopping lists and communiqués about payment (or, mostly, nonpayment) of tuition. To include all these letters in full, with context and identifications, would require a much longer or multivolume work. Yet omitting the entire group would short-circuit the purpose and the dynamic of this collection. What others knew (or thought they knew) and what they thought and said provide a vital way of knowing the person whom they addressed.

An editorial decision was made, therefore, not to include all the letters to Catherine in full, but rather to include such excerpts as especially reveal their context or illumine the culture and writing style of the era and the writers' expectations and attitudes toward Catherine and her mission. Some parts of these letters are startling in their boldness or humor (for today's reader), or their bizarre comments. A few letters are simply summarized briefly, but all extant letters are given some space and notice; none are simply omitted. Any letters not given in full are marked "abridged" or "summarized." All may be examined in transcripts in the Nazareth Archives.

Another editorial challenge involved whether to include footnotes or endnotes to identify or explain persons, events, and common or cultural attitudes. Although the liveliness of the letters often flowed from such details, in the end it was felt that the burden of notes would so enlarge and clog the text as to make it almost unreadable. Many notes would of necessity merely cite the lack of current information or offer citations only to remote sources or bits of common community memory and tradition. The text, therefore, is without footnotes; instead, source information is included in the editorial commentary following the letter.

Finally, letters in this volume have been labeled, both for cross-referencing here and to locate them in the Nazareth Archives. To indicate their time period and to distinguish Catherine's letters from those written to her, all letters carry the number of their chapter as they appear in this book (i.e., Chapters 1 through 5). Catherine's own letters are then numbered within that period (1-4, 3-2, etc.); letters to her carry letters rather than numbers within each chapter (1-D, 3-B, 4-AA).

Over the years, letters by and to Catherine Spalding and others were found and arranged in varied archival collections. All letters by Mother Catherine—originals, copies, typed transcripts—are now in the Collected Letters of Mother Catherine Spalding in the Nazareth Archives. A researcher will find all Catherine's letters in that collection, so no location is cited at the head of each letter here. A few originals remain with another owner, and Nazareth holds only verified copies. Most letters to Catherine are in a multivolume collection of Duplicate Letter Books; others may be found in a collection of Original (or Old) Letter Books, or in the collected letters of a single person—Mothers Frances Gardiner and Columba Carroll, Bishops Flaget and David.

The following abbreviations are used in this edition:

CLMCS:	Collected Letters of Mother Catherine Spalding
DLB:	Duplicate Letter Book
OLB:	Original (Old) Letter Book
CLMFG:	Collected Letters of Mother Frances Gardiner
CLMCC:	Collected Letters of Mother Columba Carroll
FDL:	Flaget David Letters
FL:	Flaget Letters

Overview of the Letters

The good news is that the scarcity of extant letters is offset by their variety. Mother Catherine's letters went to various Sisters as well as to students, friends, a niece, bishops and clergy, lay collaborators in mission, and even to the mayor of Louisville. Necessarily they vary greatly in purpose, content, style, and tone. To Sisters, Mother Catherine may offer spiritual wisdom or a better coffee pot and soft gloves; she may counsel mutual charity or tease about a "muly cow." To Bishop Flaget, she offers both sincere deference and dissent with a challenging review of SCN service in the early years of his diocese. The letter to the mayor (Letter 1-5) might be called "the essential Catherine," a first statement of SCN's mission and its inviolable purpose. Those seeking to know Catherine Spalding cannot do better than feed on this rich and various fare.

Variety in recipients, situations, and purpose is matched by variety in style. Until her early twenties, Catherine had had only an informal frontier education; it was expanded by the coming of Sister Ellen O'Connell, a Baltimore teacher educated by her father, a professor, and by the free use of his library. Some of Ellen's surviving writing exhibits the rather florid rhetoric of the nineteenth century. Catherine never adopted it. Her essential style is straightforward, her vocabulary basic, but literate and sufficient for her varied intentions; her sentence structure is usually simple or a sequence of simple clauses. She was an educated, but never showy, writer. Most letters exhibit spontaneity, either coming quickly to the point or leisurely dispensing news, reflections, and words of affection just as they came to her. To Bishop Flaget, however, when a crisis created the need to be factual and persuasive, she wrote a letter whose every line shows careful and complex construction, governed by knowledge, logical thought, and controlled emotion.

Whether to a bishop, a student, or a Sister, any letter of Catherine Spalding reveals something of her strong emotional nature and its influence on her way of relating and writing. Her affections ran deep and flowed easily in letters to Sisters, especially a friend like Claudia Elliott. To a collaborator and friend like Mrs. Maria Crozier, she is warm, teasing, and newsy. To young Sisters whose formation and profession she had confirmed, she is warmly affectionate and maternal, dispensing good counsel and asking for continued correspondence. In contrast, her one letter to her niece is almost shocking in its severity. The clergy elicited her genuine respect, with more or less formality according to the relationship and the occasion. By those same two norms, Catherine revealed her feelings to a greater or lesser degree according as she felt herself likely to be understood or as the urgency of the occasion aroused them.

The differences in style and tone to various recipients are mirrored in the variety of Catherine's signatures. To a clergyman, civic official, or businessman, she signs herself as "your obedient servant" or with a term of esteem or respect; yet to Bishops Flaget and Spalding, she may wind up with a full sentence of emotional expression and a simple "Catherine." Clergymen, former students, and lay collaborators receive her surname and sometimes her title, "Mother of Nazareth." To her Sisters, however, she is typically their "sincere," their "affectionate," their "devoted as ever" Catherine. To them she may style herself a mother, but in context, not as a title. If she does sign with a title, it is usually "Sr.," used often with clergy and laity, but seldom to her Sisters. Nowhere is her simplicity and sense of her relationships more evident than in her choice of signatures.

Reading the Letters

What suggestions or cautions may be offered to the readers of Catherine Spalding's correspondence? Because the letters offer no lengthy or memorable reflections on her or the Sisters' spirituality, or on the great events of the community's early life, it is possible to trivialize them, to overlook what they do reveal and their significance. Religious life, for Mother Catherine, was a matter of relationships and service—to God, to the Church, to one's Sisters and neighbors, and above all other persons, to the poor. Relationships and service find expression in small ways—in small gifts, brief expressions of deep affection and good counsel, short statements about an event or about one's feeling for mission. Eloquent passages are not readily lifted from Catherine's letters, but one might meditate at length on such a remark as "I have lived long enough to learn to take all these things just as they come" (Letter 5-11).

A reverse temptation may be to invest Catherine with mythic dimensions and importance. A great lover of God, of "our holy religion," and of God's most vulnerable people—that she certainly was. And whom and what she loved determined what she did. She was also a simple and practical woman, who saw needs of character and action and forthrightly addressed them. Her letters directly address practicalities as well as persons she loved and respected—or with whom she experienced conflict. The rich reward of reflectively reading Catherine Spalding's letters is the discovery and inspiration of who she truly was.

The current urgency of her Sisters to have these letters again available is evidence of her lasting impact as exemplar of the call for faith, hope, and charity in a modern era so different from hers, yet so fraught with similar sufferings, joys, hopes, and needs. Their desire is shared by many others who sense the hidden treasure. Her ways of addressing life in her time can guide responses in ours. Though Catherine Spalding last wrote in 1858, she still addresses herself to us.

Chronology of Mother Catherine's Life

1793–1797: Catherine Spalding born on December 23, 1793, the third child of Edward and Juliet Boarman Spalding. Early childhood in Charles County, Maryland, where a fourth child is born. Family migrates to Nelson County, Kentucky, about 1797, leaving large extended family behind.

1798–1812: Catherine's sister Ann Spalding born; mother dies; father remarries, then deserts financial obligations and family. Girlhood with aunt, Elizabeth Spalding Elder; her husband, Thomas Elder; and their ten children. At sixteen, moves with her sisters to home of cousin Clementina Elder Clark and Clementina's husband, Richard Clark.

1813–1821: Joins religious community founded at St. Thomas Farm, Nelson County, by the Reverend John Baptist David, on January 21, 1813; is third member and second youngest. On June 2, 1813, elected first superior of six Sisters of Charity of Nazareth. 1814: establishes Nazareth Academy. 1816: makes first vows as an SCN, to be renewed annually for the rest of her life. 1818: leads expansion of academy into new brick building, large enough for fifty students and long use. 1819: opens first branch house, Bethlehem Academy, Bardstown; refuses reelection for life as Mother; is appointed Mistress of Novices.

1822–1823: Learns land under school at St. Thomas can never become SCN property. 1822: moves to new land for motherhouse and academy at Nazareth, Kentucky, near Bardstown. Severe poverty and crowding again. 1823: opens school in Scott County, near Lexington, Kentucky.

1824–1831: Recalled to leadership as Mother at Nazareth at death of Mother Agnes Higdon; discovers severe indebtedness due to construction and poor bookkeeping; leads SCN to solvency and building of new chapel and academy in 1825.

1831–1838: Opens Presentation Academy in St. Louis Church basement, Louisville, Kentucky. Sisters nurse victims of cholera epidemic and take orphans into their small home behind the church. 1834: builds orphanage beside the church; soon too crowded. 1836: locates St. Vincent Orphan Asylum and Infirmary on Jefferson Street, east of downtown.

1838–1844: Mother at Nazareth. Duties in administration of community, academy, and branch schools of SCN; struggles to maintain independent identity of SCN. July 12, 1841: death of Bishop David. See of diocese moved from Bardstown to Louisville. Presentation moved to houses on Fifth Street, near St. Louis Church, now the cathedral.

1844–1850: Superior of St. Vincent Asylum and Infirmary, Louisville. Prominent leader in developing care of homeless children in city. Witness in legal test of will of Polly Bullitt, former Nazareth student; confrontation with Henry Clay; wins commendation of judge and favorable decision in case. February 11, 1850: death of Bishop Flaget.

1850–1856: Mother at Nazareth. 1851: Sisters in Nashville separate from Nazareth. 1854–1855: Leads construction of new church and academy. Expansion of membership in both school and community; expansion of missions in Kentucky. Infirmary separated from orphanage and relocated to Fourth Street in central city, renamed St. Joseph Infirmary.

1856–1858: Returns to direct orphanage in Louisville; visits homes of sick poor. March 20, 1858: death of Catherine Spalding from pneumonia.

The Correspondence

1

Foundation Years

1812–1838

When four-year-old Catherine Spalding left Maryland with her parents, Edward and Juliet Boarman Spalding, and with her older siblings Ralph and Rosella and younger sister Louisa, the heritage of the English Maryland Catholics had already taken root in her. In the home of her grandfather, Basil Spalding, she had attended Mass, and she had imbibed something of the religious and cultural assumptions of the Maryland landowners of the 1790s. Fidelity to the Catholic faith and freedom to practice it were paramount and included a sense of obligation to serve God, Church, and neighbor. Second only to faith was love of landed homestead and stability on it. Regrettably, in that time and place, unquestioning acceptance of slavery was the means to maintain home and land. That heritage, with its inherent contradictions, came to Kentucky with the Spaldings and is reflected in Catherine's leadership and letters.

The traumas of Catherine's early life in Kentucky certainly shaped her character and the particular passion she brought to her later mission. After the birth of Ann, her fifth child, Juliet Spalding died, and Edward remarried two weeks before Catherine's sixth birthday. Edward accumulated debts; and when Catherine was nine or ten he deserted his obligations and his family and disappeared. His children became wards of their aunt, Elizabeth Spalding Elder, and her husband, Thomas Elder. In their stable home, amid their own ten children, Catherine grew up, loved and cared for. But she also saw her uncle go to debtor's prison for her father's debts, her little sister's service claimed by one of the creditors until her uncle could reclaim her, and, at fifteen, she and her siblings declared orphans. Within a year or less, she and two of her sisters went to live with their cousin Clementina Elder Clark, who had married Richard Clark. Thus, Catherine had four homes in two states, as well as three fathers and four mothers, real or surrogate, all before she was sixteen. The future mother of Louisville's orphans had been formed.

In 1807 and 1808, teenaged Catherine observed the commotion in the local Catholic colony about who should become the first bishop in Kentucky. This included a furor of vituperative letters, accusations, and counteraccusations concerning pioneer priest Stephen Badin. By the time Benedict Joseph Flaget had been appointed bishop of the new diocese of Bardstown, Catherine had learned something about how a conflict might be made worse or be amicably settled, a skill she would later employ as first Mother of the Sisters of Charity of Nazareth.

Bishop Flaget and his friend and collaborator, the Reverend John Baptist David, desired a religious community of Sisters to educate the girls of Kentucky and in time to serve also the sick poor and orphaned in the tradition of St. Vincent de Paul. Two women began the community in December 1812. Catherine joined in January 1813, and in June was elected among the first six members as Mother. For six years, she led the development of a stable, spiritually motivated community and the establishment of a small but growing school at St. Thomas Farm in Nelson County and another, Bethlehem Academy, in Bardstown. In August 1819, she persuaded her clerical superiors that she should not be Mother for life, and was appointed Mistress of Novices. In 1822, learning that the community could never own land at St. Thomas, she cooperated in the traumatic removal of their home and school to Nazareth, north of Bardstown, losing all the resources they had already invested in them.

Catherine spent the next year establishing a school in Scott County, Kentucky; but in 1824 the sudden death of her successor, Mother Agnes Higdon, occasioned Catherine's recall to Nazareth as Mother of the growing community and Directress of Nazareth Academy. Wisely, she gave direction of the academic mission to Sister Ellen O'Connell, an experienced teacher from Baltimore, while she remained a primary collaborator. This second term as Mother entailed handling large debts Mother Agnes Higdon had incurred to build a boarding school. From 1825 into 1828 Catherine was the construction and finance manager for building a church and school, laying out gardens and a farm to support all Nazareth's dwellers. In 1829, legal incorporation guaranteed the community's right to own and acquire property in Kentucky.

The major expansion was to Louisville. In 1831, leaving her office and a stabilized Nazareth behind her, Catherine led three Sisters to establish Presentation Academy in the basement of the only Catholic church in that growing but rough city on the Ohio River. Early in her time there, cholera struck the city in late 1832. The Sisters agreed to nurse the neglected sufferers, and then gathered orphans into their small house behind the church. The way thus opening for the ministry she most desired, Catherine led the community and Louisville's citizens in building an orphanage next to the church and, only two years later, in purchasing a building large enough for fifty children with a wing to serve as an infirmary for the city's sick. From 1836 to 1838, Catherine resided in that building and first directed its ministries.

Given this twenty-five-year span of such intense activity, conducted with persons nearly always together as collaborators, it is not too surprising that only five of Catherine's letters remain from that long foundational period. Fortunately, the five are representative of what Catherine did and how she did it. To Father Joseph Rosati, CM, she appealed for pastoral care of a former student at St. Thomas. With an elderly lady desirous to live out her days in the Sisters' care, she made a careful agreement beneficial to both parties. To Bishop Flaget she wrote the first of several letters confronting him, in all respect and strong feeling, with a problem he was causing the community. A brief bill of credit is signed for money "for the use of" a new member's mother. And in one of her most notable letters, she briefly, bluntly, and forcibly defends the honor of her community to the Mayor of Louisville.

By 1838, when she was called back to office as Mother, Catherine Spalding had grown from a nineteen-year-old volunteer eager for religious service into a spiritually strong and astute woman in her early forties, initiator and leader of three forms of ministry, well able to direct, defend, and develop what she and her Sisters had begun.

Letters by Mother Catherine Spalding, 1821–1834

1-1

To Rev. Joseph Rosati, CM St. Louis, Missouri
Nazareth May 19th/1821
Rev. & Dear Sir,

You will, no doubt, be rather surprised to receive a letter from me; yet as I believe you to be a true son of St. Vincent, I confidently address you on the present subject which once so much interested your zeal and charity. I mean, Mary Rollin, who is my god-daughter and your former penitent. As I suppose you have ere this heard of her pitiful situation, I cannot doubt but that your zeal and interest have already been very active in her favor. It is now about 1 year since she left Nazareth to go to her mother in the state of Illinois, & the last letter I received from her was written not more than 5 months after she arrived there, in which she informed me that her persecutions were so great that she was obliged to leave her mother and live with her sister, who, she said, treated her well, tho' she believed it proceeded only from the hope they entertained of prevailing on her to marry one of her cousins, & of course, to give up her church. She observed also that there she had no possible means of going to confession, all being opposed to her, though she lives within 45 miles of Vincennes. Since the reception of this letter I can receive no intelligence at all of her, altho' I have written to her, but she informed me that the letters are immediately taken from the office by her mother.

Perhaps I am informing you of what you know better than I do. But in case you do not, I write this that you may, by your influence, do something for that dear soul whom I consider to be in the greatest and most imminent danger; and altho' I am truly interested, yet you know as I am but a poor Sister of Charity, it is not in my power to do anything except to pray & solicit the interest of others for her. You are acquainted with the goodness of her heart & know also her capacity to be useful in some good work, provided she is well conducted, and I know she has every confidence in you, tho' you must know as well as I, that here she would never again be happy. You may perhaps infer from this that there is some inconsistency in my conduct, since I opposed her going with you when you desired it, & now solicit you to make provisions for her. However, I hope at least, the purity of my motive will plead my excuse as well before you as before God. I knew we lived in an uncivilized, tho' criticizing part of the world. I had, therefore, many apprehensions.

I heard some time since from Father David that you had informed him that she was to be received in the monastery of Florissant. If so, I am truly glad, but I cannot think she would be so unfeeling as not to write to me, knowing how anxious I am about her.

You will, I hope, excuse the liberty I have taken, & pray often for me, my Rev. & dear friend, & may I presume to say it, Brother. I am, with the most sincere respect yours in our Lord.

Catherine Spalding

(The original is in the library of St. Louis University. A copy was procured for Nazareth by Brother David, CFX, and a second copy by Mr. Francis Clark.)

This letter involves the identities of several persons little known at the time, who left little record of their movements:

Father Joseph Rosati (see Appendix A), was one of several Vincentian priests at St. Thomas from November 1816 to September 1818. He gave spiritual ministry to the new SCN community, and evidently performed pastoral duties to their boarder students. He made one five-week trip to St. Louis in late 1817 and some ministry trips to congregations, including Vincennes, on the border of Indiana and Illinois. He would become superior of Vincentian priests in the United States, and first bishop of St. Louis in 1827.

Mary (Polly) Rollin enrolled in Nazareth Academy April 10, 1816, at age twenty, a Protestant boarder from Louisville. No date for her leaving and no "remarks" about her are given in the Academy Record Book.

On April 17, 1819, Father David wrote Rosati in part: "You do not tell me anything on the subject of Miss Rollin. I am sorry for having persuaded her to leave with Mr. Timon's family. That was the most excellent opportunity that she could find. She also seemed opposed to the voyage she had taken before: neither does she wish to attach herself to Nazareth. She had therefore written her parents to await her return. Her faith and piety are very shallow. But she is not wanting in her conduct."

Catherine's letter indicates that in 1821 Mary's mother and sister were living in Illinois, about forty-five miles from Vincennes, Indiana. No information can be given of Miss Rollin's whereabouts at that time.

John Timon (b. 1797) worked in Baltimore in the family dry goods business and moved west with his family, to Louisville in 1818 and to St. Louis a year later. Thus, in 1821 he was still a young layman engaged in the family move to Missouri, obviously known to Fathers David and Rosati. He and his family could be trusted as escorts of Miss Rollin to Missouri. After the business failed, Timon entered St. Mary of the Barrens Seminary in 1823. He was professed as a Vincentian in 1825, ordained in 1826, and in 1847 appointed the first bishop of Buffalo, New York.

The monastery of Mother Philippine Duchesne's Religious of the Sacred Heart was established in Florissant, Missouri, near St. Louis, in 1819.

It seems clear that Mary Rollin became a Catholic when of legal age with Mother Catherine as her sponsor, in opposition to parental wishes. David's letter indicates that she had taken a "voyage" before 1819 (perhaps home to Louisville?) and then returned to Nazareth; but, being discontented there, she wrote her "parents" to expect her home. Catherine mentions her "going with" Rosati (on one of his short trips? with a view to some permanent placement and employment?). The Timons arrived in Louisville in 1818 and went on to St. Louis a year later; that is likely when David persuaded Mary to go with them. She left Nazareth definitively about 1819–1820 "to go to her mother." The last Catherine heard from Mary, her mother, now in Illinois, had "persecuted" her; so now she was with her sister, still unable to reach Vincennes to have a sacramental life. Rosati, Catherine assumes, has heard of Mary's plight. She hopes that Mary may be with the Sisters in Florissant, which might mean either as a boarder or a prospective member.

Unanswerable questions remain: what Mary Rollin's final destination was, by what movements she reached it, and the circumstances that led to Mother Catherine's distress and her appeal to Father Rosati.

Whatever the wanderings and final settlement of Mary Rollin, her situation was not atypical for young unmarried women who could not or would not reside with their families. Their best hopes were protection and employment in another's household as maid or child caregiver, perhaps as a servant in a boarding school, or acquiring the status of a religious. If young, single women such as Mary were unable to be happy with any of those options, their life maintenance was precarious indeed, and their freedom of choice in location, marriage, and religion easily compromised. Catherine Spalding had cause for her warm-hearted and persistent concern for this young woman.

1-2

Copy of Agreement

Articles of agreement made and agreed on this 22 day of
May in the year of Our Lord one thousand eight hundred
and twenty eight between Mother Catherine Spalding
of Nazareth Monastery in the county of Nelson State of
Kentucky of the one part And Elizabeth Wescott of the
County afor[ementioned] of the other Part Witnesseth
that Whereas the said Elizabeth Wescott being desirous
of retiring from the noise and bustle of the world and to

> devote the remainder of her life to the service of God in the Monastery afor. And whereas the said Elizabeth hath by certain instruments in writing bearing even date with these Presents conveyed to the Right Reverend Benedict Joseph Flaget of Bardstown a certain tract of Land and some Negroes for the benefit of the Monastery afor. The said Catherine Spalding hereby undertakes and agrees to furnish the said Elizabeth Wescott with a separate Room in said Monastery & to cause her to be boarded and taken care of as a member of the family during her life or so long as she shall choose to remain in said Monastery furnishing her with clothing as other members of the family. The said Catharine Spalding also agrees to support and bring up Elizabeth Brosius (niece of the said Elizabeth Wescott) until she shall complete the sixteenth year of her age to admit her among the boarders in the said Monastery & to give her a good education. The said Catherine Spalding also agrees to pay three hundred Dollars to Jane McCoy of Baltimore State of Maryland niece to the dec'd Husband of the said Elizabeth Wescott And also to pay two hundred Dollars for the education of John Brosius in the College of St. Thomas.
>
> In testimony whereof we have hereunto set our hands and & seals on the day & year above written
>
> Catherine Spalding Elizabeth Wescott
>
> Signed sealed and delivered in presence of us
>
> Augustine Ach. D. Robertson James Elliott

Elizabeth Wescott was evidently a widow with three dependents, one of at least five elderly women residing at Nazareth by 1828. Her needs would be met by the agreement above. Early annals name another woman still living there in 1847; if Mrs. Wescott lived that long, she had indeed made a good bargain.

The agreement accompanies a bill of sale identifying the three slaves as "female" Louisa and two "boys," William and Henry; no ages or relationships are indicated. They were sold to Bishop Flaget for $1,000 "for the use of the Sisters of Charity of Nazareth Kentucky" with legal language to "warrant and forever defend" the validity of the sale and ownership. Robertson and Elliott witnessed both documents.

Bardstown Courthouse records show 136.5 acres in the Wescott tract of land. Flaget could transfer ownership of land and slaves to Nazareth after it was incorporated in 1829.

As Elizabeth Brosius is identified as Mrs. Wescott's niece, who is to be educated at Nazareth, John Brosius, to be educated at the men's college, was almost certainly brother and nephew to these women. Jane McCoy, niece of the deceased Mr. Wescott and to be recipient of $300, is not otherwise identifiable. A notation attached to the original Agreement cites receipts for two payments of $100 each, dated May 8, 1832, and July 30, 1833. Perhaps a first payment was made between 1828 and 1832.

Augustine Robertson was a young lawyer from Detroit who had led a revision of the laws of Michigan, been made a judge, and been lawyer for Father Gabriel Richard in a lawsuit. He came to Kentucky in November 1827, calling himself "still a pagan" and desiring to convert. Flaget baptized him; David confirmed him in January 1828. Robertson was studying French, Latin, and theology and helping at St. Joseph College when he served as witness to the Wescott Agreement.

James Elliott was brother of Sister Claudia Elliott (see Appendix A). Their parents, Stephen and Mary Dant Elliott, were migrants from Maryland. A letter from his sister Juliette in 1843 names seven other siblings. In 1828, he would have been a deacon anticipating ordination in 1829. His entire ministry was at St. Michael Church in Fairfield, Kentucky, where he died suddenly on April 9, 1871. He is mentioned in many of Mother Catherine's letters to Sister Claudia.

1-3

To Bishop Benedict Joseph Flaget
Nazareth May 9th 1829
Most Rev. & dear Father,

We are now ready to adopt generally the white collar or reject it entirely, just as you & Father David please to say & decide; I beg you then dear Father, on my knees and for the love of God that both of you will say to me decidedly what you wish me to do & what you wish me not to do. Ah, would that you could both see my heart just as it is known to my God. I know indeed that it would be seen full of miseries, but I believe it would be seen far from sentiments that may now be apprehended to exist in it, which apprehensions may cause much uneasiness to some to whom I would fain give satisfaction & prefer any sufferings rather than willfully give one moment's pain, I think that same God of mercy knows that I never wished to act in anything independently of any superior. But, Oh, if I only could always know immediately from my Superior what is disapproved in me & what he wishes me to correct, how much happier would be my wretched pilgrimage, how much lighter my burden! Tho' I know I do not deserve such a consolation in my pains; did I only receive them & profit by them as I ought! If my superiors could only always know things as they are with all their circumstances! But when I sometimes try to do this, I dare say I may often appear to wish to extenuate, to disguise. I know and repeat that I am very capable of erring & that I may often err both in my judgment & conduct. But it seems to me, if I know my own heart, that my superiors have only to say "I will this" or "I will it not" and I have no other desire than to do what they will. Tho' I sometime try to represent things as I conceive them to be, this again may appear like opposition on my side,—but, dear Father, perhaps it would be much better and more perfect in me, always to let everyone think & believe according to the first impressions or representations that have been made; if so, with the grace of God, I will labor daily more & more to bow down & submit to all things, hoping that that God who knows the clay of which I am formed, will know how to compassionate his frail creature, if I sometimes on those occasions yield too much to the feelings of nature.

As to the collar, I shall certainly await your joint answer before you will see another worn in the Community. If you only knew how little choice I have in such a thing; but I conceived that it might have some good effects, such as uniformity, decency, & modesty; moreover, the idea I had, that in most religious costumes, something white is worn close about the neck. & so after what Father observed to me in presence of several Sisters who all remember, either for or against, he then sanctioned it & told me I could introduce it. It was only then that I gave the least encouragement for it in the house by permitting some sisters to make some & make a trial of it before we decided on the precise form and dimensions. In this again I have erred, but I hope it is not unpardonable, & the effects may in the end turn to the good of my soul—for if wearing them had ever been found a Subject of temptation, it will now ever be a penance. If I have said anything improper, I hope, dear Father, it will be pardoned & believe it was not designed, for in the beginning this, I sincerely begged the light and grace to say nothing improper. & my only determination is to do in everything, as far as I can know it, the wishes of my superiors, no matter how I may come to the knowledge of it.—I feel that my life has been spent & my peace sacrificed to the good of the Community; my better days are gone, and it would now, even according to the world, be foolish in me to wish to introduce what now would serve for the vanity & enjoyment of those who come after me. Moreover, dear father, we are not unmindful that if there are now splendid buildings, comfortable lodgings, &c ., it is not precisely for us who " have borne the heat and burden of the day," but for those who will perhaps never appreciate what has been undergone to produce the comforts & advantages that they will enjoy.—But vain & foolish would I be if I expected my reward in the acknowledgments of mortals. No, I do not. I ask for nothing, I desire nothing but the grace & mercy of my God.

You may Think, dear Father, that my feelings are too deeply wounded to be healed, but believe me I am not. I have expressed my sentiments, but probably in too awkward a manner to be well understood. I shall now endeavor to be tranquil whatever may be the result.—I leave the favorable interpretation of it all to your own fatherly indulgence,—my intention I trust was good,—

You are entirely welcome, dear Father, to show this to Father David; I have no secret in it for him. I conclude by begging the prayers & blessing of you both that after passing through the many & various storms & trials of this wretched life, I may at least be at eternal peace & rest in the next, Alas, my God, I fear much the contrary.

The weakest, most unworthy, but not the least devoted of your children in our Lord,—

Catherine

The background of this letter has to be pieced together from its parts. The "decency" and practicality of a white collar seem to have occurred to Catherine, perhaps from some remarks of David in the presence of other Sisters. She then presented a request and reasons to him, received approval, and introduced trial designs. How so small an issue became a tempest, just how the sensible Flaget became disturbed, and what he had said to produce such a passionate response from Catherine all remain a puzzle. The letter suggests that some Sisters must have not merely disagreed with the change but interpreted Catherine's motives, spoken to one or both bishops, and reported to her their views of the episcopal response.

Though the letter begins with the community's ("We") readiness to obey Flaget's decision, Catherine has a good deal more to say. Her direct and honest character, as well as her vulnerable feelings and bold capacity to express them, are all present in her appeal to her own better knowledge of the circumstances and her virtual demand to know Flaget's wishes without ambiguity, delay, or indirection. She wishes to be indifferent to others' views of her while implying her right to be heard as one who knows the truth. The letter has a dash of anger, of sarcasm, even of self-pity (her "better days are gone" at age thirty-five!); and she herself introduces the extraneous subject of the 1825 buildings whose cost in sacrifice may never be appreciated. Though she pulls herself in at the end, with a sort of apology for her intensity, she does not renege on her position, and she seems quite unafraid of Flaget's response. Her expressed devotion to him, by all evidence, was genuine, as was his respect for her. This letter would be the first of several in which she would engage him in issues far more significant than a collar.

As for the outcome, the Sisters of Charity of Nazareth wore a white collar from this era until the 1970s.

1-4

Bill of Credit

Due Ann Bamber one hundred ten dollars, to be paid in small sums for the use of her mother Elizabeth Bamber & without interest, being a deposit in the hands of said Ann Bamber for her mother

Nazareth, O[ctober] 28th 1830—Catherine Spalding, M.S.

Rec'd of Mother Angela Spink $18 1/2 of the above amt.

(signed) Ann Bamber
Joanna Lewis Tr.

Research has not yet uncovered the full circumstances of this bill of credit. Ann Bamber was the baptismal name of Sister Margaret Bamber, an important figure in the early history of the SCN's mission. In October 1830 she was a novice at Nazareth, having entered in June 1829 and received the habit that August, an unusually quick reception. She did not, however, make vows in the usual one year but did so in August 1831. Any financial arrangements during her novitiate would be duly recorded so that both her own and the community's obligations would be understood and honored.

Two possibilities (among others) may be suggested:

1. The $110 was a deposit given by Ann or by someone else for the care of her mother, which she put in the hands of the SCN for the community's use while small amounts were paid back without interest to Elizabeth, her mother. The $18 1/2 was indeed a "small sum," though probably sufficient for Mrs. Bamber's needs if dispensed regularly.

2. Ann might have simply deposited money with the SCN to be dispensed back to her in increments she would use for her mother. As a religious, she could no longer use the money for herself or at her own discretion.

Either way, the document makes clear in writing, with signatures, the financial terms and limited responsibility of the SCN congregation. It is part of the management skills Catherine was rapidly developing. It is also a witness to the care an early member was allowed to exercise toward an aging, otherwise solitary parent.

Mother Angela Spink succeeded Mother Catherine in 1831. Evidently, payments continued after Catherine left office and went to Louisville, and after Ann made vows.

1-5

To the Mayor & Council of the City of Louisville

Gentlemen,

At that gloomy period, when the Cholera threatened to lay our city desolate, & nurses for the sick poor could not be obtained on any terms, Rev'd Mr. Abell, in the name of the Society of which I have the honor to be a member, proffered the gratuitous services of as many of our Sisters as might be necessary in the then existing distress: requiring merely, that their expenses should be paid.—This offer was accepted; as the order from your

honorable board, inviting the Sisters, will now show.—
But, when the money was ordered from your Treasury to
defray those expenses, I had the mortification to remark
that instead of saying: "the expenses of the Sisters
of Charity," the word "services" was substituted.—I
immediately remonstrated against it,—& even mentioned
the circumstances to the Mayor & another gentleman
of the Council.—& upon being promised that the error
should be corrected, I remained satisfied that it had
been attended to; until a late assertion from one of the
pulpits of the city leads me to believe that it stands yet
uncorrected on your books, as these same books were
referred to, in proof of the assertion.—If so, Gentlemen,
pardon the liberty I take in refunding you the amount
paid for the above named expenses, well convinced that
our Community, for whom I have acted in this case,
would far prefer incurring the expense themselves rather
than submit to so unjust an odium.—

Gentlemen, be pleased to understand, that we are not
hirelings—& if we are, in practice, the Servants of the
poor, the sick & the orphan;—we are voluntarily so: But
we look for our reward, in another & a better World.

With sincere respect,
Gentlemen,
Your obt. Sert.
Catherine Spalding,
Sister of Charity.
Feb. 10th 1834———

The cholera that struck Louisville in 1832 was part of a severe pandemic that had spread from Europe to Canada and into the United States through New York into the South. (For the story of the SCN's voluntary service culminating in the letter to the mayor, see Doyle, *Pioneer Spirit,* pp. 100–105.)

After the Nazareth Council agreed to the request for Sister nurses, four Sisters were sent from Nazareth to Louisville: Margaret Bamber, her sister Hilaria Bamber, Martha Drury, and Martina Beaven. In the stagecoach, they encountered a young student for the Lutheran ministry, Charles Schaeffer, who described them in a letter to his sister as "influenced by the power of the Divine principle" and about to "offer themselves as sacrifices . . . all meek and gentle like a lamb to the slaughter." He was put off by the Sisters' "gloomy appearance," all "clothed in Black and veiled," but when they had unveiled in the daylight, he discovered two of them "considerably advanced in life/say 35/" and the other two "young & beautiful." After conversing during the long day's ride, he described them "as sociable as old friends" and the day his happiest since leaving his sister's home. The Sisters had cordially invited him to visit Nazareth; he intended to accept.

Charles Schaeffer (1813–1896) was the son and grandson of Lutheran ministers and, in his own career, very influential as pastor, professor at a Lutheran seminary, administrator and trustee, translator, and author of theological, historical, and devotional works. Born in Maryland, he was ordained in 1836 and lived nearly all his life in Pennsylvania. It is not known why he was traveling to Louisville from Bardstown; he may have been visiting his sister. Schaeffer's letter to his sister, quoted here, appeared on Ebay and was purchased by Martha Birchfield of Lexington, Kentucky, and sent to the Sisters of Charity of Nazareth on December 12, 2012, as a gift for their bicentennial.

The four Sisters from Nazareth joined Sisters already in Louisville as teachers at Presentation: Clare Gardiner, Appolonia McGill, Serena Carney, and Catherine Spalding. They closed the school and assisted in the nursing. The risk taken by all the Sisters sufficiently accounts for Catherine's dismay at the slur on them and the tone of her letter. Emphases by underlining are hers, apt evidence of her capacity to be blunt and assertive of rights and justice even to higher authorities than herself. The final paragraph constitutes what may be called her manifesto, or the first "mission statement" of the SCN congregation.

The mayor of Louisville was John Bucklin (see Appendix A). The city charter at the time gave the mayor not even a vote on the City Council; he had to "give information and recommendations." In response to Catherine's letter, the Council did decide to correct the wording on the city books and to return the $75. That fact suggests that Mayor Bucklin and the Council members were not without a sense of honor and justice. Catherine had won their respect, and she retained it through a long career in Louisville.

Letters to Mother Catherine Spalding, 1832–1838

There are no extant letters to Catherine Spalding while she was still at St. Thomas or at her first residence at Nazareth. From the period of her first residence in Louisville, however, six letters to her are extant. None of them connects directly to any extant letter written by her before 1838—a puzzle that merely suggests how many letters must be lost to her history.

The six letters to her reveal that Catherine maintained a relationship with her relatives in Maryland despite their inability to meet, and that she had formed some cordial friendships with laywomen, who felt a freedom to call on her services. These women also were her main supporters, donors, and public fundraisers for St. Vincent Orphan Asylum; their suggestion of taking management and even ownership prompted an exchange of letters between Mother Catherine and Bishop Rosati of St. Louis. Three letters from relatives of students of Nazareth Academy, enrolled or prospective, may have been forwarded to her from Nazareth. When St. Joseph College in Bardstown began to receive male students from Louisiana in 1825 following a school fire there, their sisters were often sent to Nazareth to receive a "finished" education. Many more letters from parents or guardians were received in later years; these generally reveal the same cordial respect and freedom of request or requirement for financial assistance or for services to a student.

1-A
From F. Hertsog
DLB 21, p. 17

Isle Brevelle
January 22, 1832

Madam Spalding
Honored Sister,

With the program which gives me details of the studies of my dear Desiree and Suzette, you have the kindness of telling me that you are satisfied with their application and their character. Their father is always happy to hear such praise and it pleases me to think that with your honorable kindness my dear children are enjoying your friendship.

In regard to their studies, I fear that they do not apply themselves enough in arithmetic and geography. I presume that you will help them to grow stronger in these two branches.

I am enclosing the amount of the bill that I owe you. Our worthy Mr. Etio kindly took upon himself the care of this matter. After this, please send the bill to him.

In the care of my dear children, you will be a second mother: that is for me a very happy feeling of security. Please, Madam, do not let them lack anything necessary.

Believe the great consideration with which I am Your very humble servant,

F. Hertsog
We rarely receive letters from Desiree and Suzette
Addressee, Madam Spalding,
Superior of Nazareth College
Bardstown, Ky.
Postage- .25

Suzette Herzog, aged twelve, and Desiree, aged fourteen, were registered at Nazareth on April 22, 1831. Both left on March 25, 1834. Their address was given as Nachitoches, Louisiana. In the academy record book, the name is spelled Herzog.

No letters to Catherine exist to verify if these girls were among the earliest students from the Deep South. It is not perfectly clear whether this letter was sent by the girls' father or their mother. If the father, he may have been a widower; no mention is made of their mother, but the role of "second mother" is given to Mother

Catherine. The tone of the letter is less demanding than that of many later letters concerning payment and students' needs. The dates of the letter and the girls' enrollment indicate they had already completed a spring–summer session and the fall semester. By 1832, Catherine was already in Louisville, which they evidently had not told their parents.

1-B
From B. R. Spalding
DLB 1, p. 33

Pleasant Hill
January 18, 1833
My dear Cousin,

It is with the most painful feelings that I announce to you the illness of my poor brother John. He was taken on Saturday last, and has not been able to leave his bed since; and I fear from the ill action of the medicine he has taken, a long and painful illness may be anticipated, although the doctor apprehends no immediate danger. I trust your prayers and those of the community over which you govern will ascend to the throne of Mercy in his behalf.

He told me a few weeks ago that he had written to you and had given permission to draw on us and our mutual friend Mrs. Elder for assistance (I forget how much) in educating some little orphans whom you, in your universal benevolence and charity, wished to bring up in the knowledge of God and his religion. You have our best wishes to succeed in your benevolent design, and shall have, as long as we are able, our most ardent cooperation.

Mrs. Turner, I am told, has reached her father's house. She has sent word that you are anxious to hear of Uncle Hilary Spalding's family. I will give you the details in a hurry this morning, as the Rev. Mr. Coomes has just called. Cousin Maria, the oldest daughter, married shortly after Uncle's death, Ed. J. Hamilton, and died about two years since. Her husband has married again and, it pains me to inform you, has married Cousin Ann, the youngest of the girls. They are both well and living, I fear, in splendid misery on the Potomac River, about ten miles from hence. Cousin Henrietta also married shortly after her father's death a D. Jamieson, who survived his marriage about 18 months.—Cousin H has married again, and she and her husband, John Hamilton, live about 8 miles off on the Zachiah Swamp. Cousin H is in bad health and is not likely to recover. The boys, Rufus, Ferdinand and Dinnis, are at home with their mother. They are all well and I believe doing well. The first attends the farm and the second is a doctor and is in attendance on our poor brother, and the third, I believe, is undecided in selecting a pursuit of life. This is all that my present hurry will permit giving you this time, my dear Cousin, but I will with pleasure return to this subject whenever you wish it.

I believe our sisters and their families are all well now. Ann had her second son ill for some time, but he has since recovered. Lizzy, our youngest, has had a second child born. Sister Polly, our eldest, is well and perfectly contented with home in Prince Georges. Hoping to hear from you shortly, I remain, dear Cousin, Sincerely, etc.

B. R. Spalding

(Note added: "The letter cost 25 cents and was addressed to Mother Catherine Spalding of the Convent Louisville, Ky.")

At this time, Mother Catherine was resident at the home of the Sisters and orphans on Fifth Street, adjacent to St. Louis Church, in Louisville. The first separate orphanage had not yet been established.

See Doyle, *Pioneer Spirit*, Appendix A for the known relations of Catherine Spalding and other descendants of Basil Spalding, her grandfather. Basil had seven sons (Henry, John, William, James, Basil Jr., Edward, and George Hilary) and six daughters (Christine, Ann, Mary, Mary E., Elizabeth, and Catherine). Henry, Elizabeth, and Catherine all married an Elder; either of the two women could thus be "our mutual friend Mrs. Elder"; Elizabeth, as Catherine's past foster mother, may be the likeliest. Not much more about Basil's grandchildren can be verified from the archives at Nazareth.

From the letter, it is possible to conclude that "Uncle Hilary" is Basil's son George Hilary and that Maria, Henrietta, and Ann are his daughters, thus Mother Catherine's cousins. The letter writer, B. R. Spalding, may have been the son of Basil Jr., since he also refers to Hilary as "Uncle." Polly, Ann, Lizzy, and John seem to be his siblings. It is evident that Mother Catherine had made an effort to keep contact with these cousins, out of real family interest as much as hope for their support of her mission. The letter reflects much about the way large families in the mostly rural areas of Maryland intermarried and sought to prosper, as well as the importance they placed on familial connections and loyalty.

No positive identification can be made of the Reverend Coomes mentioned in this letter. However, the Catholic Almanacs of 1833 and 1834 list one priest, the Reverend Ignatius Coomes, stationed in Pomfret, Maryland, the area of the Spalding family land. He would very likely have been pastor of Catherine's relative there. All the priests named Coomes in John Lyons's sketches of the priests of the Bardstown diocese were reared and lived their clerical lives in Kentucky. It is possible, though unlikely, that one of them was visiting Maryland and the Spalding family at the time of this letter. The writer seems to assume Catherine will know who this "Rev. Mr. Coomes" is.

1-C
From Bishop Joseph Rosati
OLB 16, pp. 23–24

June 1833
Dear Sister,

You wish to know my opinion about the manner in which your orphan establishment should be established; if it would be more conducive to its prosperity that the good pious ladies by whose exertions some funds have already been procured for this charitable institution, should form themselves into a corporate body, own all the property, and have the management of its economical concerns. We have certainly innumerable examples of such corporations in our country, by which many excellent charitable institutions have been created and are actually administered and supported. And indeed, in cases where there is no means of having a religious Community to whom these establishments may be safely entrusted, corporations of charitable persons afford the only way of creating and supporting them. But such is not the case with the contemplated asylum. Very happily for the poor orphans of your city, there are Sisters of Charity to whose care the institution is to be entrusted. I do not see therefore any necessity for having another body. On the contrary, we have examples by which it appears that very often these corporate bodies, composed of many different members, animated no doubt by good intentions, but not agreeing to adopt the same measures, have not well succeeded in promoting the welfare of the institution; and the religious Community, who had to conduct it under their direction, have been placed in the impossibility of doing all the good they might have done, if left more free in the management of things with which they are better acquainted than those, who having had no hand in the labor, have no experience about it. In St. Louis, the hospital and asylum of the Sisters of Charity have prospered exceedingly, because the generous founder of these institutions has left the management of them altogether to the Sisters. Therefore, I do not hesitate one minute to say that the best way should be for the asylum to be conducted by the Sisters of Nazareth, without the interference of any other body. As to the means of procuring funds, and providing for the support of the orphans, no doubt the charitable ladies of your city will not desist from such a good work; they will continue to exert their zeal, and will perfect what they have so happily begun.

I am sincerely,
Your most humble Servant in J. C.
Joseph, Bishop of St. Louis

By 1833, Father Joseph Rosati, to whom Catherine had appealed in 1821 on behalf of a former student, had become Bishop Rosati of St. Louis (see letter 1-1 and Appendix A). Her respect for him and for his experience and judgment seems never to have waned. When the group of ladies who were her principal donors and volunteer workers for the orphans conceived the idea that they should not only support the orphanage but form a corporation to own and manage it, Catherine's intuitive wisdom warned her of possible damage to the mission. She had also the wisdom to withhold her own judgment until she conferred with a more experienced observer of such lay projects regarding their benefits or failures. She presented the issue and her questions to her friend and former mentor at St. Thomas, Bishop Rosati. Her letter to him is not extant, but its contents are clear from his summary preceding his reply. Both were wise enough to see the advantage of a "both-and" approach to the mission: the Sisters retain ownership and oversight; the ladies continue to support it. They did so.

1-D
From Catherine Frazer
DLB 1, p. 60 (abridged)

On envelope: To Mother Catherine Spalding
Infirmary and Orphan Asylum Louisville
Favoured by Rev. Mr. Magill
Lexington, January 17, 1837
Dear Mother Catherine,

Mr. Magill has kindly offered to take a letter to you and I am about to trouble you concerning the contents of the book case and secretary which you have—I had so little time to think and was so bewildered while in Louisville that I am aware I gave you little satisfaction concerning the things left under your charge, and if you believe me, I have not the slightest recollection of many things which I have, on inquiring from Catherine concerning them. Found I really packed in a box and trunk at Mrs. Anderson's. I would be very much indebted to you if in your leisure hours you would look over and select from the bookcase such books as you think will be useful to the children and lay them aside till a convenient opportunity offers of sending them to Mrs. Anderson's to be put in the box there: there are a great many handsome and useful children's works, made presents to the children at different times, which I should like to have, though I am sure that many are scattered and lost—there are several school books both English and French and some music of Catherine's in a box at Mrs. Anderson's, which would now be really of use to Catherine, but which I disliked writing for to Mrs. Anderson, fearing she would give herself trouble about them and she has already so much and Mr. Anderson also. I am sure they are tired out with us.

[A paragraph discusses the alarming health of "dear old Mrs. Anderson" and concern for the health of the younger Mrs. Sidney Anderson.]

Sister Ann is very well and I suppose will write you by Mr. Magill. They have the largest and best school decidedly in town, and people seem every day to open their eyes to its merits for I think it increases in size. I am very pleased with the improvement Catherine makes in all her studies. She herself is as happy as she could be away from us. She is very fond of her home and wishes no better than to spend her Saturdays and Sundays after Church with us, which she always does.

She recommenced her school the first of the year. She was with us under a physician's constant care for between six and seven weeks . . . until medicine restored her health. She is now very well. She always speaks of you, dear Mother Catherine, with affection and respect, and I am happy to tell you that the Sisters all appear to be pleased with Catherine in every respect and even hold her up as an example to others.

[Mrs. Frazer reports further about her two sons, one successful in business with "one of the first men in Lexington," the other a failure for lack of "industry and perseverance."]

Catherine made her first Communion last All Saints Day. Neither of the boys ever made theirs. When you see Mrs. Matthews will you give my best love to her and good Miss Ann, and to Miss Rosaline Mallan, whom I am sure from the deep interest she takes in you and yours, you often see, give my best love and wishes. I regretted much to hear of Mrs. Marshall's recent illness from Mr. Magill. I did not like to question him concerning her disease, but hope she is better.

I am sure, dear Mother Catherine, you will be pleased to know that my dearest sister Mary Ann will be married on the 23rd of this month to a Mr. Lane, a worthy clever young Louisiana planter. . . . They say he is a very wealthy man. . . . But I have tired out your patience, dear Mother Catherine, and will conclude by begging you to remember me affectionately to dear Sisters Hilaria and Appolonia, whom I shall ever remember with gratitude and affection. It is my wish, dear Mother Catherine, that if the book case and secretary will be of any service to you, that you should keep them; and if Mr. Kearney, who attends to the settling of the affairs of the Estate, should speak of them as belonging to the estate, I would wish you to show him this part of the letter. They could bring but a few dollars were they sold toward the payment of any debt, and as they stand, they may be of service to you, if you will accept them as a debt of truest gratitude. Mr. Frazer, whom you may not remember, does not forget you, joins me together with Catherine and boys whom I have just seen, in the best wishes for your prosperity and happiness and believe me, dear Mother Catherine,

Your sincerest friend,
Catherine Frazer

Very few positive identifications can be made of persons named in this letter. The Nazareth Archives have no information on Catherine Frazer the writer, and no girl of that name is in the Academy's Register. The letter suggests that Catherine the mother may have been a patient at St. Vincent Infirmary or else a visitor for some duration of time, and that her daughter Catherine and her husband Robert may have also visited and become acquainted with Mother Catherine and the other Sisters. The Andersons and the Frazers seem to have been related through the two sisters mentioned. Mrs. Frazer may have known Mother Catherine in some other context before her period at the Infirmary; that would likely be the "Lady Managers," women who regularly assisted in the financial or service needs of the orphanage. The women Mrs. Frazer names, accurately or not, are very likely Lady Managers. Rosalie Mallon Smith, wife of a physician, was a frequent visitor and assistant at the orphanage. At the time she wrote this letter, Mrs. Frazer seems to be living in Lexington with her husband and two sons and to have her daughter Catherine in boarding school at St. Catherine's Academy in that city.

This possible scenario is supported by some possible identifications: Sisters Hilaria Bamber and Appolonia McGill were both missioned at St. Vincent Infirmary at the time of this letter. Both were considered skilled nurses; both had nursed in the cholera epidemic of 1832–33. Sister Appolonia became known as the best nurse in the city; in the Civil War she nursed in a Louisville army camp and died while on duty.

Mr. Magill is evidently the Reverend John McGill, then assistant pastor at St. Peter's parish in Lexington. Born in Philadelphia in 1809, of Irish immigrant parents, he had come to Bardstown with his family in 1819, received a B.A. from St. Joseph College in 1828, studied law and practiced in New Orleans, then returned to Kentucky. After theology at St. Thomas Seminary in Bardstown and St. Mary's in Baltimore, he was ordained by Bishop David in 1835 and missioned in Lexington. Later, he served in Louisville at St. Louis Church and as editor of the *Catholic Advocate*. In 1850 he became the third bishop of Richmond, survived yellow fever, cholera, and the Civil War there, and died in 1872.

Her connection to Father McGill would assure serious consideration of any letter from Mrs. Frazer—despite its length, detail, tone, style, repetition, and general verbosity. But why she had visited the infirmary, brought furniture with her, and left it behind is a mystery. Still more puzzling is the nature and extent of the friendship with Mother Catherine, which allowed her to assume that Catherine had "leisure hours" and would gladly use them to sort out books for the Frazer children and send them, at her own expense, to Mrs. Anderson for further safekeeping. No letter of response from Catherine is extant, nor is there any record of what finally became of the secretary and bookcase—or of the friendship.

1-E
From Mr. Briscoe
DLB 11, p. 58b

To Rev. Mother Superior
August 15, 1838
Madam,

In leaving my daughter with you, I have thought proper to leave such instructions in writing as I look upon as indispensable for her health and comfort. From, I fear, a predisposition to suffer under colds it is expected that she shall lodge in a room during winter, where she shall have a fire night and morning. I have also thought proper to appoint Mr. John M. Mackin as my agent to supply her with anything she may need, and it is also my request that at such times as holidays and at such other times that will not interfere with her studies, that she may be allowed to visit at Mr. M. Mackin's; and if she should, from sickness, require a physician, I wish the more able employed and for Mr. M. Mackin to be made acquainted with her illness. Mr. M. Mackin will also pay or furnish any money that may become due for her education, in my absence.

Mr. Briscoe

The academy register lists three girls named Briscoe, all from Port Gibson, Mississippi. Two were enrolled only from May 1835 to November 1836. The third, however, was Indiana Briscoe, daughter of Mr. and Mrs. William Briscoe, enrolled from May 1835 to July 1839. This letter may be presumed to refer to her. Her father must have brought her back from a vacation at home and felt urged and free to state his requirements for her individual care and privileges. Letters from the 1840s will often be similar in their concerns and even more assertive in tone.

Of Mr. Mackin nothing is known beyond his agency for Mr. Briscoe.

1-F
From William Clark
OLB 17, p. 2.

Lebanon, Ohio
Aug. 30, 1838
Mother Superior,

Permit me to introduce to you my sister and brother. While at Nazareth in company with Mrs. Dorden and Mr. Hughes of Mississippi, I was so much pleased with your Academy and with the college at Bardstown, on account of the healthy location and the admirable regulations of each as to be desirous that my brother and sister should attend them. Enclosed, my father sends

> $30, which he hopes will be all sufficient to pay her bill for the first quarter or until he shall be able to make another remittance. He wishes her to be entirely under your directions with regards to her studies. But is desirous for her to complete them in the course of two years. He wishes you to have the disposal of her time, but hopes that when her brother calls for her she may be permitted to accompany him to town, unless contrary to the rules of the seminary, to which he desires her in every respect entirely to conform. He wishes her to study music in connection with her other studies. Unless you think it best to defer it for a while.
>
> Very respectfully,
> Wm. Clark

Of three girls named Clark registered at Nazareth Academy in 1838, two had already been there since 1830, having entered very young; they were not residents of Ohio. The third girl, listed as Harriet Clarke, entered September 2, 1838, and remained until July 1839. Her parents were Dr. and Mrs. Clark from Lebanon, Ohio. The discrepancy in the spelling of the last name may be attributed to an error of the registrar or simply to the casual spelling of names in the nineteenth century, which is evident in various contexts and documents.

William may have attended St. Joseph's College in Bardstown; he was at least a visitor there and acquainted with some of the Southerners who were frequenting the school and sending girls to Nazareth. In this case, the role of the brother/son seems to have been primary and influential on the expectations and allowances for the girl. Harriet seems to have completed her education at Nazareth in two years; whether the payments were timely cannot be asserted. The letter suggests they may have been chancy. Nothing is recorded of Harriet's later life.

Nothing is known of either Mrs. Dorden or Mr. Hughes. They may have been among the Mississippi families who began to patronize St. Joseph College in Bardstown and then Nazareth Academy.

Conclusion

With the election of August 1838 and Catherine's return to leadership as Mother and headmistress of Nazareth Academy, one may say that the foundation years of the SCN and its mission were accomplished. The community had survived the loss of home and school at St. Thomas and the crowding and false debts of the move to Nazareth, as well as the divisions of opinion and charity of the early 1830s. The mission in Louisville was firmly established and had won local approval and support. Reconciliation with Bishop David would soon be under way, and he would note happily that Nazareth Academy was soon to reach "130-odd boarders." These young women would be Mother Catherine's call to mission for the next six years, a mission requiring collaboration of Sisters, agents, and parents, whose surviving letters testify to a general public awareness of the school and its reputation for offering a solid curriculum and training in religion and morals to young women.

2

Mother and Administrator

1838–1844

A glaring discrepancy confronts a reader of Mother Catherine's biography and also her extant letters from her third term as Mother at Nazareth, 1838–1844. The period confronted her with enormously important and demanding events, duties, and moral issues as administrator of both growing school and expanding congregation. Yet only one of these crises, the confrontation with Bishop Flaget over SCN identity, is found in her existing letters.

No sooner had she returned to Nazareth than she became critically ill from "congestive fever," the nineteenth-century term for malaria. She very nearly died, was not really well for eight months, and suffered lingering headaches from treatment of quinine with mercury. She returned to a school diminished by cholera that had discouraged enrollment and claimed the lives of several key Sisters. The farm had suffered much from neglect and frequent change of overseers. An effort to restore it led to the first known direct purchase of slave labor. No letters deal with any of these events; they do not express concern for the school's survival, grief for the Sisters lost, nor moral qualms about the purchase of humans in slavery. She may well have felt all three emotions and expressed them in writing—but not in still-existing letters.

Even more drastic, Catherine resumed leadership of a community in conflict, with divisions that had been festering since the early 1830s. Bishop David had been displeased with Sister Ellen O'Connell's influence on Mother Angela Spink, and some of the young Sisters considered Ellen's teacher training and supervision too severe. Sensitivities, loose comments and reports, misunderstandings, and misinterpretations all contributed to Bishop David's decision to remove Sister Ellen from the Nazareth campus, which had caused Mother Angela's resignation and David's own move to residence in Bardstown. He had also roused differing opinions in the Sisters on other matters. Catherine had to lead in reconciliation with Bishop David and reunification of the Sisters. In 1841 she brought David home to Nazareth, where he died, ending the era of their co-leadership of the congregation and causing her grief for the loss of a genuinely loved friend. One short written request remains that expresses Catherine's deep feeling for David and his relation to the congregation.

While David was dying, Bishop Flaget initiated his ill-conceived plans to unite the SCNs first with Mother Seton's Sisters in Emmitsburg, Maryland, and then with the Daughters of Charity in France. It may be considered an act of Providence that this threat to the community's identity and local mission only served to reunite the Sisters in a huge effort to preserve their community. This proved to be the major effort of Catherine's life and her most successful, expressed in two masterfully written letters that made her truly a Mother, a lifesaver to her battered community.

Once that crisis had passed, Catherine could devote herself more to her ordinary duties as Mother: admitting new members, supervising their novitiate, and accepting them for vows; promoting the health and spiritual well-being of Sisters; participating in Council and Board meetings; overseeing the campus; welcoming visitors; attending the sick and burying the dead; and visiting the branch houses in Louisville, Bardstown, Lexington, and Union County. In 1843, she negotiated the opening of another mission in Nashville, Tennessee. The pressure on her to send Sisters to Nashville is expressed in letters to her from the bishop of that city, Richard Pius Miles, who was himself under duress to expand the Church and its mission in a new diocese with very few Catholics and almost no churches or clergy.

Finally, Catherine was again headmistress of Nazareth Academy, responsible for its overall program, maintenance, and advancement. She had invaluable assistance in Sister Columba

Carroll, successor to Ellen O'Connell in direction of the academic program. But Catherine was the "mother," the guardian who knew each student, the ultimate arbiter of her needs, wants, and well-being. The woman who was so fond of orphans, so willing to beg for their necessities, was now forced to spend much of her energy in ordering school supplies and trying to collect tuition to pay for them. To do business, she had to have agents in Louisville and New Orleans. Here, her letters are again missing; what she ordered or requested, what demands and complaints she had to endure, what satisfaction or praises she elicited—all these are found or hinted at only in the collection of letters written to her by agents, or by parents or guardians of students.

Unfortunately, there is no one-to-one correspondence between any of Catherine's letters and those sent to her. Comments often indicate that she had initiated or responded to a communication, but her letter was not preserved. Because the surviving letters to Catherine are numerous, some very long and repetitious, what are given here are generous samples, with some letters transcribed in full and some excerpted to highlight content or tone. Others are simply summarized or listed. All may be found in full in the Nazareth archives.

The letters to Catherine provide another important, sometimes pathetic, sometimes amusing view into her life as Mother and headmistress at Nazareth. Hard-pressed parents did have real difficulties: no common national currency then existed, and state banks could accept or reject the currency of another state. Cotton crops and small businesses did fail; some parents had their own delinquent debtors. But others reveal themselves as being simply reluctant to pay. Catherine had to pursue delinquents through her agent. In addition to financial pursuits, she had to explain what she could or could not do to meet parents' wishes for their daughters' course work, clothing, comfort, or entertainment. All this labor was compounded by the rapid turnover in enrollment; many students remained at Nazareth only a year or two. That meant quick turnover in record-keeping, debt collection, purchase of clothing, and reports to parents. It is regrettable that, although parental letters are plentiful, no direct letters from Catherine to them are extant.

The compilation of letters in this chapter, though small for six such busy years, lets readers know Catherine more intimately and understand her labors, stresses, and accomplishments, her warm personality and managerial skills, the love she gave, and the admiration she elicited from so many varied persons. In August 1844, she finished her term of office and expressed to Claudia Elliott (Letters 2-9 and 2-10 below) her enormous relief from its burden and her satisfaction as she returned to her other loved charges at St. Vincent Asylum and Infirmary in Louisville.

Letters by Mother Catherine Spalding, 1839–1844

2-1

To Sister Louisa Dorsey
Nazareth August 31st 1839
Orphan Asylum
Louisville, Kentucky
My dear Sister,

I received your message by Sister Ambrosia; & altho' I laughed when she told me & replied that you would have to do as I did & turn about & get funds—(This you know was a mere joke) yet rest assured you will always find in me a heart that will know how to sympathize with you in any difficulties; which comfort, I never had in all that I had to encounter in establishing that house.—But God be praised! I hope His holy will has been done—& He will not abandon his own.—if your heart beats friendly towards my Dear Orphans, be assured it is a new claim you have on me & an additional tie full[ly] as strong as the one that unites us in the sacred bonds of religion. I enclose you here $10, which I had the good luck to obtain the other day from a stranger to appropriate to the benefit of the orphans.—I shall continue, as I have done to procure for them all that I can.—I feel uncertain at this time when I shall be able to see you but hope you will have no difficulty as the Sisters there are acquainted with the place.—Ah! my dear Sister, could you only read in my heart you would soon know with what delight I would now change situations with you—for in the whole universe there is not a spot to which my heart clings but to that.—

If our good & venerable Bishop calls there as he passes through Louisville be sure to tell him from me that I wish him to give that place his Special Benediction.— My kindest love to all the Sisters & God bless you all is my humble & sincere prayer.—

Catherine

(The envelope addressed to Sister Louisa by Mother Catherine bears the notation "Politeness of Mr. [or Wm.] Davis.")

Sister Louisa Dorsey had been a Sister in the SCN since 1821, having come with Mrs. Ann O'Connor (Sister Scholastica) from Baltimore, escorted by Father Guy Ignatius Chabrat. In 1839, after Mother Catherine had returned to office at Nazareth, the capable Sister Louisa was made superior at the Louisville orphanage, responsible for its maintenance and the welfare and education of the children. She had evidently sent a plea for assistance to Catherine. The letter reveals both the financial constraints she experienced and Catherine's own love for the children and desire to support them.

Since the letter was written in 1839, Sister Ambrosia is Sr. Ambrosia Foy, not Ambrosia Abbott, who entered in 1842. Ambrosia Foy was missioned in Lexington and left the community in 1841.

Bishop Flaget had gone to Europe in 1835. Due to a papal request that he preach throughout France to stimulate interest in the Association for the Propagation of the Faith, he remained abroad for four years. When he returned to the United States in August 1839, Mother Catherine must have thought he would stop in Louisville en route to Bardstown. It is not known whether he did so; he arrived in Bardstown in September and was welcomed at Nazareth with a ceremonial banquet on October 9. The crisis over SCN's independent identity or its merger with Emmitsburg was soon to follow.

No particulars about a William Davis are available. He could have been any local citizen-friend of Nazareth doing a courier service, a common practice at the time. Or he may have been the father of Nazareth students listed in the Academy Register: Dorinda, Frances, and Mary Jane. Mary Jane was still at school in 1839; her father may have visited Nazareth and returned home to Jefferson County, Mississippi, by way of Louisville and the orphanage.

2-2

Emancipation papers for slave Luke
August 15, 1840

Know all men by these presents, that We J. Haseltine & Catharine Spalding have manumitted and set free and by these presents, do manumit and set free our Negro Man Luke, aged about forty eight years, about five feet six or seven inches high, heavy made and quite black with a scar over the right eye and one on the left wrist.—In Testimony whereof we have hereto Set our hands this fifteenth of August Eighteen hundred and forty.

J. Haseltine, Genl. Sup. of Nazareth,
Catherine Spalding M. Supr of Nazareth

(The instruction given below is pasted in OLB 3, p. 23.)

15 /Aug. / 40
Dr Sir,

Mother Catherine & myself have signed our names on a blank sheet—Over which we wish you to write free papers for Luke. I would do it myself but do not know the form of such an instrument. Y[ou]r attention to this will [be] much oblige[d.]

Yr obt. Servt.
J. Haseltine

This is the only documented evidence of emancipation of one of the slaves of Nazareth. Little is known of Luke beyond the description of him here. He had lived at both Nazareth and the Louisville orphanage, and the issue of family separation was not new. Council minutes of December 10, 1834, record a resolution that Luke was not to be sold but "continue the property of Nazareth" and "remain at the Orphan Asylum in Louisville or any other house not more than two days' journey from his wife, provided his future conduct did not require a change in the resolution." Apparently he was a "gift" to the orphanage, as no monetary exchange with the Motherhouse is noted.

Why Catherine chose to emancipate him after her return to office at Nazareth is not known. His conduct may have been deemed meritorious enough to earn his freedom, or it may have been given in sympathy with his desire to be near his wife. Recognition of marriages of slaves and appropriate accommodations for them were part of Nazareth's policy, though no other action this generous is recorded. That at least one emancipation is certain in Nazareth's history is some relief to later members of the SCN family.

John Kearney, Esq. was a prominent citizen of Louisville, involved in the opening of the second Catholic church structure in 1830. Historian Ben Webb describes him as a "lawyer of high standing and an earnest Catholic." He is mentioned in the letter of January 14, 1837, from Catherine Frazer to Mother Catherine as active in settling the Frazer estate in Lexington. Catherine was to show him that letter as proof of Mrs. Frazer's offer of her bookcase. Kearney was called on to validate Luke's emancipation in 1840. He may have given regular legal service to Nazareth.

2-3

To Rt. Rev. Bishop Flaget
Bardstown, Kentucky
Nazareth April 17th 1841
Rt. Rev'd dear Bishop & Father,

I do not know that you required any answer to your letter of yesterday.—I have read it with all the attention of which I am capable—& I have spent not only 1qr before the adorable Sacrament, where in fact I find my only comfort, but quarters have been spent there.—& I feel now as I did at first.—I can only say to the best of my power I will endeavor to comply with your orders—If you believe that Almighty God will be more glorified by our wearing a black cap instead of a white one—I hope you will do me the justice to believe that I attach no importance to those little articles of our clothes—If we have worn the white head dress for these 25 years, we have done so by the decision of the Council & that of our Revered founder & 1st Supr & one among the reasons that then decided this was, that white was the color worn by the Sisters since the days of St. Vincent.—But this matters not—white or black is the same to me.—& for any thing further I forbear to make any remark.—May God's holy will be done!—& may he in mercy, grant me the grace to save my poor soul, it shall be my only aim.—I feel consoled, dear Father, that in your visit the other day, from what you remarked to me, you found the Community happy & contented & in the regular observance of the rules & religious duties. which I do think to be the case as far as can be; & I fondly trust with the blessing of God, it may continue to improve.—On my part, Rt. Rev'd Father; if I have ever treated you or your Rev'd Coadjutor with anything like disrespect, I am indeed unconscious of it.—& most assuredly it was never intentional.—But if I have unconsciously acted thus—I do

> most sincerely & humbly on my knees, beg your pardon for the same.—I know I have sometimes spoken jocosely & perhaps too freely with Bishop Chabrat, but as all was in joke I thought no harm; still it may be wrong—& I shall of course endeavor to correct it entirely.—I have written more lengthily than I intended & perhaps I have not expressed myself as I should.—But my God, I trust, knows the purity of my intention—& I leave it all in his Divine hands.—I did think I had experienced every kind of trial.—This is entirely new.—God be praised for all, & have mercy on me his humble & unworthy handmaid.—Please bless & pray for—
>
> Your ever obt. but unworthy
> Catherine

This letter and the following are the record of Mother Catherine's thought, feeling, and action in the "crisis of independence." The facts of this event are these: Both Bishops Flaget and David were members of the Order of St. Sulpice, whose specific charism was the formation of priests. To administer religious communities of women was outside their normal mission, and in the late 1830s, the Provincial of the Sulpicians wrote from France that their priests should cease such responsibilities and devote themselves to seminaries. To comply, the Sulpician ecclesiastical superiors both in Emmitsburg, Maryland, and in Kentucky would have to find other superiors for the Sisters of Charity.

Since the 1820s, Bishop Flaget had experienced tensions with his Sulpician superiors over their perceived indifference to the Kentucky mission. He had wanted his seminary affiliated with the Sulpician seminary in France and Sulpician priests sent to assist in Kentucky. No such requests had been honored. Nevertheless, Flaget was Sulpician at heart and well disposed to have another arrangement for supervision of his Sisters of Charity. He began to collaborate in the proposal of Father Louis Deluol, superior of the U.S. Sulpicians and of the Sisters of Charity in Emmitsburg, to join the Sisters there to the Daughters of Charity in Paris and thus place them under a superior from the Vincentian priests. In

1850, Father Deluol did accomplish the union of Mother Seton's Sisters of Charity with France—without consulting them and by orders that created enough opposition to cause one group to separate and become an independent community under the bishop of Cincinnati.

The Deluol-Flaget plan for the Kentucky Sisters of Charity of Nazareth was that they would first merge with Emmitsburg, then with France. The process would begin by a change from the white cap in Kentucky to the black one worn in Maryland and proceed with removal of the SCN's local ecclesiastical superior, Father Joseph Haseltine. Whether Catherine knew the full implication of the change of color cannot be said, but she clearly did not want it and felt free to make that known. By her second letter in July, she was deeply distressed at the proposed loss of Father Haseltine and clearly knew that the distinct identity of the SCN was at stake.

That the community was vulnerable to such authoritative interference could not be denied. Financial troubles and debts resulting from inability or reluctance of parents to pay tuition; departures of members, even three Sisters together and the bishop's own niece, Eulalia Flaget; and five deaths in recent months, including that of pioneer Ellen O'Connell—all suggested a dangerous instability and perhaps inadequate leadership for so important an enterprise. Both David and Flaget seem to have experienced a dampening of their confidence in the SCN's ability to manage its own life, and to have felt a need and right to plan a remedy by consultations in secrecy from the Sisters themselves.

The proposed measures would constitute a drastic change in identity that would impact the SCN's governance, membership, and mission. It would break with its past history and commit to a very uncertain, unpredictable future. Catherine clearly viewed the essential elements of past SCN life as still valid and foresaw the effects of the change as destructive to any hope of future growth. Any attempt at resolution would have to combine respectful dissent with obedience and intent of harmony, to achieve a stable union of Sisters, clergy, and all collaborators in the mission.

When writing letters in times of serious challenge, Catherine seems to have used generous underlining of words for emphasis or contrast. To follow these underlinings and to note implied questions in her text ("If you believe . . ." [but do you, really?]) is to feel the level of her conviction and emotion, also to perceive her boldness. She was, in fact, challenging her bishop and major superior even as she expressed her genuine respect and intent to cooperate with him.

What incident caused Catherine's reference to Bishop Chabrat in this letter is not known. But it was a well-known fact that he was sensitive to his clerical station and dignity, easily enough offended. Guy Ignatius Chabrat had come from France to Maryland, then to Kentucky as a seminarian with Bishop Flaget, who ordained him. He was ever "first son" in Flaget's mind and affection, though the bishop could describe him in introductory letters as a "zealous and fervent missionary" and also as "a quibbler and a fighter of the first class" (FL, vol. 2, February 11 and 12, 1820). Over the opposition of priests and laity, Chabrat was made coadjutor bishop of Bardstown in July 1834. Many considered him too rigid, demanding in his asceticism, deficient in poise and graciousness, and devoid of humor. Some expressed displeasure at having "another French bishop." When Bishop Flaget went to Europe, Bishop Chabrat was, in effect, the bishop of Bardstown. Catherine, well endowed with wit, wisely maintained caution and propriety in her relationship with him, and seems to have been generally successful.

2-4

(A typed copy bears the notation "The Humble remonstrance and earnest petition of the Sisters of [Charity of] Nazareth, addressed to their Rt. Rev. Bishop and App. Father, Dr. Flaget, Bishop of Bardstown.")

July 6, 1841 [date on back of letter]
Right Reverend Father,

Since the reception of your letter containing your late orders relative to the changes you required in our

Community, we have unitedly spent much time in meditation and prayer to God for his light and grace;—we have repeatedly offered up novenas, supplicating that his holy will might be done in regard to our dear Community. And now, most beloved and venerated Father; it is with sentiments of the deepest respect, and true filial regard, together with a profound regret, that we have come to the conclusion to lay before you, our Bishop and Father, our humble and earnest entreaty, that we may be allowed to continue unchanged in the manner in which we have been established in your Diocese by your zealous co-laborer, our revered Father and Founder in Kentucky.

We entered the house of Nazareth and embraced, with our whole hearts, the practices, rules and constitutions given to us by him, being assured that they were dictated by the Blessed Vincent of Paul, solemnly authorized and approved of by yourself, and sanctioned at the court of Rome; and we were always left under the firm conviction that they were sacred, and never to be liable to any change.

Father David (whom you have so frequently and so warmly recommended to our confidence and reverence, as being one of the greatest divines and holiest clergymen) has, on numerous occasions, expressed it to us as his decided opinion, that it was much better, both for our happiness and spiritual good, that we should exist always, as you and he had thought proper to institute us,—a separate and distinct body;—and that he felt most grateful to God for so directing and ordaining it. And, surely, Religion in Kentucky can be more extensively and effectually served by us, as we now exist.

And here, we may be permitted to express our humble thanks to Divine Providence, and to yours and our revered Founder's protection and instruction, that Nazareth, as you acknowledge, with parental joy, has never given any scandal in your diocese, but has constantly labored to do good,—the success of which efforts, facts attest.

Permit us, too, dear Father, to recall to your parental recollection, those primitive days of our poor, afflicted community when with simple heartedness of devoted children, we zealously and cheerfully spent the energies of our youth, in the fields, looms, spinning rooms, kitchens, &c—at St. Thomas,—rejoicing that we could thus by our humble labors in the most servile and lowest occupations, contribute our poor mite to the support of the seminaries and churches in your diocese; while, at the same time, we were struggling in the commencement of our own little community. Afterwards, we labored with the same zeal for the college, seminary and cathedral in Bardstown. And oh! Father, those were happy days, because we looked forward with delight, to the rise and progress of these works of Religion; believing that we ourselves were settled in the way of life to which we were convinced we were called, by our common Father. We never dreamed that a change would be required of us; otherwise our zeal and energy would have been paralyzed as they now are.

With due humility and a deep sense of the over ruling care of Heaven, allow us to call to your mind the number of respectable families added to the church, by the education and religious impressions, which individuals receive at Nazareth: every year brings with it conversions either in the school or after young ladies have left our Institution; and you know far better than we do, the immense weight of prejudice which has been removed by Nazareth's humble efforts, aided by the blessing of God. Add to this, the baptisms and first communions for which children are regularly instructed and prepared each year, both in the branch houses and at Nazareth. Many scholars are also educated gratuitously every year in each one of the houses; and alms largely distributed to the surrounding poor. Of these things we do not boast, for it is only our duty; but we merely wish to give your paternal heart consoling proof that Nazareth is, as it has ever been, devoted to the interests of charity and Religion.

And the Orphan Asylum which it was your most ardent wish to see established (all who do justice must acknowledge) would not exist at this time, had it not been for the untiring exertions and labors of the Sisters of Nazareth; who moreover aided the good work by pecuniary means drawn from the resources of the Society.

It is true, many members have left our community; but we have every reason to believe and to know that the same occurs, and perhaps more frequently, in other communities where the vows are simple and yearly; and, as you are aware, such defections do sometimes take place, and not unfrequently, in monasteries where vows are taken for life. We read in the discourses of St. Vincent of Paul, addressed to the first Sisters of Charity, that, even during his lifetime and in the first fervor of the company, many members left, and, after leaving, spoke in the most disparaging terms of the order. During the last six years, only three have gone from among us,—and they returned not to the world.

We need not remind you, beloved Father, that we commenced in a new country, and not even in the most Catholic settlement of the country; and, therefore, owing to that cause, and perhaps some others, our community is comparatively small. But we have always been taught to believe that the strength of a religious body depended not so much upon its numbers as upon the fervor, zeal and devotedness of those who composed it; and especially upon the blessing of our good God, who seems to delight in effecting good by instruments few and feeble. Still, we have five houses in your diocese, all doing well, the members of which are happy in their state; and each house is doing not an inconsiderable portion of charity, from the resources and labors of the Sisters.

You have already had the unanimous testimony of the Sisters that the community was never happier, more orderly, more united, or more zealous in the observance of their rules,—that all are most desirous to live up to the spirit of their state. For all this we humbly and thankfully bless God. And although our schools and houses are flourishing, and favored by the Almighty with success; yet God forbid that we should glory in being the instrument; but we feel, as every Christian heart would feel, an anxious wish to maintain our society unchanged, as our revered and holy Founder and Father first established it, and as he wished and believed it would, under your paternal care, continue.

We are accustomed to our manner of life, and feel thoroughly convinced that we could not find happiness, by being connected with, or mixed in any other community or family;—and, furthermore, that we might, by so doing, jeopardize our eternal salvation, for which alone we embraced our state of life.

Honored and dear Father, though we do urgently and humbly implore to be still allowed to continue unchanged, as we began, in the practices, rules, and constitutions, as given to us by yourself and Father David; yet we beg you to be assured that it is our most earnest desire, as we know it to be your right, should disorders creep in, that you should administer your fatherly advice and correction. We always have cheerfully and gladly acknowledged you as our first Superior, but we believe that the interests of the Society, and our constitutional rights, require an immediate ecclesiastical Superior. We cordially wish, and urge, frequent visits from you, and that those visits should be of such a length as to enable you to be intimately and personally acquainted with the general interests and business of the house, and with each individual in particular. And we candidly assure you that it is, and has ever been, our fixed determination to persevere in our holy vocation, and to labor sedulously to advance constantly in the virtues, required by our state of life.

In itself, we attach little importance to the article of dress, yet we think changes so striking as that you propose in our cap, hazardous and calculated to arouse public observation, to elicit surmises, and occasion prejudices, which may be highly detrimental to Nazareth, and perhaps to religion in Kentucky. Had we worn the black cap for twenty-five years as we have the white one, we should feel equally reluctant to so remarkable a change as that of the color; which undoubtedly would subject the community to animadversion and ridicule, and might thus tend to diminish public respect and confidence, which St. Vincent of Paul considered as most essential to the success of the Sisters' labors.—With regard to the two last articles of your letter, we have nothing to say, and our rules have already marked out similar restrictions respecting the visits paid to clergymen, and very few Sisters have ever been in the habit of transgressing in this point.

In terminating, most revered and cherished Father, we throw ourselves on your kind and fatherly forbearance, begging you not to consider us importunate, but to listen, with a Father's heart, to the humble, earnest, and most respectful remonstrances of your children; who feel convinced that these changes may be the laying of the axe to the root of that tree, which you and we equally believe to have been planted and watered by the hand of God. Numbers of our Sisters, whose deaths have been most holy and edifying, have asserted such to have been their dying belief; and no one who is acquainted with the commencement and progress of Nazareth, can doubt it being the work of the Most High.

In the presence of our good and merciful God, and kneeling before the sacred image of his crucified Son, we hereto affix our names—earnestly imploring you, our dear and truly revered Father, in the name and for the sake of Him, whose place you hold in our regard, to yield to our entreaties, and once more restore to your children that happiness and quiet of mind they have so long enjoyed at Nazareth—promising you in all the sincerity

> of our hearts that we shall, by the grace of God, redouble our efforts to advance in the virtues of our state of life, and to do good in your diocese.
>
> Sister Catherine, M. Sup.
> Personal signatures of twenty-eight Sisters
> (see Appendix B)
>
> The Sisters of the branch houses have also written & expressed their cordial wish to unite with the Motherhouse in petitioning that their Society should remain a distinct body, with their Constitutions, Rules, Dress, &c. unchanged.—
>
> Signatures of twenty-three additional Sisters

This letter followed the previous by nearly three months, during which Flaget had been in frequent and secret contact with Father Deluol in Emmitsburg. He was determined on the change in headdress; in June he wrote that three American prelates had been "almost scandalized by the elegance of the round white bonnet" of the SCN, and he had ordered the change to the black cap, effective in August. But he now had heard that the Sisters in Maryland would adopt the white cornette worn by the Daughters of Charity in France, and he was sure the Kentucky Sisters would prefer it to the black cap. More seriously, he was unsure about the exact dimensions of authority of a bishop and a bishop's authority as an ecclesiastical superior of religious women and wanted Deluol's counsel.

Catherine, meanwhile, had been making her own contacts. She had called on Father Stephen Badin as collaborator; he had visited Nazareth, met with the Sisters and listened to their wishes, questioned them as he felt appropriate, and then written his "Observations" to Flaget, essentially advising him to back off from his intent to change the cap or dismiss their ecclesiastical superior.

What exact orders Flaget wrote to Catherine to precipitate this July reply is uncertain, as no letters from him to her about the whole episode have been found. But her reply makes clear that he had registered some distress about the lessened membership of the SCN and what he perceived as a decline in the Sisters' fervor. He had also expressed his intent to remove their well-loved and very helpful ecclesiastical superior, Father Joseph Haseltine, and to join the community to another congregation. The density and detail of Catherine's replies to these points, as well as her defense of the history and religious spirit of her Sisters and of their desire to remain distinct and to do even more good in his diocese, all deflated any valid reasons for Bishop Flaget to change their communal and corporate identity.

This letter is both the longest and surely the most important that Catherine Spalding ever wrote. On it depended the outcome of her and the community's dissent and plea. Weak arguments would leave Flaget's decisions in full strength; too strong a dissent might rouse his anger and provoke a full assertion of his authority and right to command. Yet simple submission would, she and the others felt sure, destroy their community's mission and its likelihood of further growth in members or works.

Appendix B identifies the Sisters who cosigned this letter. The number of those who signed makes very clear that the protest and petition came from the community as a whole and not only from its leader. (For more on these events and the issue of independence or merger, including an analysis of Catherine's letters, see Doyle, *Pioneer Spirit,* pp. 137–145.)

2-5

AGREEMENT with Catharine Smyth

This agreement made this _____ day of February 1843
between the Council of the Community of the Sisters
of Charity of Nazareth Ky. And Catharine Smyth of
Louisville Ky. Witnesseth, that the aforesaid Council
of Nazareth engages to furnish the said Catharine
Smyth during her life a Home either at the Infirmary
& Orphan Asylum in Louisville Ky. or at some of the
other Establishments belonging to the said Community

of Nazareth as may be mutually agreed upon by the parties, that is, by the Superiors of Nazareth and the said Catharine Smyth; and, with a home, Nazareth engages to furnish the said Catharine Smyth with all the necessaries of life as long as she shall live. In consideration of which the said Catharine Smyth relinquishes all right or claim to five hundred dollars which she loaned to the conductors of the Infirmary & Orphan Asylum above named and she furthermore will faithfully pay over to the Superior of Nazareth all money or monies she may hereafter make by her own services or industry.

In witness whereof we the parties have hereunto signed our names & affixed our seals this day & year first above written.

Catharine Smyth
Catherine Spalding M. Supr. of Nazareth

No extant evidence establishes the identity of Catharine Smyth; she is not in the Register of Nazareth students, nor can her age at the time of the contract above be determined. It seems clear from the contract that she was at some time a supporter of the Louisville orphanage, as were many of the ladies of that city. Whatever her need was in 1843 or later, she seems to have been motivated by foresight and care for her own retired years by agreeing to move into an SCN establishment.

Either her concern was premature or she simply changed her mind about what she really wanted, for on the back of the contract, the following notation is made:

"I Rescind this contract December 23d 1845 and acknowledge the receipt of five hundred dollars in full of all debt and demands against Mother Catherine Spalding superior of Nazareth." Signed: Catherine t Smyth, witnessed by Wm. Colgan.

In 1845, Mother Catherine was back in Louisville at the orphanage, and the superior of Nazareth was Mother Frances Gardiner. Which of them agreed that the contract was not a good arrangement and obtained Ms. Smyth's official rescission is not known. Nor is it known whether she had ever lived, even briefly, in an

SCN house, nor what arrangements she made for her living after the rescission. It cannot have been easy for either Mother Catherine or Frances to raise and return the $500 previously loaned by Ms. Smyth.

William Colgan must have been a citizen of Louisville, probably a lawyer. It is possible, though less probable, that his name was actually Coleman; four gentlemen of that name are listed in the Louisville Directory in 1832; they appear to have been merchants in the city.

Letters to Sister Claudia Elliot

The following letters are clustered in order to create a composite picture of Mother Catherine's character and her collaborators as they are revealed in her relationship to one Sister and in the story of the mission to Nashville, Tennessee. In 1843 the SCN opened a boarding school, St. Mary's Academy, which had been promoted by Bishop Pius Miles and a member of his clergy and supported by various laypersons, who wanted a quality education for their daughters in a developing city. This event occasioned the start of a series of letters from Catherine to Sister Claudia Elliot, one of the most active Sisters at Nazareth, who was sent to help in the new mission with her numerous domestic skills, her native intelligence, and her selfless, warm personality (see Appendix A). These letters indicate that Catherine and Claudia had a close personal and collaborative relationship. They reveal not only the duties Catherine was fulfilling but also the feelings she had for her Sisters and their concerns. Through Claudia, readers come to know Catherine as a tender, even vulnerable, friend.

Dating of these letters is often incomplete and must be reconstructed by internal evidence matched with the known movements of both women. Claudia was sent to Nashville in January 1844; Catherine was then in her third full term as Mother at Nazareth. After completion of her term in August 1844, she soon returned to the orphanage in Louisville. The five letters here were sent either during this period of her office or very soon after her return to Louisville.

2-6

To Sister Claudia Elliott
St. Mary's Academy
Nashville, Tenn.

Nazareth Feb. 23d 1844
My dear Sister,

I received your letter from Louisville, & have heard from you twice since.—I am glad to hear you are so pleased with your new home, for you know, dear Sister, that my desire is to see you always happy.—Your brother James was here a few days ago; he did not know you were gone until he got here, but of course, he was satisfied.—He has lately got a letter from your brother in Misouri, your friends there were all well.—I suppose you know we have buried poor old aunt Winny.—She was the greatest object you ever saw, before she died.—Jane has another son—Matilda also.—We have had several short attacks of sickness lately, both with the girls & Sisters.—Give my best love to all the Sisters.—Does Sister Alice & you practice writing & reading together sometime; you must be sure to write to me as I told you. Our school is increasing.—Pray for me & believe me yours with sincere affection

Sr. Catherine

Rev. James Elliott, Claudia's brother, was a diocesan priest, pastor of St. Michael Church in Fairfield, responsible also for some mission parishes in surrounding counties. From there, he could visit Nazareth without great difficulty and apparently did so with some frequency for that time. Father James remained in Fairfield until the end of his life in 1871.

Winny, Jane, and Matilda were slaves, as was Uncle Solomon, cited in the next letter. The frequency of Catherine's reports to Claudia about slaves has been taken as evidence that their supervision had been Claudia's responsibility and that she had exercised it with kindness and much personal care for individuals. Other letters indicate that various slaves were fond of her, even wished to be sent to Nashville to work under her again.

Sister Alice Drury became an SCN in 1838 and made vows in 1840. Her missions are not listed before 1846, so she was probably at Nazareth. This letter puts her at Nashville in 1844, and she later served in St. Catherine, St. Vincent, Bethlehem, and La Salette Academies. Before her death in 1870, she held Catherine's role as superior of the Louisville orphanage.

2-7

Sister Claudia Elliot
St. Mary's Academy
Nashville, Tenn.

Nazareth, May 20th. 1844
My dear Sister,

I received your letter a few days ago, & you know how sincerely glad I was to get it, for I began to fear that you was not going to write at all. You need not be uneasy, I can read your writing very well. I think indeed that you have enough to keep you very busy. Still you must try & find time to write me a little letter sometimes. I wish I could give you gumelastic legs or some kind with which you could step even back to Nazareth for I assure you, I never did miss one so much in my life, & if the thing were to do over again, I believe I would not consent to it. But I suppose others are gratified, & it does not matter for me.

Your brother James came here the week after you left & was surprised to find you gone, but said he knew you were contented anywhere. He was well. & I gave him our old organ for his church in Taylorsville. They are very proud of it. He had a letter from your sister Julietta lately; all your relations were then well, but your brother

> Stephen had lost two of his children, & poor Eliza Hagar is left a widow. I will send you the letter by the first opportunity. Pray often for me, my dear Sister, & be sure I never will forget you. I don't have the headache very often of late. Thank God the family is very healthy at this time except uncle Solomon who is no better.—Our garden is beautiful at this time.—Do write again very soon.— Give my love [to] all who ask for me.—Your sincere friend Catherine

This letter reveals Catherine's attitude to personal friendship in relation to community life and mission. She evidently valued friendship highly and did not hesitate to share the pain of separation from a confidante whom she knew to share her selfless priorities.

Claudia and James Elliott had numerous siblings; he made a point to send her, through Nazareth, any news he got of them. Taylorsville, a small town near Fairfield, was one of his mission parishes, whose church he erected in 1830 and where he served until ill health forced his resignation from this mission in 1862.

Eliza Hagar cannot be positively identified. She may have been an alumna, a neighbor well known to the Nazareth Sisters, or possibly one of the Elliott family whose poor health was being reported to Claudia.

2-8

> Nazareth Nov. 15th
> My dear good Sister,
>
> I cannot let the Bishop go without scratching you a few lines—for such neglect always seems unkind or ungrateful on my part,—tho' I feel sure that you know I never forget you. Oh! It hardly seems right for me to be here without you. But so it is.—But in heart & soul we can be united. Your brother James was here lately & we always speak of you.—He was well & I think said you must write to

> him.—He looks to me, more like old times than anyone else. Give my love to Sis. Christine. I'll be glad to hear from her when she has time to write.—I hope your health is good.—Remember me to Mr. & Mrs. Mateer—& to all who ask for me.—We have a good many apples this year & are trying to keep them through the winter. Pray always for your old & sincere friend & Mother in Our Lord. Catharine

No year is given for this letter, and a year is hard to determine. Catherine obviously is writing from Nazareth, where an apple crop could be raised and consumed; yet in November 1843 Claudia was not yet in Nashville, and by November 1844 Catherine herself had left office and returned to Louisville.

The unidentified bishop was possibly Flaget, en route to visit Miles in Nashville, but is more likely Miles himself, still negotiating conditions for the SCN mission there. Sending letters in care of travelers was a common practice at this time, as it was generally more reliable than the postal service.

Sister Christine Coomes entered the SCN in 1825 and made vows in September 1826. After missions in Lexington and Louisville, she went to St. Mary's Academy in Nashville in August 1843 and stayed until the separation in August 1851, when she returned to Louisville. Her will in the Nazareth Archives shows that her part of her father's estate, once settled, was to go to Nazareth.

Mr. and Mrs. Mateer were evidently a Catholic couple in Nashville who had assisted the first Sisters on their arrival. They are mentioned in letters, as here, but the popular histories of the Leavenworth Sisters do not include their names. Catherine seems to hold them in continuing esteem.

2-9

> August 10, 1844
> Nazareth
> My very dear Sister,

I have only time to write you a few lines—to tell you how much I was delighted to get your long letter & to see you have improved so much in your writing & spelling.—You see now I was right when I told you practice was all you needed.—You need never be afraid to write. I can read your letters with great ease & always with much pleasure.—But don't write to me any more until you hear where I am stationed, for at this time I am but [a] loose piece of furniture. But I am truly glad to be so.—I never felt so much relieved in all my life.—I am sorry I could not finish your stockings. Sister Alice can finish them for you.—Give her my love & all the other Sisters too. Now pray for me.—& be sure I am not changed, but for you, I will ever be the same old friend.—Catherine
(Reverse) The thread left of your stockings

2-10

Sister Vincentia &
Sister Claudia
St. Mary Academy
Nashville, Tenn.
[no date except Dec. 12 on
Louisville Post Office Stamp]

My dear old friend & Sister Claudia,

Could you think for one moment that I had forgotten you?—No, you have been too faithful & untiring in your many acts of kindness to me, for me ever to forget you. & so far, I have never been deceived in you.—Therefore I must ever value your friendship.—I am now at the asylum with more than fifty orphans, one sweet little babe, most of the children are small.—It is now fixed for us to have Mass every Sunday & Wednesday, & very often we have it on other days too.—So you see times are getting better with us for spiritual help—& quite often we have a little sermon.—Pray for us that good [God?] may still provide for so many poor & destitute ones.—Give my best love to Sister Alice, I suppose she knows her sister is married.—I have not seen your brother for a good while.—You must be sure to write to me soon; if you neglect to practice, you will soon forget. My best respects to Mr. Mateer & his wife.—

Yours as I ever have been
Catherine

The year of this letter is almost surely 1844, three to four months after Catherine left office in August and returned to take charge of St. Vincent Asylum in Louisville. She is reconnecting with Claudia, describing fairly new conditions, so it is unlikely that a whole year has passed, to December 1845. Together, the two previous letters depict her emotional as well as geographic transition on leaving office as she revealed her feelings to a trusted friend. She had seen the community expand, had saved its distinct identity, and had guided it across the state line to Tennessee. She could now follow both her heart and her assignment to the place and little people where her heart was most at home.

2-11

Message on the back of a picture

This picture hung many years in the room of our venerable Father & Founder Bishop David. I now beg as a favor that it may always hang in the room of the Mother Supr. as a remembrance of his many virtues & his zeal for the spiritual & temporal good of Nazareth. July 1844—Pray for—

Sr. Catherine Spalding Mother of Nazareth

This request of Mother Catherine Spalding was pasted on the back of a picture of the Blessed Virgin Mary. Bishop David died in July 1841; it seems that Catherine had claimed and treasured the picture herself until the final month of her term of office, which would end in August 1844. Then, rather than take personal and permanent possession, she made it a memorial of David's role and counsel in the foundation and leadership of the congregation. Her request has been honored; the picture may still be seen in the office of the president of the SCN.

Letters to Mother Catherine Spalding, 1839–1844

While Mother Catherine's own letters in this period of her leadership are mainly concerned with the life and development of the congregation, of individual Sisters and the mission, the letters written to her form a record of her daily practical concerns for basic survival and support of all these entities. Of the letters printed here, six are from bishops, two from Academy alumnae; most are from Nazareth's agent and from parents of students dealing with their own concerns about curriculum or costs/payments. Read in groups, these letters create a context in which we may discover Catherine as busy administrator and capable manager, kind, compassionate, and firm. Within each group, chronology of the letters reveals their frequency, and in some cases even their tone of harassment.

2-A

Letter of Bishop Guy Ignatius Chabrat to Mother
Catherine Spalding
DLB 2, p. 45

January, 1839
My dear Mother Catherine,

I return you most sincere thanks for the good wishes you have expressed in your letter in my behalf. May the Lord in His mercy bless me and my labors this present year, but all for His greater honor and glory, for I do not desire to live unless His name be glorified by all I will do or say.

Permit me at the same time to assure you that it is from the bottom of my heart I wish you and all under your care all kinds of good success and prosperity, but above all an increase of zeal and fervor in the discharge of your religious duties—being well convinced that if you are all true sincere religious, temporal and spiritual blessings will never be wanting to anyone of you, whatever may be the obstacles and difficulties you may have to encounter. If God is for us, we need not care who is against us.

May the Lord then bless you all and make you prosper in all things, according to His will.

Recommending myself to your prayers, I remain, dear Mother Catherine,

Truly yours in Jesus Christ,

Guy Ig. Chabrat, Bsp. Coadjutor of Bardstown

Letter 2-3 above offers an account of Bishop Chabrat's character, role, and relationships within the diocese, including his apparent tiff with Catherine. In 1839, he was in charge during Bishop Flaget's absence in Europe. Catherine had evidently written him New Year's good wishes. His reply is not only cordial but clearly respectful of her character. Any friction between them had not yet occurred or must have been set aside in favor of friendly collaboration in the diocesan mission. That challenge would not last long, as Bishop Chabrat's eyesight began to fail so seriously that he returned to France for special treatment and finally stayed there in 1845.

Letters from Bishop Pius Miles in Nashville

The following three letters offer a record of the opening of the mission in Nashville, Tennessee. No letters of Catherine to Bishop Miles are extant, but his letters to her reveal the urgency he felt and tried to impose on her, as well as issues involved and negotiations required (or omitted) before the Sisters would be sent. The letters from Miles have been grouped for ease of reference in pursuing the story of this mission, which was not destined to endure but did occasion the move of some of Catherine's Sisters to the West as the first Sisters of Charity of Leavenworth, Kansas.

Richard Pius Miles, OP, was a Kentuckian by birth. His family was part of the Catholic congregation in Cox's Creek; he may well have known Catherine as she attended Mass and sacraments there with the Elder family. Ordained in 1816 as a Kentucky Dominican, Miles was reputed to be a devout, efficient, kind, and just priest and teacher. In 1838, he was appointed the first bishop of Nashville, a new diocese that included the entire state of Tennessee. Miles's task was truly a hardship mission, as he had very few Catholics and no diocesan priests at first, no fellow Dominicans, no money, and only one small, deteriorating brick church. Lonely, poor, and often ill, he rode circuit until, in 1841, he could predict that Catholic institutions might succeed—if only he could obtain religious personnel. Catherine the pioneer was favorably inclined to his request; but as a prudent manager, she was not hurried. Nashville is now a three-hour drive from Nazareth; it was then a journey of several days to a city of much anti-Catholicism and few material or spiritual resources.

2-B

Letter from Richard Pius Miles, Bishop of Nashville
DLB 1, p. 97 (abridged)

Nashville, Nov. 2nd, 1841
Dear Mother Catharine,

I reached home on the Saturday week after I had the pleasure of seeing you, in good health and much delighted as you may easily imagine to meet my affectionate children: you have seen the account of my reception, it will serve as an example for the diocese of Bardstown on some future occasion.

Your intention to make an establishment in Tennessee

. . . has excited great interest & I have every reason to believe that an establishment of the Sisters of Charity would be generally patronized. Several fine farms from one to five miles distant from Nashville have been offered for sale; if you could prevail on Father Haseltine . . . to call and see these farms, he would probably be able to select one that would suit you. . . . Come soon, as most of them will be sold at auction if not disposed of at private sale.

Be kind enough to write me and let me know what is your decision on this subject. I hope you will not disappoint me.

[Here the bishop details his meeting "an English lady of the order of St. Francis," his invitation to her to "come with me," and her letter reporting permission for "a colony" to establish themselves in his diocese. He has no obligation to the English "ladies" and greatly prefers the Americans from Nazareth. He puts the onus of choice on Catherine: "it remains with you to decide what shall be my reply to this letter. . . . I wish to hear from you as soon as convenient in order that I may know what to say to my lady. . . ."]

I have an offer from another part of Kentucky not far from you, but the authority under which they live are too complicated and their rule has been so often changed that I fear neither they nor I should be able to understand it.

Please remember me kindly to Rev. Mr. Haseltine & accept for yourself and community my Benediction together with my best wishes for your prosperity.

I am Madam, Sincerely yours in Christ,
Richard Pius,
Bishop of Nashville

P.S.: There are some valuable houses & lots for sale in the city, should you prefer that to the country.

2-C

Letter from Richard Pius Miles to Mother Catherine Spalding
DLB 1, p. 98

Nashville, Dec. 15, 1841
Dear Mother Catharine,

Your long expected and much esteemed favor of the 3rd ult. came to hand last evening, which I hasten to acknowledge.

I am greatly gratified to learn that you have resolved on establishing a branch of your institute among us, and I beg it as a favour that it be done as soon as possible. I think it would be better to establish yourselves first in the City and begin with a day school, and you will then have an opportunity of making future arrangements with more precision, and if possible I would wish you to begin at latest in the spring; the people are demanding your presence on all sides, and I would like to see them gratified while they are in the humour. They are disgusted with the want of discipline in the female institute of this City . . . , and could you come soon you would be in time to rescue the disappointed of that institute. I hope you will be able to come in the Spring, if so you would do well to rent a house, which should be attended to very soon; get some good judge to come and procure you one, the sooner the better; you could also make an establishment at Memphis, where they are very anxious to have you established.

Be kind enough to give this matter as early attention as possible and let me know the result. I am so frequently asked when you are coming that I am wearied with giving them the same indefinite answer: I don't know.

I am glad you consulted the Bishop on this matter as I would wish everything to be done with as much [illegible] as the nature of the case will admit.

If I had time I would beg your indulgence for the imperfect scrawl. . . . but the goodness of your heart will easily pardon the errors I have committed.

I recommend myself and my poor diocese to the pious prayers of your community.

With sentiments of highest esteem I am sincerely yours,

(Signed) + Richard Pius
Bishop of Nashville

The bishop Catherine consulted had to be Flaget, as he was the ultimate superior of the SCN, and the Sisters could hardly go outside his diocese without his approval. Had he not approved, friction could have developed between the two bishops as well as with the Sisters. Miles's letters clearly suggest his determination to have the mission and the polite pressure he put on Mother Catherine to accede to his wishes. The Nazareth Council voted on August 17, 1842, to open an Academy in Nashville with Sister Serena Carney as superior. St. Mary's Academy won patronage despite anti-Catholic opposition, and the bishop began to urge purchase of property. The SCN did not go to Memphis until many years later.

These early letters are a prelude to the drama that would develop later and cause the separation of the Nashville SCN from Nazareth.

2-D

Letter to Mother Catherine Spalding from Bishop Richard Pius Miles
DLB 1, pp. 108–109 (abridged)

Nashville (Tenn.)
Oct. 6th, 1843
Dear Mother Catherine,

Your much esteemed favor by Mr. Maguire has been duly received. I am much gratified in finding that you are disposed to come into the most important part of my proposition, that of helping us to pay for a house for the Sisters, and am glad to have it in my power to inform you that all the objections made on your part against the house, location, etc. of Judge Grundy, have been obviated by our having purchased another house.

[Bishop Miles then details the story of the purchase. Two months before, a Mr. Stephenson "pointed out to me a house which he thought would suit the Sisters, which house was to be sold on a certain day to the highest bidder; during your visit here I did not think of informing you about this" due to his illness and bewildered mind. Mr. Stephenson asked if he should bid on the desirable house, "assuring me at the same time that it was one of the best houses in the town for the Sisters, and that it could be had, as he thought on good terms. I told him without hesitation to bid for it, which he did and it was knocked off to him for $11,050, to be paid in one, two and three years without interest." He extols the location of the house near the church and near the Sisters' previous residence.]

The Sisters have got possession and are delighted with their new home, and even Sister Serena is convinced of its superiority over their former residence, although they thought before seeing it there was not one in Nashville that could equal it.

I have had many offers to take it off my hands and it is the universal opinion that we have made a most excellent and cheap purchase.

The first payment becomes due on the 25th of September next, at which time I sincerely hope you will be able to give us the assistance we ask: Mr. Conroy has kindly lent his name as our security, to whom and to Mr. Stephenson we shall never be able to be sufficiently grateful.

My health is pretty well restored and all the rest are well.

Allow me to thank you for the fine present you sent me. The idea must have originated in the poverty of my robe de chambre, which you saw during my sickness.

My compliments to Fr. Haseltine and all the community, whom I beg constantly to pray for me.

Yours sincerely in Christ,
Richard Pius Miles, Bp. of Nashville

Several Sisters went to Nashville in late 1842. They first lived in the home of the Stephensons; Mrs. Stephenson was a graduate of Nazareth Academy. They occupied a commodious house that had been the residence of Captain John Williams. The letter above, from October 1843, reveals that Catherine Spalding had visited Nashville herself to engage in the housing selection and that she had for some reason objected to Judge Grundy's house (too big or small? condition? location? price?). Only after the action of the bishop and Mr. Stephenson is Catherine informed of the purchase of yet another house and the three-year indebtedness. Miles's assurance that everyone is pleased and others are offering to buy the house seems a hint that he might sell it if Catherine does not agree to help pay for it. Miles has thus left Mother Catherine and the Council in a trap. They can't leave the Sisters homeless; the SCN are in a dilemma if they cannot readily pay for or do not approve the house for use as convent or school. Early annals record that the Sisters thus "reluctantly" became the owners of the property and were burdened with the inevitable financial worry.

"Mr. Maguire" refers to Father John Maguire, who in 1843 was pastor of the Cathedral of the Holy Rosary in Nashville. Sister Serena Carney remained superior of the Sisters until 1847. No specific description of Judge Grundy has been found; he must have been a fairly prosperous citizen and legal person, if his house was now considered big enough for consideration as an academy and convent.

Letters from Bishop Flaget

With all necessary authorization from Rome, Bishop Flaget moved the see city of his diocese from Bardstown to Louisville in 1841. He moved to the city himself in December, but was too ill to celebrate Christmas at St. Louis Church. In January 1842, he and Bishop Chabrat moved their residence to the rectory of that church, now the cathedral. Only in 1850 would it be replaced by the Cathedral of the Assumption, which still stands.

Evidently Catherine had healed any remnants of distress and division left from the 1841 independence crisis and had restored good feelings with the Sisters and their bishop. At this time, Flaget's health was declining seriously. He would soon need the aid of Martin John Spalding as his coadjutor bishop and overseer of the construction of the Louisville cathedral. Flaget's last public act would be the blessing of the cornerstone. Both his decline in health and his affection for Catherine, which only grew stronger, are reflected in this and the next letter. Coming as they did in the midst of the correspondence with Bishop Miles, these late letters from Flaget, the bishop with whom Catherine had collaborated for all the previous SCN missions, must have been a sort of balm, soothing and encouraging to her spirit.

Father Pruyere, named in the July letter, is certainly John M. Bruyere, listed in John Lyons's book of the archdiocesan priests. He was ordained in his native France, volunteered for the Bardstown diocese in 1841, moved with Flaget and Chabrat to Louisville, and was soon appointed professor at the diocesan seminary. Later he assisted Father Haseltine at the motherhouse and academy at Nazareth.

2-E

Letter to Mother Catherine Spalding from Bishop Flaget
DLB 1, p. 119b (written in French)

January 25, 1842
Very dear Mother Catherine,

I thank you very cordially for the new year's wishes you were so kind as to send me, on my arrival in Louisville.

It is at the Orphan Asylum I received them, and it is from this holy infirmary that I forward my thanks to you. Scarcely had I reached Louisville when a heavy cold settled in my chest occasioning blood spitting and violent pain in my side, but thanks to the care and prayers of your daughters, who are also mine, and to the prescriptions of the Doctor, I am out of danger and tolerably well. Towards the end of the week, I will probably go to my new episcopal lodging.—There I will have nothing else to do, but to pray for my dear Kentuckians, Catholics and Protestant. I bear them all in my heart, and in the thirty years that have elapsed since I came to Kentucky, I have never offered the Holy Sacrifice of the Mass without thinking of them. However, persons consecrated to God are justly recommended to Him in a very special manner.

My very dear Catherine, may God pour upon you, continually and in abundance, the spirit of St. Vincent de Paul that you may communicate it generously to your dear daughters. May your scholars and servants also receive their share.

Such are the sincere and daily invocations of—
Your old friend and very affectionate Father in God.
(signed) Benedict Joseph, Bp. of Louisville

2-F

On July 18, 1842, Bishop Flaget wrote to Mother Catherine (again in French)
DLB 1, p. 119b

Rev. and much revered Mother,

On account of the weakness of my head, and the oppression of my chest, I will be unable to go and celebrate the Feast of St. Vincent de Paul with you tomorrow. I send you a very worthy substitute, for my old person. In Mr. Pruyere, superior of my Seminary, who by his modesty and piety will repay you a hundredfold for my absence.

In the Mass which I hope to have the happiness of celebrating tomorrow, neither you, the Sisters, Mother General, nor your dear daughters of Charity will be forgotten.

I salute you all in the Sacred Heart of Jesus. I unite myself with all your family in the heart of St. Vincent, beseeching him to obtain for us, some rays of the great charity he had for the salvation of souls.

(signed) B. J. Bishop of Louisville

Letters from Former Students

Letters to Mother Catherine from Nazareth alumnae are not numerous but are revealing of the former students' typical feelings about her and her past and present relationships with them. Especially if they had received religious instruction directly from her and even been sponsored in baptism, the affection expressed is occasionally very intense. Personality and the epistolary style of the time sometimes combined to create a gush of nostalgic, florid, and even sentimental rhetoric. Other letters are more businesslike or in a friendly way transmit family news, which the writers expected her to receive with interest or concern. Few letters of Catherine to alumnae are extant; most seem to have been responses to particular situations previously narrated to her. She offers affectionate remembrance and counsel, in appropriately warm yet restrained style.

2-G

DLB 1, pp. 87–88 (abridged)

Cincinnati
June 17th, 1841

Addressed to:
Mother Catherine Spalding
Superior of Nazareth Academy
Near Bardstown, Ky.

Surely, my dear Mother, you have breathed some spell, some witching influence upon this morning's air, to chain my thoughts to Nazareth and thee. How much and how fervently I think of thee, dear Mother, only One can know.

Thy remembrance has stolen gently and silently—a brilliant and stainless gem—to the depths of my heart of hearts. Who knows that its serene light may but consecrate what is there unhallowed.

Do not suppose me extravagant in my expressions this morning—remember—I inhale my enthusiasm from the spell-frought air: but indeed at no time, in no place can I contemplate thee; or those scenes with which thou art inseparably connected by the tender ties of association, without those glowing emotions of love and friendship which even the highest language of enthusiasm will fail to embody.

Now, Mother, do not permit your imagination to present you with your humble protégé in the mock-heroine style—her eyes "in a fine frenzy rolling," for nothing could be more false. She wears the same calm, (and as some of my friends have remarked) cold exterior, your pauvre petite God-daughter always wore.

And right thankful is she to Nature for the kindly veil, which she has thrown around her heart, for it conceals affection which would seem worthless in the eyes of the many, but which are notwithstanding inexpressibly precious to her. Pardon my egotism.

Never, dearest Mother, tell me again that your friendship for me is inefficient, that it can never be, while it continues to exist. I do assure you its efficiency has been tested more than once; it has wrought, in silence and solitude, many cures.

How often in the visions of the night does Nazareth rise before me . . .

[In a long paragraph of emotive diction and imagery, she cites locations at Nazareth dear to her memory:] . . . groves of the bee-haunted locust, . . . parlor with the multitude of blushing roses peeping shyly into its open windows;—its little chapel where I laid my heart on the One true shrine, where I bound upon my soul that faith which it will carry with it into Eternity, and that quiet secluded room too called "Mother's Room" where I listened to thy gentle teachings. . . . Nazareth, thou art a spot clustering with sacred memories. Mother, do you know I am selfish enough to wish that my place at N—— should remain vacant, at least while you are its inmate. . . . I have not yet read the work you recommended but will embrace the earliest opportunity of doing so.

Do not be shocked that I should perpetrate such a scrawl as this. . . . . I have no taste for pretty letters. . . . . Please remember me to all, dear Mother. My aunts and uncles bid this "wee bit" paper bear you a heavy burden of love and respect, and I have charged it to tell you how devotedly

I remain your child in God.

A.A.L.

Often think of me in your prayers

A.A.L. is almost certainly Almira Lowe, who was a pupil of Nazareth Academy from 1838 to 1840, when she graduated. Academy records give her name, home location, academic information, and information of her later life. The Register of Baptisms at Nazareth recorded the baptism of Almira Ann Lowe, seventeen years of age, on January 27, 1840, by the Reverend S. H. Montgomery. Father Montgomery and Mother Catherine Spalding were her sponsors. Academy records further state that she married a Mr. La Boyleux and that he died in 1850.

The Catholic Directory for 1839 reveals that a Reverend Stephen Montgomery was pastor of St. Mary's in Covington, Kentucky.

Miss Lowe's circumstances as student and convert sufficiently explain her devotion to Mother Catherine. It is a fair example of other letters Catherine may have received from alumnae she had sponsored.

2-H

Letter to Mother Catherine Spalding from A. E. Crittenden
DLB 11, p. 144a

Bolivar, Tenn.
April 7, 1843
Dear Mother,

I received a note from the Treasurer of your Institution today; which took me entirely by surprise. It was a call for the am't due for my board and tuition while I enjoyed the advantages afforded by the instructions of those excellent Sisters. I will explain why it surprised me.

When I returned home, I acquainted my mother with the fact that I intended discharging the debt myself. She positively forbade my doing any such thing, and retained the Bills, insisting that she would satisfy them herself. She never mentioned anything respecting the affair after I left her, and I supposed that it was entirely settled. She is now married to a gentleman by the name of Bonomt, and resides at Metropolis City, Illinois. She has the Bills, and I have no doubt intends the payment of them.

Write to her and let me know the result. I have written by the same post to her upon the subject.

Yours respectfully,
E. Crittenden

(Addressed to: Miss Catherine Spalding, Mother Sup'r of the Institution of Nazareth, near Bardstown, Kentucky.)

Few names are more notable (and plentiful) in Kentucky history than Crittenden, but A. E., the writer of the above letter, cannot be certainly identified, nor can her story be verified. Names and dates all conflict.

The only Crittenden daughter in Nazareth's records is Ann Mary, enrolled in 1825–1826, almost twenty years before the date of A. E.'s letter and the bill she had just received. Ann Mary was the daughter of Mr. and Mrs. John J. Crittenden of Frankfort, Kentucky; her father thus was almost surely the famous Kentucky citizen and lawyer who held almost every important elective or appointed position in state and federal government, refusing only his chance for a third-party nomination to the United States presidency in 1860. His first of three wives bore seven children and died in 1824, before Ann Mary went to Nazareth. His second wife brought three children to the family and bore two more; she would hardly have been the mother cited in the letter, who in 1826 might have insisted on paying but had not done so by 1843. Nor did either of John Crittenden's later widow-wives leave him to marry someone else and move to Illinois. In 1843, Crittenden was a U.S. senator from Kentucky; his daughter Ann Mary was probably already married to Mr. Chapman Coleman (the Louisville merchant?). It is possible, of course, that Crittenden was the married name of the Miss A. E. who was educated at Nazareth.

Whose daughter then (or daughter-in-law) was A. E. Crittenden? And did the bill ever get paid? Wide conjectures among so many offspring and relationships are possible, but so far cannot advance to certainties.

Letters from Francis McKay

Francis McKay was Nazareth's agent in Louisville for purchasing many sorts of goods and for collecting payments due to Nazareth. Letters and financial reports he sent to Mother Catherine indicate that this gentleman had some importance to the developing academy and religious community.

McKay's importance in the civic and commercial community apparently made him a busy and trusted person but did not lead to his biography in an encyclopedia or any later documentation beyond such mentions as Ben Webb gives: that he was "a prominent Catholic," one of the early Irish and American-born Catholic residents of Louisville, and a large contributor to construction of the Cathedral. Fortunately, the Nazareth Archives preserves a copy of an 1845 advertisement for "Nazareth Female Academy," inviting inquiries to "Rev. J. Haseltine, Superior" or "Miss Catherine Spalding, Mother Superior" and naming "F. McKay, merchant of Louisville, Kentucky," as "agent for the Academy, to whom remittances may be made." He may have been one partner in the firm of McKay & Davy, listed in the Louisville Directory of 1832 as merchants on Main Street between Fourth and Fifth Streets. As Nazareth's purchasing agent, he dealt with many other merchants named in his reports; as debt collector, with many parents or guardians. If these persons are not further identified, no record of them has been found.

McKay's letters to Catherine are often accompanied by lists of purchases or collections made on behalf of the academy. He had to manage money carefully, arrange for delivery to Nazareth of large items and boxes sent for students, and pursue some parents for long-unpaid accounts. As the years go on, these letters and lists become numerous and repetitive, though still important as historic records. Because of their number and similarity, they have been grouped below and in subsequent chapters; some have been abridged, others merely summarized. All can be read in full in the Nazareth Archives. McKay's business relationship with Nazareth may have been quite casual and trusting or very generous; no mention is made of fees paid to him.

2-I

Letter to Mother Catherine Spalding from Francis McKay
DLB 11, p. 34

Louisville, Ky
April 19, 1842
Dear Madam,

> I send per wagon 30 bushels Blue Meshane Potatoes. Also 2 bbls. lime, called white lime for Whitewashing, and 1 bbl. of altar wine. I was buying a bbl. for the college; the Bishop also got one and recommended it so highly that I concluded to buy one for you. It is also a good table wine. Jim makes up the remainder of the load with sand. I have not been able to get you any wheat yet. There is none coming to market, it will be very scarce and will advance in price as well also flour. If there is any wheat in your neighborhood, buy it, for it will certainly rise in price. I will buy any that offers here; if you do not want sugar or coffee for two weeks, you need not send Jim down next week. Sugar has taken a sudden rise of one cent a pound. I see no good reason for the advance and think it will recede again. Kavanaugh planted the trees; they will decorate my little plantation very much and I am under obligation to you for them. I bought the loaf sugar from Cody. He showed me a good sample. I will send you another bbl. of good sugar.
>
> Very respectfully etc.
> Fras. McKay

As purchasing agent, McKay evidently had significant room for his own judgment about quality and cost of goods and freedom to offer his counsel and to make purchases at his own discretion. In the economy of the era, and in the uncertainty of tuition payments, the concern about the rise of a single penny in price is revealing and understandable, and he clearly felt accountable to Catherine for his selections.

Transportation of bushels and barrels to Nazareth was evidently done by "Jim," perhaps a white workman or a slave of Nazareth, considered reliable enough to drive the wagon back and forth on these errands and to deliver the whole purchase or shipment intact. "Kavanaugh" is not a typical slave name; he was probably a gardener on McKay's "little plantation," which was probably on the outskirts of Louisville, near enough for the merchant to conduct his business and send his reports, these probably also by Jim.

2-J

Letter to Mother Catherine Spalding from Francis McKay
DLB 11, p. 33

Louisville, Ky.
Oct. 4, 1842
Nazareth Academy,
To Francis McKay Dr.

2 bbls. Lard oil 81½ Galls. @ 62½	$50.94
½ chest of G.P. Tea	41.60
4 kegs white lard	9.00
012 bxs. Gloss	6.50
2 " "	8.50
129 lbs. iron assorted	6.89
	123.43

Dear Madam,

Above is a bill of sundries sent by you, the balance of the lard, he will take in sand, the account of Martin & Griswold was paid long ago. I have not paid the balance due Oldham, but suppose it was paid in settlement with Speed for work on 5th Street House.

Very respectfully etc.,
Fras. McKay

This letter piques one's curiosity about the nature, cost, and use of the goods listed: the quantity of lard used in cooking at the time, "gloss" (furniture polish or a product for ladies' personal adornment?), and the uses of so much iron (at about five cents a pound—for railings, porch steps, fireplaces, kitchenware?). Who needed or provided sand, and for what purpose?

Martin and Griswold have not been identified. Oldham seems to have been a merchant; he may also have been the father of Penelope Oldham, who entered Nazareth from Louisville at twelve years old, but stayed less than a year. James S. Speed is noted in the archives for writing Mother Catherine a letter in 1839 concerning Miss Oldham's admission as student at Nazareth. Nothing else is clear about the Oldham–Speed connection except that they both did something to put Nazareth in their debt.

The *Louisville Encyclopedia* cites two James Speeds. The better known was a lawyer, politician, and great friend of Abraham Lincoln. James Stephens Speed, however, is more likely the person named by McKay, as he was first an employee and then a partner in the firm of Pickett and Speed, in building and railroad contracting. He became mayor of Louisville, then the target of the Know-Nothing party for his Catholicism (he was a convert). He was displaced in the election of 1855, occasion of the Bloody Monday riots.

The Fifth Street House must have referred to the property bought when Presentation (or the "Fifth St. School") came up from the basement of St. Louis Church. What work was done is unknown, but transferring a school to an old residential building must have necessitated some repairs and renovations, for which any of these men might have been a contractor.

2-K

Letter to Mother Catherine Spalding from Francis McKay
DLB 11, p. 29

Louisville, Ky.
Oct 17, 1842
Nazareth Academy,
To Francis McKay, Dr.

2 bxs Rio coffee 331, 10¾	$35.59
3 bbls molasses 112 cents	28.12
1 keg nails	6.25
1 bucket	.38
	$70.34

Dear Madam:

Above is a bill of coffee, molasses, etc., sent by Jim; the camphine has not arrived yet, it is a very difficult article to get. I had to send to New York for it, will send it as soon as it arrives.

Very respectfully, etc.,
(Signed) Fras. McKay

This notice, only two weeks after the previous one, suggests the consumption and expense of a quantity of food and other goods. The supplies listed are practical; and coffee at little more than ten cents a pound seems remarkable to the modern eye. A dictionary definition of camphene as a "solid terpene" that looks and smells like camphor is not very helpful; such compounds are variant hydrocarbons distilled from evergreen and fir trees into a form of oil used for medicinal purposes. In the nineteenth century, camphene was also used as lamp fuel, but was limited in use because it was explosive. If so used at Nazareth, it is understandable that prayer for protection against fire became a community custom.

2-L

Letter to Mother Catherine Spalding from Francis McKay
DLB 11, p. 25

Louisville, Ky.
Dec. 21, 1842
Dear Madam

I got the parlor stove at Bridgeford's, and also got the seven plate stove there. He took your description of the pipes and (said) he will send the exact length etc. The note I gave for Mallet was $30. I send a box from John McCauley for his niece, Miss James. I have not yet seen Murphy.

Very respectfully etc.,
Fras. McKay

Does the tea please you?

Given the date of this letter, one sees the need for adequate heating and cooking equipment, and consideration of the details of size and cost required for the numbers of people at Nazareth. Catherine and McKay had limited choices of suppliers. James Bridgeford established in 1829 a small foundry at Seventh Street and the river; it remained there until 1900, manufacturing high-quality stoves, ranges, tinware, mantels, and grates. Obviously, details of such equipment had to be specified and noted for durability and economy. Mallet and Murphy have not been identified; a John McCauley worked in Louisville in printing, but the only recorded student named James did not enter Nazareth until 1844.

2-M

Letter to Mother Catherine Spalding from Francis McKay
DLB 11, p. 20 (abridged)

Payments made to Francis McKay on account of
Nazareth Academy from
19 July 1842 to Jan. 18, 1843.

July 24	Amt.Miss Ware's acct.	$28.75
Aug. 4	" " Belknap "	24.07
" 9	" " Hirnsobn	24.29
Oct. 12	Rec. on acct. Gen. Rawlins	100.00
"	"From Bill New Orleans	100.00
"	"Rec. from E. Dorsey on acct.	100.00
Pd. Bk. Ky for 94 collecting sum		187.39
Nov. 28 Jas. D. Breckenridge acct. __		82.00
		$954.18

Dear Madam,

I enclose [for] you Sander's notes and above you have a list of collections. Mr. Frabue says he will pay in two weeks. Mr. Hewitt will be here next month. Cody gave me a draft on New Orleans for $200 which I sent for collection. S. Owen has given a draft on the South which I have also sent for collection.

Very respectfully etc.,
Fras. McKay

McKay evidently sent an annual summation of the student accounts he had collected (or not). This abridged list is a fair sample of his mode of accounting to Mother Catherine. The entire list gives fourteen amounts dated from July 24 to November 28, 1842; apparently no further payments were made before the New Year. The smallest amount recorded was $24.07, the largest the $187.39 deposited in the Bank of Kentucky for ninety-four collections. The largest single amounts were the three for $100 each. Even considering the greater purchasing power of a dollar in that era, the total of less than $1,000 for a year suggests the poverty and daily concern in which Catherine and the Sisters lived and conducted their mission.

It is not clear if "Sander's notes" are his bill to Nazareth or his payments for his daughter Sarah. Mr. Frabue is probably James Trabue, whose daughters Mary and Sarah had just entered Nazareth in September 1842; they left after one year. John Hewitt had opened a daguerreotype studio in Louisville in 1842; no Hewitt daughter is listed in the register then. In 1840, William Belknap started a nail and boilerplate business in Louisville. Maria Owen, daughter of Mr. and Mrs. Shapley Owen of Louisville, was a student at Nazareth in 1842. No Cody, student or parent, has been located, but he evidently was in debt to Nazareth. Cody and Owen had given McKay drafts (or checks) on two Southern banks, which he then had to send to them for collection and deposit in Nazareth's Kentucky bank.

2-N

Letter to Mother Catherine Spalding from Francis McKay
DLB 11, p. 13 (abridged)

Louisville, Ky.
June 10, 1843

[The initial—and confusing—portion of this letter concerns notes presented and partial payments made to, or to be expected from, two men, Crayier and Weyell. The rest details the difficulties of getting payment from Mr. Phillips and Mr. Rudd.]

I spoke to Mr. Phillips twice about [the accounts]. He said that Mr. Rudd was sole executor, and would pay them. I also spoke to Rudd and he said he had not yet seen any money from the estate but would pay it when he did receive the money. . . . Mr. Rudd likes to hold on to money as long as he can. . . .

Very respectfully etc.,
Fras. McKay

Few of the persons named in this letter or the next can be identified. But they present a fine mix of the issues and annoyances that dogged the struggle to keep Nazareth solvent: minuscule payments on big debts, counterfeit money, failed fortunes and bankruptcy, unsettled estates and inheritances, pleasant manners smoothing unexplained delays in payments needed to support both education at Nazareth and the orphans in Louisville. The connection of the Phillips and the Rudds is surely that James Rudd's wife was Nannie Phillips Rudd, a prominent and outspoken woman among Louisville's Catholics. Mr. and Mrs. Rudd were both leaders in the Catholic community. James Rudd was a city councilman, a trustee of the St. Louis Church built in 1830, a delegate to the Kentucky Constitutional Convention of 1849, where he defended Catholic immigrants against restrictive measures, and a contributor to the construction of the Cathedral in 1850. Mrs. Rudd was among those women most supportive in the founding of the orphanage. That they should cause Catherine any financial distress seems surprising.

2-O

Letter to Mother Catherine Spalding from Francis McKay
DLB 11, p. 14 (summarized)

Louisville, Ky.
June 22, 1843

5 bales mops	1536/75—1460 @ 3 cents	$43.80
L box stearin candles	32 @ 25 cents	8.00
		$51.80

[The letter accompanying this bill concerns the price of candles and payment issues. Fifteen persons are named. Some seem to be recipients of payments from Nazareth; most are debtors to Nazareth. Reasons given for delay include a recent marriage, a possible lawsuit, and a failed attempt to get a bankruptcy.] These Phillips, etc., are a strange set.

Very respectfully etc.,
Fras. McKay

I send per wagon a box for Miss Indiana Hughes, a box for Miss M. McGuire, and a bundle for Miss A. Shrader.

Stearin, a solid white compound made from several chemical processes and reactions from animal and vegetable fats, was used in candles. Since it was not cheap by any standard, the candles in this purchase were probably destined for altar use in the chapel.

Some of the names cited in this letter can be found in the register of students, though not all coincide with the 1843 date. Assessing indebtedness would have been made more difficult by the departure of some students after only a few months or even less. Reasons for these very short stays are not given, only excuses for nonpayment. Reading these, Father Haseltine, at least, may have found some amusement in making an analogy to Luke 14:20: "I have married a wife and therefore I cannot come."

2-P

Letter to Mother Catherine Spalding from Francis McKay
DLB 11, p. 19 (summarized)

Louisville, Ky.
Sept. 28, 1843
Nazareth Academy,

2hhds. of sugar	1933 63/84	$123.23
½ chest G.P. Tea	77/12 65/90	58.50
½ do y hysado	71—12 59—65	38.35
1bbl. No. 3 macker[e]l		10.00
LBu. Pepper		2.82
2kegs nails		10.00
1cask cheese		11.83
		$254.73

Dear Madam.

[The letter comments on the quality and comparative prices of items purchased, indicating that McKay was regularly employing his wisdom and freedom in decision to select goods and foods to be sent to Nazareth. He also reports on two delinquent accounts.]

Very respectfully etc.,
Francis McKay

I send a box for Miss Harper.

2-Q

Letter to Mother Catherine Spalding from Francis McKay
DLB 11, p. 11 (summary)

[The letter, dated July 18, 1844, lists purchases of sugar, salt, and wine, and drayage for loading the wagon; total charges: $215.49. It also reports on the possible purchase of a mangle and the making of a marble tombstone.]

2-R.

Letter to Mother Catherine Spalding from Frances McKay
DLB 11, p. 12

List of unpaid accounts from Nazareth Academy since 20th July, 1843 to July 20, 1844.

rend. Oct. 18, 1843	Balance
Miss America Shrader " " " "	$ 24.25
" Matilda Bland " " " "	40.16
" Ophelia Harper " " " "	104.59
" Margaret & A. Gaines " " " "	65.00
" Do " Mar. 4, 1844	163.87
" Ophelia Harper" " " "	79.00
" Ann & M. Dorsey " " " "	142.39
" Sophia Taylor " " " "	57.81
" Mary Agnes Hamilton " " " "	.63
" Florida Rawlins " " " "	90.09
	$767.79

Louisville, Ky.
July 20, 1844
Madam C. Spalding.
Dear Madam,

Enclosed you will find my account with Nazareth Academy for the past year, showing a balance to Credit of Academy of $520.80, . . . which I think you will find to be correct. The deduction made on Miss Krasey's account was for a Prayer book and ribbon returned and the time from which she left school until the end of the session. . . . G. Rawlins . . . has not yet paid after deduction from the

> account $16 for French and dancing lesson[s], which he said he had prohibited to you in person. You will perceive that $100 more has been made on the claim against Murray Phillips, which reduces it to a small balance. . . . . Should there be any error in the account, they will be promptly corrected. . . . . I bespeak you a happy and creditable examination, exhibition etc.,
>
> Very respectfully etc.,
> Francis McKay

However much the multiple details of the annual accounts may have wearied Mother Catherine (when they did not amuse), they must have renewed her sense of gratitude for her agent and the wisdom of hiring him to handle these complex and unpredictable accountings.

Two men named Phillips had daughters at Nazareth. Henry Phillips enrolled his very young Emma twice, with three years between enrollments, in the 1850s. Murray Phillips had three daughters at Nazareth, but not until the 1870s. McKay has cited the Phillips as unreliable for payments; here Murray Phillips seems to have made strides in handling his debts, whatever their source.

Letters from Parents and Guardians

Though Nazareth Academy had been growing in numbers and quality ever since its transplant to the new motherhouse campus, the early 1840s was a significant period in its development and in Mother Catherine's life as its leader. The influx of young women from Louisiana and other Deep South states was now an established expectation, and some adaptations to their culture and to the expectations of their parents had to be negotiated. One attraction of Nazareth was the promise of instruction in "the solid branches," accompanied by such "accomplishments" as music, dancing, fluency in French, and gracious deportment. Letters to Catherine often specify a parent's values and requirements for the daughter's curriculum. Specific considerations for her comfort, clothing, personal economy, and travel home may be added. The one overriding topic, however, is the issue of payment—its possibility, timing, and entanglement with debtors, agents, and banks. While these letters reveal the difficulties and stresses that were Mother Catherine's daily fare, they also show the general success of the mission, the satisfaction with the education offered, and the parents' appreciation of her maternal care of her young charges.

2-S

Letter from Stephen Sanders
DLB 11, p. 73 (abridged)

Louisville, Ky.
Sept. 8, 1840
(Miss) Catherine Spalding,

Having this favorable opportunity of sending my daughter Sarah Ann in the care of the Rev. Mr. Coomes, I embrace it the more freely knowing that she will directly be under your care; and if it accords with your will and I live, I wish her to remain with you until she finishes her education. I have the misfortune to inform you that I am in bad health and . . . I am at the present without money and am unable to say at this time when I will have; upon this subject I spoke to Mr. Haseltine. He promised to have a conversation with you and write to me. . . . If it should please Providence to restore my health again I will satisfy you promptly, if not, I have a sufficiency of permanent property out of which you will be paid to the utmost farthing and this you may keep in your possession, which will be good to you as my note for whatever her expenses may amount to. . . . After reading this if you are not aprized of my situation in life, I hope you will enquire to your satisfaction and answer this by the first opportunity. If you receive her, I will leave her education principally to your superior judgment, except the French language that

I think will be of little use to her, at any rate until she has finished her other studies.

Yours with respect,
Stephen Sanders

Sarah Ann Sanders, daughter of Catholic parents in Louisville, entered Nazareth Academy in October 1839 at age twelve; in 1840 she must have been returning with the escort of a priest. She remained at the academy until July 1842. No other Sanders is listed in the academy register.

Her father's letter is one of many sent to Catherine about nonpayment of the school debt, yet one of the few that specify an alternative mode of payment or that invite investigation of the writer's finances and probabilities. An academy financial ledger of the era indicates that Sarah's account was eventually paid in full. Sanders's letter also suggests the era's idea of a parent's rights to specify curriculum. In this case the issue is the often disputed value of fluency in French: was it the mark of a completely educated lady or a mere waste of study time and tuition?

The Reverend Coomes who escorted Sarah to school could be any of the several priests of that name who were in Louisville about this time; the likeliest is the Reverend Walter S. Coomes, who had served in Nelson County and in 1840 was assistant at the soon-to-be Cathedral in Louisville.

2-T

Letter from J. S. Silsbee to Mother Catherine Spalding
DLB 11b, p. 67

Columbus, Ohio
January 11, 1842
Dear Madam,

Your letter came safe to hand yesterday. I am very sorry things have turned out as they have. You should have received your money long since, but we were most sadly

> disappointed in this town. We have not made enough here to pay our board. I was certain after we had been open here for a week or two, I should be able to pay you; but the money did not come in, and I have tried every way to raise it for you so far, but in vain. On the 22nd of February, we have a large Whig convention here which will bring some 10 or 12ppp [12,000?] strangers in town, and then most certainly we shall receive some good houses, and I will take the money out and send it to you. I should be sorry to have Frank sent away, for it would cost us considerable trouble to go and get her, besides she might be misused, and until the 22nd we should not have money to go after her, and people would remark saying that our child was sent away from school because we could not pay our debts. I know 'tis unpleasant for you as the trustees look to you for pay, but I do assure you most truly we have not been able to pay you so far at any hazard. However you, of course, will have to use your own privilege either to keep her or send her away, but if unfortunately you should be obliged to send her away, let us know by letter when you intend to do so, and if you should do so of course I'll pay the arrears as soon as possible. There is no offence. We feel much indebted to you for what you have already done for us. Mrs. Silsbee sends you her best love. Tell Frank that pa and ma is well, and wish much to see her. Our best regards to Sister Emily and Father. There, I've forgot his name.
>
> Yours truly,
> J. S. Silsbee
>
> P.S. We had a democratic convention here last week. It was a failure. They held their meetings at night, and did not come to the Theatre.

The Internet offers a long and amusing article about a Joshua S. Silsbee (or Silsby), a stand-up comedian who traveled and performed throughout the United States and British Isles. Originally from New York, he was billed as a "Yankee comedian" and assures a prospective employer and manager, "I have new Yankee pieces and would be a strong card for you." This letter to Catherine seems to be from this "Josh Silsbee," written after several unsuccessful performances.

On August 10, 1840, Silsbee married Martha M. Trowbridge, a widow and actress who traveled and often performed with him. Martha Trowbridge's daughter Frances ("Frank"), would be Joshua's stepdaughter. She is registered at Nazareth Academy from November 1840 to November 1841; the letter, however, indicates a later stay and a debt of longer standing. Given their lifestyle, her itinerant parents were very likely anxious to have her securely cared for in a boarding school, even if beyond their means. The academy financial ledger for 1837–1854 satisfies one's curiosity, however, by indicating that the account for Frances Trowbridge was paid in full. Silsbee apparently was sincere in his desire to pay his debt to Nazareth.

This letter is evidence that Mother Catherine had to make some hard decisions about appropriate enrollment, by the girl's need rather than the respectability and financial or social situation of her parents.

2-U

Letter to Mother Catherine Spalding from D. Comstock
DLB 11, p. 68

New Orleans
July 18, 1842
Mother Catherine Spalding.
Madam,

I have taken the liberty to inclose herein a letter containing a small remittance to Sarah Barker for the purpose of paying her expenses home. Will you please place her under the care of someone who will take charge of her and will see to placing her under the charge of one of the captains of the mail boat at Louisville. I had intended to have come up myself but cannot possibly do so. I am sorry I could not have sent someone for Sarah, but this was out of my power, also I hope she will get home safe. I regret more than anything that has occurred in my life perhaps that I am all this time unable to pay my account at Nazareth. I have never since I have been poor, until now, seen the time that I could not raise a few hundred dollars, but it is a mortifying truth, altho. I do not owe one hundred dollars in the world besides my account at Nazareth. I cannot at this time raise that amount. I have steamboat stock. I have payments and attachments against property, but I cannot raise money on any of them now. I hope, however, to be able to pay you in full in a short time; and feel assured I shall, the moment that I can raise it, forward the same to you without the least delay.

Very respectfully your obt. servant,
D. Comstock

Sarah Barker entered Nazareth Academy at age twelve in November 1839; she left on July 27, 1842, shortly after the date of this letter. It is not clear whether she had completed a course of study or was withdrawn for lack of ability to pay, or what was her relation to D. Comstock of New Orleans. She was a Protestant, daughter of parents resident in Madison, Indiana. Comstock may have been her appointed guardian or a relation or family friend. He evidently felt himself rather than her parents to be responsible for her outstanding account. Old financial records at Nazareth list her account as paid in full.

2-V

Letter to Mother Catherine Spalding from A. Harper
DLB 11, p. 69

St. Louis
August 15, 1842

Miss Catherine Spalding,

I leave here tomorrow for Louisville for my daughter and am sorry my time will not admit of my visiting Nazareth. You will please forward my bill to Mr. McKay and I will call on him and settle it.

I will determine about Ophelia's returning again when I reach Louisville; the times are now so hard that I feel like I shall not be able to pay for her education at Nazareth. Write me what you will take her for per annum, including the making of her clothes payable at the expiration of each year. I will write you from Louisville again.

My respects to all my friends,
In haste your friend,
A. Harper

Forward my bill immediately on receipt of this as my stay will be but a few days in the city.

The Academy Register offers names of three students named Harper—Isabella, Ann, and Ophelia. All began at ages twelve or thirteen, remained for several years, and are cited as Catholic graduates. Ophelia, the subject of this letter, did remain at Nazareth from 1840 to 1845, and her account is listed as paid in full. She became a Religious of the Sacred Heart and died in 1850. The parents—of one or all three?—were Captain and Mrs. Andrew Harper, residents of Scott County, Kentucky. Harper's letter to Catherine may well serve as an example of the nineteenth-century form of an application for financial aid: he pleads his need but offers no specific financial figures to support it.

2-W

Letter to Mother Catherine Spalding from Mary Lyle
DLB 11, p. 144

Natchez, March 6, 1843

Dear Madam

As our girls are on the eve of leaving for Nazareth to be placed under your maternal care, I shall just write you a few general directions with regards to their studies and other little matters.

We wish them to have a thorough knowledge of the solid branches before they pay much attention to the accomplishments or extra branches. I do not consider a young lady accomplished unless she is well versed in History, Geography, Arithmetic, and Grammar, practical as well as theoretical. They both have a habit of expressing themselves very incorrectly; they are acquainted with the rules. I am pleased generally with the progress they have made; their penmanship is pretty good, but sadly deficient in Orthography. Mary Ann says she never could spell well, and thinks she never will, but she is mistaken in that matter; they read pretty well. I wish particular attention paid to the vocal part of Mary Ann's music. I think if her teacher will insist upon her opening her mouth, she will in time sing pretty well, but as it is she leaves too much of the labor for her nose to perform; with regard to Jane, her papa says, if her teacher finds she cannot learn, to discontinue it, but if possible, he would rather she would perform French. Now for the externals. The doctor wishes them taught to dance. Mary Ann has a habit of sitting too much bent over, or rather has what is called the "Grecian bend," which I wish corrected if possible. Hoping that they may do well the next year as they did the last, I conclude by wishing you health, happiness and prosperity.

Respectfully your friend,
Mary Lyle

P.S. Doctor wishes you to furnish them with whatever clothes they may need. We think it a better plan than to get them here, for you know best what quality of dress is suitable. M. L.

Mary Ann and Martha Jane Lyle both entered Nazareth in November 1841, at ages twelve and ten; they left in July 1844. Dr. and Mrs. Hugh Lyle of Natchez, Mississippi, were prosperous Protestant parents who wanted their daughters to flourish as examples of finely educated and accomplished young Southern ladies. Many or most parents who sent their daughters up from the Deep South held similar expectations of what a Nazareth education would accomplish.

2-X

Letter to Mother Catherine Spalding from James Trabue
DLB 11, p. 83

Louisville
March 11, 1843

Bed
2 pillows
4 pillow slips
2 prs. Sheets
1 pr. Blankets
1 quilt
1 spread

Should it be convenient the outside covering can be laid away until the bed returns when it can be used again.

James Trabue

This communication was not bizarre for its time. Bed and bedding were often sent with a student if the parents could afford the materials and shipping and were sufficiently concerned for the comfort of their student daughter. This custom may have been more welcome as Nazareth's enrollment of boarders increased.

2-Y

Letter to Mother Catherine Spalding from T. Jules Fazende
DLB 11, p. 84

New Orleans, Parish of Jefferson
May 6, 1843
Miss C. Spalding,

I have been honored with your esteemed favor of the 28th March last, I have taken due notice of its interesting contents concerning my daughter, Aglazir. I see with pleasure that not only she has enjoyed a good health until now, but deserving also by her assiduity in study, some praises of you. I beg of you to do your utmost in maintaining her in so good dispositions; and may she receive by your assistance, a wholesome education with which she may appear with some advantage in society. I sincerely approve the different clothes; she follows and remarks her improvement in every one. But I am disappointed of your silence regarding the French which language here is as useful as the English for a young lady. I shall be happy if she would not discontinue it. In payment of your draft on me, the funds have been deposited into the hands of Messrs. Boulizy & Gamucheau of this city. I hope they have not spared any exertion to remit them to you as soon as possible, so as to save you any trouble of collection. I have to tender you my best thanks for your good care towards Aglazir, which in my opinion, she deserves. I would be happy if you would continue the same.

I remain your most obedient servant,
T. Jules Fazende

Aglazir Fazende entered Nazareth Academy in September 1842 at age fourteen, a Catholic child of New Orleans parents. Despite the satisfaction of her father and his readiness to pay, both expressed in this letter of May 1843, she left in July. The intent may have been a short summer visit home, but she did not return. Parental satisfaction or ability to pay may have run out; whatever the reason, Aglazir was a student at Nazareth less than a year.

2-Z

Letter to Mother Catherine Spalding from Tho. Fitzgerald
DLB 11, p. 85

Louisville
May 12, 1843
Esteemed Madam

I did myself the pleasure of addressing you a few lines yesterday under care of Mr. Haseltine, enclosing him $446 (sixty-nine of which was for Nazareth) collected at New Orleans on the 4th inst., all of which I hope will reach you in safety. Late last evening I received your esteemed favor of the 8th inst., with their inclosures. I shall feel the greatest pleasure in doing everything you require in the matter and hope most sincerely I'll be more successful than I have been upon other occasions. I have very little faith, however, in Messrs. Keys and Roberts['s] promises. Please tell Mary in reply to her letters which I received yesterday that I will be up (God willing) to see her in July next. Her Aunt, cousins, and brother, are in good health. I leave here tomorrow evening or Sunday morning for New Orleans and expect to be back on the 29th. I have the pleasure to be, esteemed Madam,

Your much obliged and obedient servant,
Tho. Fitzgerald

The main content of this letter suggests that Thomas Fitzgerald was an agent for Nazareth, collecting mainly in New Orleans. His distinction between the full sum sent to Father Haseltine and the part that was "for Nazareth" remains a puzzle. Congregational and school expenses may have been kept in separate accounts, but it would seem that any sums collected in New Orleans would be due for the students who increasingly enrolled from there. As for Mary, she might have been Fitzgerald's niece or his ward, as he cites her aunt, cousins, and brother but makes no mention of her mother. Yet the only Fitzgerald in the Register is Mary Ann, daughter of Mr. and Mrs. Thomas Fitzgerald of Louisville; she was enrolled in 1838 at five years old and remained until 1849. Small wonder if she wanted to see her relatives in 1843.

2-AA

Letter to Mother Catherine Spalding from L. B. Flournoy
DLB 11, p. 145

Sept. 3, 1843
Miss Catherine Spalding,
Lady Superior,

I am prevented by indisposition from coming in person with the young ladies to Nazareth as I had wished. . . . .
The improvement in my daughter, Cassandra, has not been in accordance with expectations. I therefore request that you will be more strict, even to chastisement if found necessary, with her. Lavinia has hardly equaled my expectation, but they promise to do a heap better. I send the institution two hundred and five dollars. This will pay my own children's account and the balance of Miss Hale's account over one hundred dollars. . . . . On Miss Hale's account I have to ask the indulgence of a few months as I have been unable to collect her funds.

Very respectfully,
L. B. Flournoy

No information has been found for any of the persons named in this letter. It does reveal some issues that must have occurred with more girls than just the Flournoys: how to handle a recalcitrant student, how to satisfy parents with the school's methods of instruction and discipline, how to get proper charges paid.

There is no evidence to suggest that "chastisement" was ever used as a means of discipline at the academy. Mr. Flournoy seems to stand by older Biblical interpretations of how not to "spoil the child." Nor is he familiar with the sort of salutation usual for Catholic religious women such as Catherine. He appears to have been either an agent for collection or perhaps a friend or neighbor of the Hale family who managed their daughter's account. In his monetary dealings he is respectful and upright.

2-BB

Letter to Mother Catherine Spalding from John Fulton
DLB 11, p. 74

Washington City
May 18, 1844
Miss Catherine Spalding
Dear Miss,

Mr. and Mrs. Egg, the bearer of this, visits your place for the purpose of taking their daughters to school. It will be a favorable opportunity for me to send for Mary Crow, as Mr. & Mrs. Egg are her uncle and aunt, for any expenses that may have accrued. You can draw upon Messrs. S. T. Chenowith & Co., Louisville, and it will be paid also for Eliza Crow's tuition. I will want her to board with you in vacation. I have no objection to her going anyplace where any of you are going, also otherwise I have any clothing that Eliza may stand in need of, get them and forward the account to Messrs. Chenowith for payment. I want Eliza to have all that she actually stands in need of; you know better than I do. I leave that to yourselves. I want nothing extravagant but that is necessary. I have wrote to Mary & Eliza; give my respects to all.

Respectfully your obedient servant,
John Fulton

Mr. and Mrs. Joseph Egg, a Protestant couple in Washington County, Mississippi, enrolled three daughters at Nazareth on June 24, 1844: Mary, fifteen; Ann, twelve; and Sarah, also twelve. All three left in June 1845. All three eventually married. Ann and Sarah became Catholic; Mary presumably remained Protestant. Two other daughters, who enrolled ten years earlier, in 1834, also became Catholic. These baptisms were registered at Nazareth. Records like these hint at a family drama that played out at Nazareth, as school policy forbade conversion of underage daughters without parental consent.

What daughters, if any, John Fulton had, or what was his business and level of livelihood, remains unknown. Whether guardian, family friend, or agent, he makes himself responsible for the two Crowe girls, Eliza, fourteen, and Mary, sixteen, enrolled since September 1, 1843, getting them to school and paying their way. Eliza and Mary remained until 1844 and 1845; both subsequently married. Why it devolved on Fulton to see to their arrangements and tuition remains unclear, but he seems most conscientious about the duties and debts incurred. The Chenoweth family in Louisville originated with a Richard Chenoweth, who came with George Rogers Clark in 1778 and eventually established Chenoweth Station, an area near contemporary Middletown in Jefferson County. By 1843, members of the Chenoweth family were clearly important in the civic community, agents in the management of funds and business.

2-CC

Letter to Mother Catherine Spalding from Gabriel James
DLB 11, p. 72

Eggs Point, Miss.
May 24, 1844
Miss Catherine Spalding,

Relying on the many good reports I have heard concerning your school which I have heard from various sources, as well as the good character which it has abroad, I entrust

> to your care my daughter with the full confidence that you will use all necessary exertions in instructing her during one year . . . in those branches which your judgment will be most serviceable to her in after life. I wish particular attention to be paid to her moral as well as mental culture, I wish it to be perfectly understood that I want her to be to no unnecessary expense, and nothing to be purchased for her use except those things absolutely necessary, for her comfort and advancement in her studies. I am thus particular with regard to her expenses, because many children sent from this country to school in Kentucky have imbibed expensive habits, and run into many useless extravagances. I am not speaking with reference to your school, which I understand is conducted on a very economical plan. I send her up under the care of Mr. Egg, a neighbor of mine, to whom you are referred for particulars. He will also arrange with you the expenses of her tuition and board.
>
> Respectfully yours,
> Gabriel James

Susan James entered Nazareth the same day as the three Egg girls cited above and also left the same day a year later. It is tempting to speculate whether the neighborly arrangements and the brevity of the girls' tenure at the academy reflect financial issues or shared dissatisfaction with the lifestyle or the religion they experienced there. Certainly most students from Mississippi came from firmly Protestant backgrounds and were seeking only a proper education for young ladies of the South. But whatever religious beliefs they imbibed, the conversions that occurred did not stop the flow of enrollment from that state until the era of the Civil War.

Conclusion

Throughout the expansion of the early 1840s, varied and numerous demands, duties, and heavy challenges were imposed on Catherine as leader of the community, its branch missions, and the academy. She met and survived them all. Much as she loved the persons with and for whom she lived and labored, she had to be well worn out, if not exhausted, by her term's end.

In August 1844 she counseled her beloved Claudia Elliott not to write again till she knew where her next assignment would take her; where that would be, she cared not. She was but a "loose piece of furniture," she wrote, and "truly glad to be so. I have never felt so relieved in all my life" (Letter 2-9 above).

She would soon have the true gladness of returning to her beloved orphans.

3

Louisville Mission

1844–1850

Catherine returned in 1844 to a Louisville doubled in size, to over twenty thousand; it would nearly double again before she left in 1850. The surge was due to the developing business of a river city, and even more to immigrants pouring in from Germany and Ireland. Both groups, but especially the famine-stricken Irish—poor, uneducated, and Catholic—roused anti-immigrant and anti-Catholic bigotry not seen before to such an extent in Louisville. The *Louisville Journal* fanned the flames; the new weekly *Catholic Advocate* responded with both satiric and doctrinal articles. It was a risky time for a group of women religious to be maintaining a Catholic institution for the sick poor and homeless children dependent on public charity.

But the orphan population grew with the general numbers. These were children of parents who had died on the boats; impoverished immigrants; the destitute, widowed, divorced; or simply "a poor unfortunate mother." Some of these children came home with Catherine from the wharves where she found them. Many were simply unwanted in any extended family that might have existed. In addition, priests regularly appealed to Catherine to take children, even sent them from outside the city or state without first asking if she had room for them, promising charitable sermons and funds when they could provide them.

Somehow Catherine and the Sisters made room. During this period they had to expand the orphanage/hospital building at Jefferson and Wenzel Streets, and once they had to rebuild after an arsonist destroyed their stable and a cow, a priceless source of milk for children. Catherine and the Ladies of the Catholic Orphan Society held an annual six-day fair for which the Sisters labored and she wrote appeals. She went begging to local merchants for food and supplies, and thus became a recognized figure on the streets, the mother on whom every orphan could lay a claim. Her visits extended to the homes of the destitute, where she sometimes donated her own warm garments, and to the wharves, where Mother Frances reported that she had assisted an arriving Irish family of seven, all sick and destitute.

Orphans required not only room and board, but education and religious and moral training as well. In this period, Catherine could expect six years out of office in which to establish a lifestyle rooted in suitable policies. Ever a collaborator and learner, she sought the counsel of Sister Margaret George, SC, Directress of the orphanage in Cincinnati. And while she gave to experienced SCN nurses the care of the sick in the infirmary, she guided its policies, including the first instance of care of a mentally ill woman. In that case especially, one would seriously wish to see Catherine's letters that elicited the existing replies from the woman's husband.

Catherine's heart was in the ministry to the orphans, a source of much fatigue certainly, but even more of joy. Other situations gave her the crosses inevitable for the Savior's follower. News would come of Sisters dear to her dying of the tuberculosis and typhus that continued to diminish an otherwise flourishing community. And in 1848, she was stricken by the murder of her own sister, Sister Ann Spalding, poisoned in Lexington by a slave girl. No reason was ever recorded for this attack, and the girl was not handed over to a vengeful authority but sent away. Tradition holds that Catherine wanted no retribution, but references in letters reveal her grief.

Perhaps it was the death of Ann that brought about contacts with her relatives in the Spalding, Elder, and Clark families, as well as with persons from her early Nazareth days and Sisters who wanted to maintain a personal friendship and supply her with community news. In these years, with the startling exception of one letter to a niece, an immature and unstable woman, Catherine wrote and received warm letters to and from Sisters, lay and clerical friends, and relatives.

By 1850 Catherine could look forward to separating the infirmary from the expanded orphanage. In that year she also saw the cornerstone laid for a new cathedral, with the aged Flaget blessing it from the balcony of his residence. When she followed his remains to the grave in 1850, she knew another era in her life and mission had ended. That August, she was again recalled to Nazareth to lead in new developments there.

Letters by Mother Catherine Spalding, 1844–1850

3-1

Infirmary & Orphan Asylum
Nov. 21/44
Dr. Rev'd Sir,

Upon reflection I find I did not finish my reply to your question about our taking the poor little orphan in Bardstown. Altho' our number is considerable, for our means, yet I had no intention finally to refuse that child.—I merely began to explain to you the state of things with us, that you might form your own opinion as to whether it would be better for the child to come.—On my part, I assure you, I am perfectly willing to take her & do the best we can for her, & you can direct her friend to send her at any time.—I trust, Divine Providence will provide for them all.—Hoping we shall have the pleasure of seeing you here again soon, I am as ever

With sincere esteem & regard
Your ob't. Sert.
Catherine Spalding

(Addressed to "Very Revd Dr. [Martin John] Spalding.")

Appendix A provides accounts of Martin John Spalding and his brother, Benedict Joseph Spalding. Though Catherine was their distant cousin, she seems never to have had a close or even casual relationship with either. Their clerical state engendered a reverence and measure of distance; both were active in diocesan affairs and management. Martin was Vicar General of the diocese at this time and clearly destined to succeed Flaget as bishop. Catherine's respect and liking for these brothers, however, was genuine; only later would Bishop Martin put her feeling to the test. The letter above serves mainly to reveal the sort of decision-making with diplomacy that she had to observe in managing the enrollment of the orphanage at this time of huge demand, limited resources, and other people's expectations of her.

3-2

Sr. Claudia Elliott
St. Mary's Academy
Nashville, Tennessee
August 1st
My very dear Sister,

I received your kind letter by Rev. Wm. M'Guire.—Could you, my good friend & Sister, doubt me for one moment, or think I am changed? No, believe me, I am always the same for you. & often do I think of the many happy days & hours we have spent together—& if Providence so disposed it I would gladly spend as many more with you, for I never forget old friends unless they change first toward me.—Thank God, we are all in good health here now with plenty children & we have had the happiness to have Mass nearly every day this summer.—In a day or two four of the Sisters will go up to Nazareth for the retreat. Sister Julia & I will remain alone to take care of the place & family.—I hope you will pray often for us.—Your dear little pin-cushion was very pretty.—Did you hear Till's fine boy George Washington was dead?—I have not seen your brother James for some weeks; but I often hear from him, he is well & still in Fairfield.—I will try

> & get him to write to you soon.—You must never think hard of my not writing to you oftener.—I have not much time & I am afraid of giving trouble.—Give my best love to Sister Christine & to all who ask for me.—& do write to me whenever you can.—& be sure I will never forget you.—Catherine—
> [On reverse:]
> Your brother often said Mass for us when he was in Louisville.

This letter, clearly written from the asylum in Louisville after Catherine had spent most of the summer there, must be dated 1845. On August 1, 1844, she was still at Nazareth completing her term of office.

Research has so far not found a Father William M'Guire in the Louisville, Nashville, or any other diocese. There may be a confusion of first names; Father John D. Maguire was ordained in 1840, offered his services to Bishop Miles, ministered in Nashville, and was pastor of the cathedral there from 1842 to 1846, when he went to Kentucky. He might easily have carried Claudia's letter to Catherine.

Sister Julia Hobbs is first named here in connection with St. Vincent Asylum; she would devote most of her years of ministry there. Probably no one after Catherine is more responsible for its flourishing work for homeless children. She is also important in SCN history for her part in her family's migration to Graves County, Kentucky, and the development of Fancy Farm as the locus of Catholic life there. She and her brothers are said to have given the land for the church. After Catherine's death, Julia was assistant to both Mothers Frances and Columba, also a member of the Board of Trustees. Only for a few months did she return from the orphanage to Nazareth before her death in 1881.

Till was a nickname for Matilda, a slave at Nazareth. The list of slaves notes her three children: John Francis, George Washington, and Ann Sodieska, born in 1842, 1844, and 1845. Only John lived to young adulthood. George Washington, born in February 1844, died before the year was out. Ann survived a year, dying in 1846.

3-3

To Mrs. Maria Crozier
Bardstown, Kentucky
Infirmary & Orphan Asylum
Louisville Feb. 25th/45

Will then you permit me, my own, dear & much esteemed friend, to recall to your remembrance, one who still entertains for you the most cordial sincere regard.—I am now deprived of the pleasure I once enjoyed of having you with me, occasionally, for a time; yet, rest assured you are often present to my mind, & my inquiries for you have been oft repeated. I have generally been answered: "She is in town, She is well," which you know, is ever grateful news to me. But you must pardon me, when I tell you that this thought has often presented itself to me. Well, it is strange, that I scarcely ever receive even a kind message from Mrs. Crozier.—Today I had a call from Mrs. Judge Marshall & an hour's conversation, or rather I listened to her for that length of time; of course, you were not forgotten: She remembers you, & I can never forget. Poor lady, things are different with her from what they were in times of yore—when you knew her; but her spirit is the same.

I am here in the midst of near sixty destitute little beings who have few to think of or love them & I am content; if I can only be useful, I ask no more.—Well, I have said enough of myself & now wish to hear something of others.—& first, your own dear self. how are you? The winter being so mild I trust you have not suffered from it.—& dear Mrs. Booker, how often do I think of her & love her as ever. Still, I feel a kind of self-reproach that I have not prayed for her as I ought.—Don't forget me with one of your family. Dear good Mrs. Slaughter first, Mrs. Ben Alice[,] Mr. Crozier—all, all, I suppose little Edward is almost a man.—I am delighted

> to hear Mary Jane continues at Nazareth, My love to her, with best wishes for her success.—Best respects to Mr. Slaughter.—Two days have elapsed since I commenced this letter, & this morning I have the happiness to assist, in our humble little chapel, at the Mass of the persecuted priest of Evensville, Just released from the state prison.—Justice is sometimes tardy; but it comes at last.—I shall probably send this by that good man who leaves soon for Springfield.—Our little family of Charity are at this time generally in good health, the Sisters also. Three inmates in the Infirmary, but none dangerous.—Please remember me kindly to Miss Margaret Wickham, Mr. and Mrs. Baker Smith, Mrs. Charles Haydon, Mrs. Kemp—in a word, to all who may ask for me. & pray often for one who ever remembers you.
>
> Sr. Catherine Spalding

Maria Crozier was the mother of an early student, Eliza Crozier, and became Catherine's steadfast friend (see Appendix A). This sole extant letter to her reveals how Catherine valued and sustained her friendships and retained her interest in those who had been her valued supporters in mission. It offers a very personal perspective on her beyond the image of efficient businesswoman and manager of institutions.

The "flexible" spelling and the duplication of names in this era complicate the effort to make positive identifications. No Mrs. Judge Marshall, no Margaret Wickham have been found, nor a Mrs. Kemp. But old records report a Mrs. Mary Kamp, elderly and widowed, who operated a family grocery in Bardstown, where she died in 1874. Mrs. Ben Alice cannot be found under that family name. But Mr. and Mrs. Benjamin Ellis of Bardstown sent three daughters, preteen and Protestant, to Nazareth Academy in 1857 and 1862. At this letter's date, the eldest would have been an infant.

Mr. E. Baker Smith, husband of Nancy, was treasurer of the Bardstown and Louisville Railroad, also a Nelson County merchant listed in the newspaper abstracts. He seems to have owned a dry goods store that was the forerunner of the Spalding and Sons on Third Street today. He and Mr. Thomas Crozier were trustees on the Board of St. Joseph College in Bardstown.

Two possibilities are found for the often mentioned "Mrs. Slaughter": (1) Mrs. Anna Eliza Slaughter, age thirty, appears in the 1850 Federal Census for Nelson County, Kentucky, as wife of Daniel S. Slaughter, a lawyer. They had eight children. In 1845, Mrs. Slaughter would have been a young wife, probably starting her family. She may have known Catherine from previously volunteering at the orphanage or at Nazareth, but it is unlikely she would already have had a daughter at Nazareth. (2) Mr. and Mrs. James Slaughter, probably of Louisville, enrolled two daughters at Nazareth: Mary Jane in May 1844, and Maria in September 1850. Mother Catherine would have known Mary Jane by the time of this letter and been glad of her perseverance in school. Nothing more is known of the parents or family.

Mr. Charles Haydon appears in the same 1850 census, age forty-four, a merchant in Nelson County. In 1830 he had married Matilda Rose Smith. They lived in a large Bardstown home called Anatok, long a historic mansion; they had there a slave named Daniel Rudd, who later became a prominent black journalist and a leader in the black Catholic community and antislavery movement.

As this letter is addressed to Mrs. Crozier in Bardstown and reads as though Catherine assumes she is in contact with all the ladies named, it may be that they were early Bardstown ladies, former students at Nazareth or wives of early professional men there, all interested in the school and its needs and development. Or the women may have been active members of the Catholic Orphan Society, and for that cause were endeared to Mother Catherine.

The "persecuted priest" was Father Roman Weinzaepfel of the diocese of Vincennes, Indiana, stationed at Assumption Parish in Evansville, Indiana. He was from France and was described as gentle and zealous in ministry, yet imbued with the rigid views on faith and morals characteristic of many French Catholics. In May 1842 he conducted the marriage ceremony of Martin Schmoll and Anna Maria Long, a young woman of dubious reputation. Her father insisted on a Catholic ceremony, and Schmoll agreed. But he soon accused the priest of raping his wife when she fainted in the confessional. This "news" led into a lurid tale of nativist and religious bigotry, street riots, drunken mobs bent on lynching, attempted escapes from prison, rumors of disreputable pasts, financial efforts to aid or destroy both sides, changes of venue, legal appeals, national publicity, and vociferous opinions in both civic and religious papers, including Louisville's *Catholic Advocate*. Finally the Schmolls divorced. (See the Gollar and McCutchan articles listed in the bibliography.) After two trials in 1844, Father Weinzaepfel was sentenced to five years in the state penitentiary, but in less than a year, his accusers became even more publicly disreputable and his defenders more numerous, highly placed, and vocal. The case against him disintegrated, and he was released. He spent a year in rest and retreat in Marion County, Kentucky, then returned to ministry in Indiana; he lived his last years as a monk at St. Meinrad Abbey.

Catherine's comment suggests that while she had no direct role in this sensational tale, she was not so sheltered as to be ignorant of it, and that it impelled her to further reflection on the good and inevitable justice of God. She offers here another small insight on her own relation to the society around her.

3-4

To Rev. B. J. Spalding
(A note on the photocopy in Nazareth archives reads, "This transcript is taken from a photocopy of the original letter in possession of Mr. Francis P. Clark. The photocopy is very faint and parts of the letter are illegible.")

St. Vincent Infirmary, Louisville
July 24/56
Dear Rev'd Sir,

I am now thankful that I can tell you your brother is, I think, better in every way, tho he is very sensible of debility.

He is now perspiring naturally.

His liver has been [illegible] tho there are still occasional returning symptoms of the disease—& he complains much of weakness but Dr. Gross says he is better this morning than he has found him yet. Major Hanley saw him and seems to think he is mending. His recovery, however, may be very slow.

I will write you again in a few days.

With sincere esteem Yours in Our Lord
Catharine Spalding

The date of 1856 is an error, as Catherine Spalding was superior of St. Vincent Infirmary during her interim in Louisville from 1844 to 1850; and after her 1850–1856 term of office, she did not return to Louisville until August. The correct date is almost certainly 1846; the Reverend Martin John Spalding was then pastor of St. Louis Cathedral in Louisville and Vicar General of the diocese. His brother, the Reverend Benedict Joseph Spalding, was pastor of St. Joseph Church in Bardstown, at just enough distance to prevent stable attendance at his brother's sickbed, causing concern for any serious illness. That illness could have been any of the dangerous, fever-inducing diseases that afflicted so many Louisvillians; in late 1847 Catherine will note that Rev. Martin Spalding is "suffering again from derangement of the liver." Catherine would see that her cousin was given the best available treatment and would herself provide the best possible news of a progressing recovery. With both her Spalding cousins, she had at the time a cordial and genuinely interested relationship.

Dr. Samuel David Gross was undoubtedly the best physician available to the need. He had his medical education and early practice in Philadelphia and became an educator, a translator of French and German medical books, and an author of at least three major treatises on anatomy, physiology, treatment of diseases, and surgical techniques. In 1840, he became chair of surgery at the University of Louisville and spent sixteen years in the position, while he also helped establish the Kentucky State Medical Society. His advice and judgment would be a major source of assurance to all involved in any case.

James and Frances Hanly (or Hanley) are mentioned in several letters; but it is possible the male reference is to two different men named James. Major J. H. Hanly is listed as parent of Miss Ann Hanly, age thirteen, who attended Nazareth Academy from 1844 to 1848. It is impossible to assert what "Major" tells of his identity or occupation, or if he is also James Hanly, husband of Frances. A James Hanly married Frances Pierce on August 19, 1841; she died on September 8, 1846, leaving two small sons (see Letter 3-5 below). No daughter is mentioned, and Frances could not have borne one as old as thirteen in 1844. If Major J. H. Hanly and James are the same man, then he must have had a previous marriage; his first wife could have borne Ann in about 1831 and then died before the second marriage in 1841. Other letters of Mother Catherine refer to James and "poor Frances"; she seems intimately acquainted with this family.

3-5

Asylum Nov. 2nd/1846

Perhaps, my very dear Sister Claudia, you may have some reason to complain of my not writing, altho' I am not, I think, behind hand in numbers, still I know it is harder for you to write than me; & it always is a pleasure for me to write to you, or, to hear from you.—Sister, I know you could never do me the injustice to suppose that I could ever forget you or your many kind attentions for me; you are one of the few that always seemed to understand my feelings & sentiments, & you never changed. Could I then, dearest Sister change in your regard. No, never.—Dear Sister, did you hear of the death of poor Frances Hanly? She died on the 8th of Sept. after a few days illness, leaving her two dear little boys motherless.—She was in her senses to the last moment, knew her danger, but had no dread of death, all say that her death was one of the most calm, resigned & pious that you can conceive of. She exacted of James the promise to prepare to meet

> her in heaven & entreated her mother in law to watch over the morals of her little boys, as she was so anxious to meet them in heaven—her last request was for prayers & masses to be offered for her soul. & this my dear Sister I beg you will not forget pray for her, & if you can get a Mass said for her.—Sister Seraphine is with us this year, tho' she felt a great deal to leave Lexington. Sisters Alice & Theodora are gone in her place. I hear they are pleased & doing well.—From what I hear the school is as about as large up there as it is in Nashville.—I hear sometimes from your brother, he is well, tho' I don't see him often.—I hope my dear Sister you pray for me & think of me often as I do of you.—My love to all the Sisters, tell Sister Christine I saw Sara Ann Sanders & her mother lately they were well—& I would write & tell Christine more of her mother's death but they told me her brother had done so.—Poor James Hanly is the most afflicted man you ever saw. He has written me two long letters of poor Frank's death, he thinks he will visit me in the spring & bring his children to see me.—Do write sometimes.—I am as ever yours Catherine

Catherine was writing from her mission at the orphanage, and since Sister Claudia was in Nashville, this letter was purely for personal connections and sending of news, not related to any business either had to manage. It is one of the letters most revelatory of Catherine's value for friendship and desire to experience it in a mutual fidelity. It hints that she had experienced a fine sensitivity from Claudia, all the more appreciated as she may have felt its lack and a change in others.

For information on Frances and James Hanly, see Letter 3-5 above.

Sister Seraphine Buckman and her very young sister, Sister Generose Buckman, were both directed before entry by Father Pius Miles, O.P., the future bishop. Seraphine made vows in 1825 and was at St. Catherine's, Lexington, 1832–1842. Generose died suddenly and unexpectedly while nursing in Bardstown during the 1833 cholera. In 1846, Seraphine joined Catherine on the staff of the orphanage. She seems to have spent many later years at Nazareth; she died there in 1891. Catherine's comment about her indicates a common difficulty for Sisters if they stayed a long time at one mission and were then uprooted for another. Seraphine was also leaving the Sisters who had consoled her for the loss of Generose.

Sister Alice Drury made vows in August 1840, so she was less than a year professed when she signed the 1841 appeal to Bishop Flaget. A letter indicates that she was in Nashville in 1844; the 1846 letter above says she had been recently sent to Lexington to replace Sister Christine.

Sister Theodora Crowe and two of her sisters were children at St. Vincent Orphanage. Theodora entered the SCN in 1841 and made vows in 1843. She was at Nashville in 1842, presumably as a novice. She was a music teacher at Nazareth in the mid-1850s, then in Lexington and Owensboro, Kentucky, and Holly Springs, Mississippi; thus she was several times a pioneer in a newly established mission. For an unknown reason, she withdrew from the community in 1880.

Sister Christine Coomes made vows in 1826 and also spent some years in mission at Lexington and then at the Fifth Street School in Louisville. In 1843 she was a pioneer at St. Mary's Academy in Nashville. That same year she made a will stating that when the estate of her father, Charles Coomes, was settled, her part should go to Nazareth. Evidently her mother died in Louisville in 1846, as Catherine speaks of it as a recent event. Christine's further loyalty to the SCN was demonstrated by her return from Nashville when the 1851 separation occurred. Her last years were spent mostly at Bethlehem in Bardstown, including two periods as local superior. She died in 1868.

Sarah Ann Sanders attended Nazareth Academy from 1839 to 1842, her early teenage years. Her mother was Mrs. Stephen Sanders of Louisville. As the family was Catholic, they may well have kept connection with Mother Catherine through the church and the asylum and helped support the orphans.

3-6

Infirmary & Orphan Asylum
Louisville, Ky
Dec 12, 1847
My dear good old friend & Sister,

Why would you think for one moment that I could be tired of your letters?—No, Claudia, if you do, it only proves that you do not know me—for I do not change. On the contrary I feel new pleasure in every letter I get from you, because, in each one I find some improvement. & that should encourage you to write often, for your own sake if not for mine.—God bless you, my old friend; altho' I miss you & often think of you, still if you are happy, I must be content.—I hope you & your nearest neighbors agree well & that their wholesome breath will protect you against all disease, & we must be very retired & quiet.—& sure enough, you have your Betty, down there.—When I went up to Naz. there was her good place on the bench, forgotten, & not a speck of her could I find even in town.—Don't you think she treated me mean to go off so & not even write me one line to say she was going or tell me she was there? But as soon as I get a leisure moment I must write to her & then she may get a scolding for she never did write half as often as she ought.—Give my love also to Sis. Christine. I will answer her letter soon. We are all well & busy too, but I don't think any one is overburdened. & God is so good that he seems to bless our poor labors. Pray for us that we may correspond with designs.—I always hear your brother James is well but don't see him often.—Our dear old Bishop is rather indisposed again this winter, says Mass in his room.—Mr. Spalding has been suffering again from derangement of the liver. Give my best love to Sister Margaret & ask her if she has forgotten me. I heard last week that Sister Hillaria had been sick for some days, but

> was better again.—Love also to Sister Euphrasia & all. & don't forget Mrs. Stevenson & Mrs. Mateer.—
>
> Ever yours in our Lord—Sr. Catharine
>
> My love to Martha. Tell her to be a good girl. I heard lately from her old master & mistress. They were well, & would be very sorry to hear Martha was a bad girl. Has she made her first Communion yet? Emily has made hers & been confirmed too.—

If no other letter to Claudia was written between this of December 1847 and the previous one of November 1846, Catherine may have been a bit obtuse in her surprise that Claudia felt an excessive gap in their correspondence. In reality, both friends were in missions that demanded a huge proportion of their time and energy; to Claudia, Catherine does not hesitate to imply that her labors exhaust her time for other pursuits of leisure or friendship.

Baptism and confirmation records at Nazareth tell of Elizabeth Jackson, daughter of Killy Jackson "f.m.c." (free male colored) and Julian, his wife, "f.w.c." (free woman colored). Elizabeth was born in 1837 and was baptized and received the sacraments at Nazareth; the record says "no sponsor." This omission seems unlikely; one conjectures that she may be "your Betty," sponsored by Sister Claudia and later sent to be with her in Nashville. The difficulty in this otherwise likely interpretation is that even a free black child would not have been instructed in writing nor expected to correspond with Catherine or the Sisters. She could have learned from her free parents, and Catherine does seem to desire her progress and correspondence. "Your Betty" also could refer to a former student or an associate in some other way with Nazareth over a period of time. By any identity, she is witness to the affection Claudia and Catherine both gave to and received from young women in any relationship.

Martha and Emily clearly are slaves; Martha must have been purchased privately for Nazareth. Both girls have been assigned from a Kentucky mission to Claudia in Nashville. Catherine's comments demonstrate the policy of providing religious instruction to servants and allowing participation in the sacraments, encouraging their rearing young ones in that faith and practice.

Bishop Flaget was by 1847 seriously failing in health and active mission. Martin John Spalding was again ill, presumably with the same illness that called for Catherine's earlier letter of July 1846 (Letter 3-4). In 1848 Flaget consecrated Spalding as his coadjutor bishop, and in 1849, his last public act was to bless the crowd at the laying of the cornerstone of the new cathedral. He died in 1850.

Sister Margaret Bamber entered in June 1829, received the habit only two months later, and made vows in August 1831. With whatever training she had as nurse, she was put to immediate service as infirmarian in Bardstown, then as leader of the team sent to confront the cholera in Louisville. After some years at St. Vincent's, Union County, she went to Nashville as housekeeper at the academy, then as nurse at St. John's Hospital. She was one of those who declined the separation from Nazareth and returned with Catherine to Kentucky, where she served until her death in 1858, only ten days after Catherine. She seems to have been one of the most influential and best loved of the early Sisters.

Hilaria Bamber entered the SCN in 1825 but for some reason did not receive the habit until 1829, four months after her sister; she did make vows with her sister on the same day. She accompanied her sister on the cholera nursing team in Louisville; both suffered the loss of the third SCN Bamber, Sister Patricia, from the 1833 cholera in Bardstown. After Hilaria served in both teaching and nursing at the academies, she was at Nazareth, where she drew pictures of the campus, the main record before photography. She died in 1852, in Catherine's lifetime.

Sister Euphrasia Mudd was one of the early members, professed in 1824. She seems to have had short spells at the openings of missions, being several times their local superior. After playing a part in Nashville's opening, 1842–1848, she opened the academy in Owensboro, then in Covington and Newport, Kentucky. Some months after Catherine's death in 1858, Euphrasia returned to Nazareth; she died there in 1863.

Mrs. Stevenson and Mrs. Mateer, women who had supported

the first Sisters in Nashville, are regularly greeted through Catherine's letters to Claudia and other Sisters.

3-7

Orphan Asylum

Now my precious good old Sister, Claudia,—& is it possible, I should leave your dear letter so long unanswered?—& that sweet nice little pious keepsake too.—Oh! dear good Claudia, if I could only send you something to convince you how Sincerely I love you & how often I think of you.—& I almost begin now to despair of ever seeing you.—Still should I never, you must continue to write to me for two reasons, your own improvement & my pleasure.—I see you improve in every letter. Do then continue to write.—We have added to our house & got every thing convenient. The kitchen for the sick people is quite separate from the asylum kitchen & Sister Phillipa has care of cooking for the sick while two Sisters take it month about to keep house for the asylum & things at large. We have Sister Mary Catharine with us now & she is one of the best Sisters I have known. Sister Martina is on 5th Street & Sister Ellen gone home to Naz.—I suppose you have become quite attached to Nashville. Do you remember old times, & how we used to talk over things?—Well, I hope you will ever be happy.—I am still plodding on the best I can.—I heard from brother James very lately, he is well, & I think changes very little, always at the same old place.—Give my best love to Mrs. Stevenson. & tell Sister Euphrasia she must take good care of her god-daughter.—My best love to all who ask for me.—The Sisters in Lexington are building a large fine house.—So you see humble beginnings come out at last. I hope they will succeed to finish it & pay for it too. Did you hear that Christine Mudd is married & doing well? She writes to me very

often.—Brother James always stops and says Mass for us when he comes to town. Adieu. Ever yours in our Lord,
Catharine

Sister Philippa Pollock made vows in 1831 and was at St. Vincent Academy, Union County, in far western Kentucky during the crisis of the 1830s. Twice Procuratrix at Nazareth, she was known for a special talent as cook, making food palatable despite poverty. She served at the Fifth Street School and Orphanage in Louisville, was Mistress of Novices for ten years, and served as an Army nurse in Louisville and Lexington in the Civil War.

Two Sisters Mary Catherine lived in a short span of the 1840s. Mary Catherine Cox entered in 1841, but died of tuberculosis as a novice, making her vows on her deathbed in 1842. The Mary Catherine of this letter must therefore be Sister Mary Catherine Tully, who made vows in 1846 and was at the orphanage in 1849. She would serve in Louisville, Lexington, Covington, and Nazareth, be elected Procuratrix in 1861, and die in 1864, also of tuberculosis.

Sister Martina Beaven, professed in 1824, was for some time in the mission in White River, Indiana, but was released from it to join Sisters Margaret and Hilaria Bamber and Martha Drury to form the cadre of SCN nursing in the 1832 Louisville cholera. Whether the stress of community issues in the early 1830s or the strain of nursing the cholera affected her cannot be known, but she withdrew from the SCN in September 1834.

Sister Ellen Davis was professed in 1843, a month after she was sent to St. Vincent Orphanage, still a novice. After further service in Louisville and Nazareth, she went to the hospital in Nashville and stayed there at the 1851 separation from the SCN. She died in Nashville in 1854. After the other Sisters had gone to Kansas, Mr. and Mrs. Thomas Farrel had her and another former SCN disinterred and buried in their family lot, the graves of both marked with one tombstone.

For Sister Euphrasia Mudd, see Letter 3-6. Her goddaughter's identity is unknown. By the sponsoring customs of the time, she might have been a child or woman in Nashville, a former student of Nazareth, or a slave sent from Nazareth to work in the Nashville mission.

Mrs. Stevenson is the Catholic woman with whom the Sisters in Nashville first stayed until their own house could be readied.

Christine Mudd, daughter of Catholics Mr. and Mrs. Mudd of Nelson County, entered the Academy in 1830 at age twelve. She remained a full fourteen years, until 1844. Small wonder she remained attached to Catherine and other Sisters who would have rejoiced in her happy Catholic marriage.

Mother Catherine rarely writes to Claudia without some mention of Rev. James Elliott, Claudia's brother and the long-term pastor of St. Michael's Church in Fairfield, Kentucky. He was not only a friend to Catherine and the SCN and one of the priests who sent orphaned children to them; he was also one of those who kindly supplied them with a celebration of the Eucharist, a blessing they could not yet receive on a daily basis.

3-8

May 24–48 Louisville
Dear Juliann,

I have received your letter & have only to say: that I have no advice to give you—for you know well that you have never followed any that I did give you—& I know you never will. I never advised you to go to Bardstown—but now that you are there I am certain that you can do far better there than you ever can in Louisville.—Why ask for such foolish advice? You know I always told you that Louisville was no place for you—have you forgot the few days you spent here?—Rest assured if you were here, in one month the Gilchrist family would be tired of you & shun you & soon you would be a public pauper.—This I am determined on, if you do come here, I will never see you nor have anything to do with you.—I will not.

With your abilities you are well able to support yourself & your two children & the expenses there are not one half of what they are here.—But all you can think of, is spending every little that you gain by begging or otherwise in roving from place to place & then "getting a start."—If you would sit down to work you would soon get through your first difficulties & people would then have some confidence in you. But No, you have no perseverance, but perpetual change.—Many have more difficulties to contend with than you, & still get along.—The advantages you speak of there, in vegetables, rent, shoes, hat trimmings &c, &c, besides the promises of work—are far above any advantages you would have here.—Be faithful to your work & nothing else is wanting to you.

Rev. Mr. McMahon cannot be candid in advising you to come here, for your good. There can be no motive in that, but to get rid of you.

Yes, poor dear Sister Ann is gone! & you can't forget all that she has suffered on your account. These sufferings have no doubt done their part in hastening her to her grave. Her remains lay now near those of poor Frances—let the remembrance of what you have caused her to suffer be now a stimulus to try hard to take care of yourself & your children.—But if you ever attempt to live in Louisville from that day, never think of me again.

May God preserve you and yours,
Catharine Spalding

[On reverse:]
It is foolish to talk of any one writing to me for consent to come here. I have no consent to give you. You must be getting crazy. All the advice on earth could not have kept you from Bardstown—& now you already think of changing. Do try to act with common sense.

(This transcript was created from a photocopy of the original letter in the possession of Mr. Frances P. Clark.)

"Juliann" was long assumed to be a cousin of Catherine, one of the large Spalding clan that had moved to Kentucky. However, after Brother Tom Spalding, CFX, established with virtual certainty that Catherine had several identifiable siblings besides Sister Ann Spalding and that her sister Louisa Spalding Pierce had a daughter named Julian, it became possible to trace her in some records of Nazareth and to give this startling letter a clearer context. (See Appendix A.)

Julian Pierce, daughter of Mr. and Mrs. Leonard Pierce (Louisa Spalding), was registered at Nazareth Academy on September 3, 1824; she was then eleven years old. Unless there were two women named Julian Pierce, Catherine's niece attempted religious life. The SCN register of members lists Julian Pierce, who entered in May 1829 and received the habit as Sister Olivia in December 1829; that would require the consent of Catherine, still at Nazareth as Mother. However, Julian left in April 1831; the pattern of instability Catherine deplores in this letter may have prevented her becoming a vowed member. The same pattern probably accounted for her subsequent unstable marriage and parenting. The academy register states that she married a B. Skinner, but no date or further information about him is given. Whether their separation or his death accounts for her single-parent status is not known.

Prior to this letter, Catherine had tried to help Julian; she had obtained an offer from their cousin John Spalding in Maryland for her to live at Pleasant Hill, the ancestral home, among her cousins and to tutor their children "as long as agreeable to her." That was not agreeable to Julian. By 1848, she had roamed with her children to Louisville, Lexington (where Sister Ann was superior), and then Bardstown, from which she proposed to return to Louisville and "get a start" once more with help from her aunt.

The severity of this letter, its scathing tone and threat of outright rejection, are all so uncharacteristic of Catherine that they beg an explanation. *Pioneer Spirit* (174–176) describes Catherine's sheer frustration with Julian's behavior and rejection of all advice; Catherine's felt need and determination to protect the scarce resources for the orphans from one who would leech from them rather than support her own children; and Catherine's fresh grief for her sister Ann, whose murder had occurred only nine days earlier.

Father McMahon, a native of Ireland, emigrated from there to the United States, was ordained by Bishop Flaget in 1825, and in 1836 was assigned to Lexington, where he would have known the SCN community and met Julian Pierce.

As for the Gilchrist family, the Federal Census of 1860 listed three women in Louisville by this name: Sarah, age fifty-one, a domestic worker; Abbey, age twenty-two, a laborer; and Alice, age seven. They were living then at the "Gautt House" (the Galt House? Louisville's fine hotel). If these are the family referred to in this 1848 letter, Alice would not yet have been born. And if Sarah is the mother of the two younger girls, Julian may have thought she could join her and earn some support by labor or child care. Practical and blunt, Catherine evidently thought she could labor in some more suitable place than Louisville.

"Poor Frances" probably refers to Mrs. Hanly, the wife of James Hanly.

3-9

Rec'd of B. J. Spalding, Exr. of Margaret Wickham Dec'd., the sum of fifty dollars bequeathed to me by the s[ai]d Margaret Wickham for the benefit of the Sisters of the Good Shepherd of Louisville Ky.—Also rec'd of the s[ai]d B. J. Spalding Exr. of M. Wickham, Dec'd., the sum of ten dollars bequeathed to me by the sd Margaret Wickham—this 13th September 1848 (Signed) M. J. Spalding

Rec'd of B. J. Spalding, Exr. of Margaret Wickham. Dec'd., the sum of fifty dollars bequeathed to me by the s[ai]d Margaret Wickham in her last will & testament—this 13th Sept. 1848 (Signed) Catharine Spalding

(Given by Mr. Francis P. Clark, July 1960.)

Margaret Wickham left no certain evidence of her relation to Mother Catherine and to Nazareth. Was she a student first or one of the ladies supportive of St. Vincent Orphan Asylum? She is mentioned as Miss Margaret Wickham in Catherine's letter to Maria Crozier in February 1845 (Letter 3-3).

The fifty-dollar legacy is said to be made to Mother Catherine rather than to an SCN institution. Religious practice and vows would have called for her to place any such personal donation at the disposal of the congregation. Her own intent and wish would have been compatible with its use for the needs at Nazareth or for the basics of life for the orphans.

3-10

Louisville Sept. 20th/48
St. Vincent's Orphan Asylum
My dear good Sister,

I thank you again & again for your kind letters. They give me so much pleasure, knowing they come from the heart, & then in each one I see you improve.—Oh! I do value your letters highly forgive then for my apparent neglect. Your good brother was here, & told me he had written to you by the Bishop.—He looks very well and I always urge him to write to you.—But your good Bishop does not give me much chance to talk to him.—We have as much as we can get along with at this time, & I hope the time is not far off when they will be able to separate the two establishments.—The new addition to our house is filled with orphans.—Good Bishop Kendrick & two others all said Mass in our little chapel for poor Sister Ann—on the same morning last week.—I thank those who said Mass for her in Nashville & hope you will continue to pray for her poor soul.—Pray also for me, my good Sister. Oh! I never can forget you. I wish I had something worth sending to you.—I am glad to hear your place is ready for the asylum & hospital & hope it will do well.—Remember when we moved to Louisville we were only 4 Sisters, to begin a poor day school.—Now see what has grown out of it.—In five years we got this place & separated.—Now there is a large pay-school & free school on 5th Street.—This asylum is full, & the

> Infirmary increasing so that we might now divide this establishment & make two of it—if we had room for it.—Besides a day school up in this end of town would be well supported.—Pray to [G]od, that all will be so done as will be for his glory, the good of our neighbor & our holy religion.—My love to Sister Christine & to each one of all the Sisters.—Kind remembrance to all acquaintances. Ever your sincere friend & Sister—Catharine

The opening remarks indicate that Sister Claudia is the recipient: the personal warmth of Catherine's tone, the improvement in her friend's writing skills, the reference to her brother (Father James Elliott), and to "your good bishop" (Pius Miles in Nashville, who evidently came on occasion to Kentucky on clerical business).

Bishop Francis P. Kenrick was a friend of many years to Catherine. A native of Ireland, brilliant and educated in Rome, he came to Kentucky in 1821 and ministered in various ways at Nazareth. His appointment as coadjutor bishop of Philadelphia in 1830 was felt by the SCN community as both a gratification and a grievous loss. Evidently he made some return journeys to his former diocese.

For Sister Christine Coomes, see Letters 2-8 and 3-5 above.

While this letter is essentially a warm outreach to a good friend, noting with pleasure the pieces of community news that are sure to gratify and encourage its recipient, it also serves to verify what growth was occurring in the SCN mission. The Fifth Street School (Presentation), begun by four Sisters in the basement of the church and then loaded with the early orphans, had branched into two schools, pay and free. Both the asylum and the infirmary on Jefferson Street now had such a numerous clientele as to need separation in locale and management. Catherine could not predict to her friend how all this might yet develop, but she saw the need for space, support, and prayer. The separate institution of St. Joseph Infirmary would become a major task of her next administration as Mother at Nazareth.

3-11

St. Vincent infirmary
Louisville, Ky.
Sept. 22nd (1848)
Dear Rev. Sir:

I write in haste to say that Mr. Jn. A M'Atee of whose illness Rev. Mr. Haseltine wrote you yesterday evening has sunk so fast that the last Sacraments have been administered to him during the night and he is now considered to be in a dying condition, can hardly last this day through.—He has been with us but two days—was sick before he left the South and took no medicine but oil until he reached here. We sincerely sympathize with his friends but fear it is now too late to hope for his life. Please convey this news to his friends as soon as possible.

Very respectfully,
Catharine Spalding

[Addressed to Rev. B. J. Spalding, St. Joseph College, Bardstown, Kentucky.]
[Notation on envelope: "Mother Frances please send these letters immediately.]
(Copy of a letter found in a trunk in the basement of the cathedral in Louisville, Kentucky, in 1967. Courtesy of Mr. Francis P. Clark.)

Mr. John McAtee resided in Nelson County with his wife. Their daughter Rebecca entered Nazareth in 1824, at age eleven. By 1848, she would have been in her twenties; her father could have been one of the many men who went South on business and came home with malaria or some other infectious disease. His outcome is not known; his daughter died young, in 1852.

The sending of the letter to Father Spalding in Bardstown and the message to the sick man's "friends" (a term used generally in letters of the time with reference to family members or very close associates) suggest that the patient had come to the infirmary from that town rather than directly from the "South." He may have been sent to the infirmary on the advice of Father Spalding, his pastor. The letter is thus an expression of both Catherine's respect for him and her genuine concern for the anxiety and probable loss to all those "friends" in Bardstown; it also indicates her compassionate character.

3-12

St. Vincent O. Asylum, Jan. 8th 1849
Dr. Rev. Sir,

I have just recd your kind favor of the 5th Inst. I cordially return all the good wishes of the season. As to the poor little orphans, I can only say that, upon reflection, I do not think we can take the Infant; we have so many small ones. If he can get any friend to keep that one until it is older, he can pay her what he would give here, & even more if he can, for we would rather take less, and even __________(?) than fill the house with those infants, & take so much of the care &c. that is necessary for older & of more importance, for any one else can nurse & feed an infant just as well.

I hope he will have no difficulty in placing it until older. The large one we will take on any terms you & he fix.—As to the bed, it is better to get a good mattress here of a suitable size & bed clothes to fit. That is easier done here, with the material we can make them.

Sincerely & respectfully yours,
Catharine Spalding

(This transcript is taken from a photocopy of the original letter, courtesy of Mr. Francis P. Clark.)

This letter is marked as directed to Father B. J. Spalding in Bardstown. He had taken his brother's former pastoral responsibility at the cathedral parish there, and that evidently included collaboration with persons who needed to place children in some suitable home. The letter indicates that he readily turned to Catherine in these situations and that she, in turn, had to make the best objective judgment she could about what was possible with the space and staffing she had to offer. It had to be a challenge to her expansive heart, touched by the needs of orphans as by nothing else.

3-13

To Sister Claudia in Nashville
April 30th—&—May 12th, 1849—Orphan Asylum

I have just read your dear kind letter, my own dear & good Sister, & the thought that your feelings toward me prompts you to write to me makes your letters even ten times more welcome & dear to me.—It is true, my good Sister, that if I fulfill all my duties I am always engaged. Still, believe me: one of my sweetest occupations is to write to you. Altho' you may not think so, as I write so seldom.—In fact Sister I write very few letters these days;—I am getting old now & ought to begin to die to this world before it dies to me.—Still I can't feel willing that my best friend should change or forget me.—& your dear letters are always truly interesting because you are so kind in giving me the news of all that I like to hear from, & how you are getting on, do then, if you love me, as I believe you do, continue to write to me.—I saw your brother in Holy Week; he always calls to see us, he was very well.—& you should write to him.—We are generally well except Sister Phillipa has been sick for six weeks & is just getting about.—Sister Appolonia was also confined to the room two months this winter. Our house is pretty full of orphans.—We have only a few sick people at this time & I would be glad if we had the two establishments in separate places. Then too we could have a pay school at this end of town, which is much needed.—Poor Mrs. James Tarleton died instantly, without time to speak one word, of apoplexy.—She had been sick two weeks, but all thought she was getting well, she could come down stairs.—Oh! what a broke up family! She was the sole tie & stay of the family.—I never saw such grief among servants.—Her son is at St. Mary's College.

My best love & kindest wishes for dear Sister Xavier, I will write her as soon as I can but she must write to me.—Since I began this, our sick strangers have increased, but some are now leaving.—Do pray much for me dearest Sister;—& give my love to each one of the Sisters.—& to all who ask for me.—

With the same unchanged feelings
I am ever yours truly
Sr. Catharine.—

Xavier, be sure to present my very best respects &c. to my good and much esteemed friend, Rev. Wm. Brown.
Eliza Breckenridge's father is dead.

This letter may register Catherine's first notice of her own aging and advancing mortality; such a sense of herself will appear in various letters of her next term. Certainly, it reinforces her often expressed devotion to Claudia and desire for contact with her, as well as the exhausting schedule of labor that prevented real leisure periods for communication. The coming separate establishment of the infirmary is foreshadowed. But, however faintly, so is the strain of her relationship with Sister Xavier Ross and the coming separation of Nashville.

For more information on Sister Philippa Pollock, see Letter 3-7 above.

Sister Appolonia McGill, professed in 1824, was one of the founders of Presentation Academy and nurses of cholera. She was briefly superior at St. Vincent Academy, Union County, 1835–1836; then served at St. Vincent Infirmary/St. Joseph Infirmary, 1836–1859. She was first superior at the new St. Joseph site and was the best-known nurse in Louisville. She nursed in the Army hospital there during the Civil War and died in service in 1862.

Sister Xavier Ross was the daughter of a Methodist minister of Cincinnati; she converted and vowed as an SCN in 1834 against his fierce opposition. Mother Catherine aided her entry to the SCN and felt deep friendship for her. Outstanding in intelligence and leadership, Xavier became superior at both Presentation and the orphanage. As Superior of St. Mary's in Nashville, she led the group that withdrew in 1851 to form a separate community there, and later formed the Sisters of Charity of Leavenworth, Kansas, in 1858.

Mrs. James Tarleton may have been the wife of James Jeremiah Tarlton, son of Alfred and Cecilia Tarlton, from the parish in White Sulphur, Kentucky. James, however, is said to have lived in New Orleans as a banker, military officer, and planter. If this is the family Mother Catherine speaks of, it is not clear why they were in Kentucky at the time Mrs. Tarleton died so suddenly.

The Reverend William Brown is one of the many clergymen whose identity is obscure. The only Rev. Brown discovered is cited in a Catholic Almanac published in Baltimore in 1851, and he is listed as the Reverend H. V. Brown, assistant in the Cathedral Church of Seven Dolors. A landmark in downtown Nashville, this church served as the city's second cathedral from 1847 to 1914. The dates agree, but the discrepancy of the first name cannot be resolved.

Eliza Breckenridge, daughter of Mr. and Mrs. James D. Breckenridge, was a student of Nazareth Academy from 1838 to 1845. As a graduate, she remained devoted to the school and her teachers. A Protestant, Eliza wished to become a Catholic, but this met with her parents' objection, so she delayed her entrance into the Church until she was married in 1857 to William Shakespeare Caldwell. After her death, his intense devotion to her led him to fund and build Saints Mary and Elizabeth Hospital in Louisville in her honor and memory. It was dedicated in 1874 during a term of Mother Columba Carroll.

Letters to Mother Catherine Spalding, 1844–1850

Catherine in this period was living at St. Vincent Asylum for Orphans, for and among children who had "few to think of or love them" (Letter 3-3). The letters she received during this time necessarily contrasted to those of the previous period, concerned with the needs and wants of students at Nazareth and their solicitous parents. At St. Vincent's, Catherine could not write or send out an agent to collect; to keep her children housed, fed, clothed, and warmed in Louisville's often severe winters, to give them even an elementary education, she had to beg for charitable donations. And she had to decide how many and which children she could take in with the resources she had. She was also responsible for oversight of the attached St. Vincent Infirmary, including its expansion in numbers of the sick and what kind of illnesses could be treated.

Not surprisingly, most of the letters sent to her in these six years concern these two organizations, located on the southeast corner of Jefferson and Wenzel Streets in Louisville. Catherine may have found relief and diversion in frequent newsletters—from Nazareth, from the new mission in Nashville, from Sisters elsewhere, from her family, and from alumnae. Taken as a group, the letters of the late 1840s contribute to the history of the developing missions; they may have been preserved for this reason. They also witness to the growing recognition of Catherine Spalding as a woman who could manage her limitations and turn challenging experiences into competence and wisdom.

A Home for the Little Ones

3-A

Letter to Mother Catherine Spalding from M. J. Jacob
DLB 1, p. 121

Louisville
Dec. 25, 1844
Dear Madam,

Your letter of the 23rd inst. I did not receive until this morning. You will please to receive the annexed check on the Bank of

Kentucky for Twenty Dollars and apply same in such way as you may think proper as a Christmas gift for the orphans.

With my best wishes for their happiness and comfort and for the success of the benevolent Asylum over which you preside I am, dear Madam,

Your obedient servant,
M. J. Jacobs

Mother Catherine Spalding returned to St. Vincent's Orphan Asylum in August 1844. She evidently sent out an appeal letter on December 23, 1844, rather too late for most donors to produce ready money. But she seems not to have received any signs of resentment for her requests or negative personal comments. No precise identity is available for either Mr. Jacobs here, or Mr. Hicks of the next letter.

3-B

Letter to Mother Catherine Spalding, Superior of St. Vincent Orphan Asylum, Louisville, from Thomas M. Hicks.
DLB 1, p. 122 (abridged)

December 31st 1844
Sister Catherine Spalding,

Yours of the 23rd did not come to hand until the 27th. I warmly approve the system of calling on our citizens to contribute to the good and charitable institution over which you and those other worthy ladies have presided with great credit to yourselves and inestimable use to society and especially to those almost friendless children.

A thousand times have I stated when a spectator of the kind and humane acts of the Sisters . . . that if there is a heaven for the blessed, . . . your reward would be in the highest order. But . . . your note, my dear Madam, does not find me in a condition to respond to the call as

I would desire—am just recovering from a load of debts, have as security over $10,200. But I do really hope that twelve months more will enable me to do as I would gladly do . . . in this good cause.

Be kind enough to receive this time the unadulterated will for the deed and believe me yours,

Thomas M. Hicks

3-C

Letter to Mother Catharine (Spalding) from Rev. A. McMahon
DLB 14, p. 6

Lexington, Ky
July 28th, 1848
Dear Mother Catharine

Enclosed I send you a bequest from Major Hanly, who is executor to John Henry, deceased. I have been directed respectfully to request the prayers of the good Sisters as well as the female innocents for the happy repose of his soul; and when you are employed in this spiritual work of mercy—may I beg of you and your saintly community, to remember him who has the honor to sign himself,

Your devoted servant in Christ,
A. McMahon

P.S. Please present my respects to Sister Seraphina. A. McM.

This letter may serve as an example of one important source of support for the orphans: bequests from friends or philanthropists who had known and admired the Sisters' work for the homeless and friendless children of a rugged society and culture.

Early in life, Abraham McMahon had been married. After his wife died childless, he followed his brother, Father Edward McMahon, from Ireland to the United States. He entered the priesthood in 1844 and a ministry in Lexington until 1851. He then affiliated with the archdiocese of Cincinnati. Father McMahon died in 1862.

Sister Seraphine Buckman made vows in 1825 and taught art at Nazareth Academy from 1848 on. She died on March 31, 1891. Her sister, Sister Generose Buckman, had died many decades earlier, nursing cholera in 1833.

3-D

Letter of Reverend John Maguire, Nashville, Tenn., to
Mother Catherine Spalding, Louisville
DLB 1, p. 132
(On envelope—"Politeness of Mother Frances")

Nashville
March 26, 1845
My Mother,

As you were so kind as to consent to take an orphan from me last Fall, I send you with Mother Frances, who is so kind as to take charge of her. The one I intended sending you is a Protestant, but as I heard some time ago that she did not go, I take the liberty of sending you this little girl. I took her from her poor unfortunate mother, and placed her with a poor woman of the city, who is not able to do Anything for her. She is a good child. I hope to do something for your poor little orphans ere long. I would send you some token now, but I am not able.

I hope you will not be angry with me for sending her without writing to you, but as I had such a good opportunity, I did not care to let it slip.

We are all well. Mother can tell you all about us. I will see you in a few months. My respects to the Sisters.

I remain your brother in Christ,
John Maguire

P.S. I shall preach a sermon on charity in order to collect some money for your orphans. I will do so in about two months. I hope to get something handsome.

Letters offering monetary support may have been scarce, but extant appeals for admission of particular children to St. Vincent's are proportionately very numerous. They came most often from clergy ministering to a disintegrating family; they pleaded on religious and humanitarian grounds and often promised to glean future funds by their preaching or other influence. A few documents of this era evidence the legal aspects of admission that Catherine had to learn and observe.

The Reverend John Maguire was born in Ireland in 1810, was ordained at Emmitsburg, Maryland, in 1840 for the Nashville diocese, and transferred to the Louisville diocese in 1846. While there, he was President of St. Mary's College in Marion County and Pastor of St. Peter's in Lexington (1849–1853). In 1855 he transferred to Chicago and returned to Ireland in 1856. He died a few years later.

Mother Frances did not forget the little girl whom she brought to Louisville from Nashville. In March 1846 she sent a pair of red mittens to Mother Catherine Spalding for her, with a note saying, "Give the mist [mits?] to little Ann—Nashville. I forget the child's name." (See OLB, p. 84; DLB 1, p. 156; and CLMFG, p. 10.)

3-E

Letter to Mother Catherine Spalding from Rev. John Maguire
DLB 14, pp. 3–4

Nashville
Jan. 29th, 1846
My dear Mother Catherine

I hope that your good Sisters and the dear little orphans are well. It rejoices me much to hear how successful you were at your fair. The smallpox is among us in its malignant form. As soon as it carried off a few of our citizens, the Sisters were called on. . . . They went forth cheerfully and their care of the sick is the theme of every tongue; even a Protestant preacher spoke highly of them last Sunday. Eight out of nine have died; not one has recovered but the first, one patient the Sisters took charge of. I have baptized all that died—adults–. . . . Not one Protestant person comes near them. I have the field clear. . . . A mother of seven children died. A virtuous Catholic on her deathbed, I promised to take care of her daughters, three in number, 4, 7 and 13 years of age; healthy girls, without a home I may say, as their father is a poor, sickly tailor, a drunkard without any energy. The little ones I pity indeed. The Protestants here have an orphan society, but it is a poor sickly affair. It must die. They take none that have a parent living.

Now, my dear Mother, If you would take the two younger ones I would forever remember you at the holy altar; that God might bless you here and hereafter. I want language to express myself as thoroughly as I feel on this subject. What a blessing it would be to take care of these little ones to preserve them from sin, ere the peach down of innocence fades from their cheeks. I beg you to take them to your asylum. I know you have many, but. . . . The Father of the orphans will not let you want. Give them a refuge from famine and danger, and they may yet be the highest jewels that will adorn the crown that our Heavenly Father has in store for you. If you take the three so much the better. I will send an abundance of clothing with them, and one hundred dollars cash that is clear of expenses. Take but the two and I will do the same. Now my dear Mother, I hope that you will do all you can for them; . . . and I may yet have it in my power to aid them more. I know that I am asked annually to preach a charity sermon, so I could send you something and this on my word, I promise to do for you.

I have said perhaps too much, . . . because I feel thoroughly on this subject. The school is out, and as well patronized as a year ago. The policy pursued by its Head, will ruin it for a certainty. It sinks fast, and I am truly sorry, but I do not and never will interfere in it, until brighter days gladden the gloom.

Srs. Margaret and Patricia have care of the hospital. Sr. Scholastica is in good health; all are well. I hope you are happy and well. Now, dear Mother, write as soon as you possibly can, as I fear that the Protestants may take them from me. Hoping and knowing that you will do all you can for me. I'll await your answer with great anxiety.

May God bless you and your household
is the prayer of your sincere friend and brother in Xst.
John Maguire

For information on Rev. John Maguire, see Letter 3-D above. Still in Nashville, he was much interested in the management and success of St. Mary Academy there. His comments are early clues to the trouble that would finally end the SCN mission there. The unnamed "Head" might be either Sister Xavier Ross or, more likely, Father Ivo Schacht. To those steeped in Vatican II's spirit of ecumenism, Father Maguire's comments on the Protestant denominations, mixing facts with his personal feelings and rivalry, are distasteful but do not obliterate his true zeal for faith and charity.

In the years before the separation of the Nashville community, it was distinguished by the tireless and fearless ministry of the Sisters during raging epidemics of cholera and smallpox. How many orphans were received at Louisville and later returned to relatives in Nashville is not known.

3-F

Letter to Mother Catherine Spalding, St. Vincent Orphan Asylum, Louisville, from Mr. Thos. M. Thruston
DLB 1, p. 159

June 25, 1846
Mother Catherine

Mrs. Clementine Allen, who will present you this, was some eight months ago divorced from her husband. I prosecuted the trial for her—all the developments in the case were greatly to her credit. She is very poor, has two children, a girl and boy, which she has thus far by the most laborious labor supported. She desires now to place her daughter under the charge of the excellent Sisters of Charity, of whom you are the principal. I advised her by all means to do so, if it be practical. Mrs. Allen, is, I doubt not in all things, a correct woman and is much to be relied on.

Be assured, Madam, of my high regard,
Thos. M. Thruston

Thomas Thruston has not been identified but was evidently a lawyer with a sense of responsibility for the ultimate welfare of his client and her child, as well as a high regard for the reputation of Mother Catherine and the Sisters' care of orphans.

Lawyers may well have been regular sources of the requests for placement of orphans.

Little can be asserted about Mrs. Clementine Allen beyond what he reports of her situation and character. She may well be the Clementine Allen in the records of St. Paul's Episcopal Church, Louisville, who had two children, Ann Amelia Theresa and William Henry Thomas. She and they were christened at St. Paul's on October 11, 1846, only a few months after Mr. Thruston's letter to Catherine. How that event links with any follow-up connection to Catherine and the asylum is a question of interest without a sure answer.

3-G

Surrender of children to Mother Catharine (Spalding) by Cerilda Cag.
DLB 1, p. 162

June 11, 1847

I, Cyrilla Cag, do hereby surrender and give up to Mother Catharine, superior of the Louisville Catholic Orphan Asylum, my two children, Ann Elizabeth, about eleven years of age, and Mary Catharine, about four years of age. I give them up because I am a widow and unable to take proper care of the said children. This step is taken by me as much for the benefit of my said children as my own. I give to the superior all the rights and power over said children, which by law, I can give and surrender. And further, if Miss Mary Gilligan will take my said child, Ann Elizabeth, I am quite willing for her to have her and I consent that she have the same right and power that I have given to Mother Catharine as specified above. I also wish my said children to be baptized and raised according to the rules of the Catholic Church.

Cerilda Cag
her X mark
Witness Ann Amiss

Cyrilla (or Cerilda) Cag is not otherwise known than by this example of the legal proceedings for placing an orphan with Catherine in St. Vincent Asylum and surrendering rights to manage her life and permit her placement with a prospective foster parent or employer. Caution was used in agreeing to such arrangements. Every girl had a right to call St. Vincent Orphanage her home till she was eighteen and to return there for counsel and sense of "family." Records of the orphanage tell that in January 1849, a Mary Catherine Cag, six years old, was placed in the orphanage. She was baptized there and died in the same year. No record explains the delay in her placement, two years after the mother's legal surrender. Nor is the placement or final outcome of Ann Elizabeth recorded.

3-H

Letter to Mother Catherine Spalding from Bishop Richard

Miles, Bishop of Nashville
DLB 14, p. 8

Nashville
March 31, 1849
Dear Mother Catharine:

We have a little girl of five years, which we wish to place under your protection; the reason why we wish to send her to you instead of taking her ourselves, is, that she is —born and the relatives [wish] to get her out of the way. The father and mother are both poor, but their relatives are in somewhat better condition, and have promised to give $30 per annum for the child's support as long as she remains with you; if not inconsistent with your established rules, you will do a great act of charity in taking this poor child, which remaining with her mother, will stand a poor chance for this world and the other, you will also have the opportunity of adding one to our Church which would otherwise be reared up in heresy or infidelity, as all the connections on both sides are protestants.

Please let me hear from you as soon as possible. We have lately had a third visit of cholera, tho I have not heard of any deaths. We are all well, both with me and the two houses of our Sisters. Sister Bernardine who has just left my house, wishes to be remembered to Sister Martina.

I am truly yours,
Richard Miles, Bp. Nashville

Sister Bernardine O'Brien directs her remembrance to Sister Martina O'Brien, her sister.

3-I

Letter to Mother Catherine Spalding from Bishop Richard Pius Miles
DLB 14, p. 8

Nashville
April 14, 1849
Dear Mother Catharine:

The bearer of this brings you the little orphan of whom I wrote you lately. The money promised is in my hands in part. I recommend the little charge to your maternal care & solicitude & myself to your prayers.

Truly yours,
Richard Pius Miles
Bishop of Nashville

3-J

Letter to Mother Catherine Spalding from Rev. John Quinn
DLB 1, p. 180

Louisville
April 9, 1849
Dear Mother Catherine,

The bearer, Mr. Roach, has just reached here after paying you a visit in order that you would receive under your hospitable roof his little children.

Every orphan in the city claims you as their mother and as they are of the number they have likewise their claim. I envy you your situation. I would feel more than happy were it in my power to do the good which you are doing. May God bless all your endeavors in trying to protect and provide for, by every possible sacrifice, these helpless and unprotected children.

I hope Mr. Roach will endeavor to assist you in the raising of his little children.

Your sincere friend,
John Quinn

The Reverend John Quinn migrated from Ireland with his brother Frank, studied at St. Thomas Seminary, and was ordained in 1838. Nearly all his ministry was at St. Louis Church in Louisville, which became the cathedral after the transfer of the see from Bardstown in 1841. He was known for prudent services to the poor. In 1852, he ministered to a cholera victim, contracted the disease, and died shortly before the new cathedral church was consecrated. He is buried in a vault beneath it. Frank Quinn bought housing for Irish immigrants, the area becoming known as "Quinn's Row." In the riots of Bloody Monday, August 6, 1855, the buildings were burned, and Frank was among those shot to death.

Several men named Roach are listed in the 1860 census for Jefferson County; they were Irish immigrant laborers; their small children would not have been born in 1849. The probable Mr. Roach mentioned in this letter is one whose two little girls, Margaret and Mary, entered St. Vincent's Asylum on the date of this letter, as recorded in St. Vincent Orphanage annals for 1849–1851. Their mother was dead. They were baptized in the asylum; Margaret died there; Mary returned to her father.

3-K

Letter to Mother Catherine Spalding from the Reverend John Quinn
DLB 1, p. 180

Louisville
April 10, 1849
Dear Mother Catherine,

I suppose there shall never be an end to the applications made to you for the reception of orphans into your asylum. Mr. Carmody who applied the other day for the admission of his own child now brings with him his stepdaughter, at my suggestion to see what you will say regarding her. She is a whole orphan—has no person under heaven to look to her. She is quite ignorant and if at her age she be tossed on this wicked world, I fear she will be lost. This induced me to have recourse to you. I know that I am more than troublesome to you, but you are our only refuge under such circumstances.

Your sincere friend,
John Quinn

This is the same Rev. John Quinn missioned at the cathedral in Louisville in 1849.

Dan Carmody, forty years old, a tailor living in Nelson County, is listed in the 1860 Federal Census. Anne, twenty-five, is also listed, along with three small children. In 1849, he would have been less than twenty, Anne in her early teens, and the others not yet born. The census facts cast doubt on his identity as the Mr. Carmody of the letter, but they also suggest the sort of unstable relationships that often caused small children to be cast on Mother Catherine's compassion and care.

3-L

Letter to Mother Catherine Spalding from (the Reverend) John Quinn
DLB 1, p. 183

Louisville, Kentucky
June 11, 1849

Dear Mother Catherine,

The bearer, John McNamara, calls upon you to see if you can possibly receive his only child. Its mother died about six weeks ago. He is an honest man. He has no money at present. He thinks he will be able to give you five dollars against the first of July and will afterwards do all he can for his child.

Do all you can to receive this little orphan and oblige your sincere friend in Christ.

John Quinn

On the date of this letter, the annals of the asylum record the reception of Mary McNamara, two years old, daughter of John McNamara, and her subsequent baptism. She was returned to her father in three months, no reason recorded. She may have been returned to the orphanage if she is the Mary McNamara, age four, who came in 1851, "mother dead, father gone." This last circumstance would have appealed to Mother Catherine as the sad echo of her own childhood.

3-M

Letter to Mother Catherine Spalding from Sister Margaret Cecilia George, S.C., Cincinnati, Ohio
DLB 1, p. 187

Cincinnati, Ohio
St. Peter's Asylum
August 26, 1849
Mother Catherine Spalding
St. Vincent's Orphan Asylum
Louisville, Ky
Dear Sister Superior,

Yours of the 16th should have been answered ere this, urgent duties interfered with my intention; this will plead my excuse. You have been more favored than we, 5 of our little ones, all under 7 left us for our Father's Home—happy little innocents secure of their immortal bliss. I trust they will not be unmindful of us, yet sojourning in this land of exile.

Usually our number through the year was generally one hundred-fifty-six; have since been added to that by the cholera which deprived some of one parent and some others of both, some few have been adopted and some placed out since, which brings our number down to 137 at present. Many of these, say 60, are under 6 years of age. All at present in good health, not one in the Infirmary. As you have heard, the epidemic has left our city, thanks be to the Almighty giver of all good gifts, and we have reason to be grateful, dear Sister, that the goodness of God has spared us the more advanced in age and only took a few of His little children for of such is His Kingdom, "suffer such to come to Me." He has them and can provide for them in His own Sweet Mercy and yet such is poor human nature, we could not give them up without a sigh, or without a tear.

Our orphans rise at 5, wash and comb during the hour

5½Morning prayers in common, after morning prayers the larger ones go to the Dormitories, presided by one of the Sisters in each dormitory, make the beds, sweep, dust, and put everything in order.

6½ Mass

7 Breakfast

8½ School commences. Three different classrooms, the ABC children and the little ones in one room, our rule is three years of age, not younger unless some particular circumstances require a dispensation.

11¾ Dinner prayers—same as the ones, which of course, you know.

12 Dinner—Silence, of course [added in margin: "reading when we are altogether"]. At this moment we cannot take our meals in the refectory on account of being crowded.

1½ School opens—at four o'clock those that are able to study employ this hour in studying lessons for the next day;—the little ones continue their lessons with one Sister, and one Sister can keep all the studies of the other; thus three Sisters are engaged during the hour the Sisters keep the studies, the two class Sisters can make their spiritual exercises. After meals, 10 or 12 of the larger children assist in washing the dishes and cleaning the refectory, etc., but must not stay longer than the commencement of school without special permission each time from myself—which I rarely grant.—The only chance these poor children have for education is while they are with us, therefore, we should do all we can do for them. We form them into bands for fine combing; this is done every day, say twenty for each Sister, in recreation or in the morning, at the convenience of the Sister.

The Externs never mix with the orphans neither in nor out of school—separate rooms and separate teachers. Sore eyes have been our torment and the only remedy I find is separate towels and basins for each one, and we have to be particular to see that this is observed. Each child is numbered, clothes, box, and everything belonging to her is marked in her number. No school on Saturdays. A general reviewing of the dormitories, etc., bathing the children in summer, etc., in the afternoon, they have sewing classes and read. I mean during the week.

Dear Sister, I have hastily sketched the above. At any time I shall feel happy to communicate any little information in my power. We are somewhat older than yours and each one's experience may add a little to the general good. Our children—such as [are] able—go to the Cathedral twice every Sunday. This keeps them before the public who love to see them and encourages them to contribute to their support. It is getting too dark and I must finish abruptly, so dear Sister, please excuse this.—My time is not my own just now—opening of schools, work new, mechanics and all the etceteras of our Martha life for Sister Servants, or as yours, Sister Superiors, you know and can feel for us.— Pray in union with us all for the accomplishing the will of our one Supreme and only good.

Yours in the adorable Heart,
Sister Margaret

> Sister Helena—quite well, heard from home a few days ago.
>
> I had forgotten to say all our bedsteads now are five feet high and have mosquito bars on them—$3.50 a piece, very good and cheap.

While the proportion of letters about reception and support of orphans exceeds those on all other topics, some letters remain to reveal Catherine's need and activity in basic management and maintenance of the asylum and the children who called it home.

This letter is a record of the best practice in Catherine's time of care of orphans by religious women. It is also the only known correspondence between Mother Catherine and the foundress of another religious community. The letter, therefore, is treasured by both the SCN and the Sisters of Charity of Cincinnati, and is given here in full.

Sister Margaret Cecilia George, SC, first Mother of the Sisters of Charity of Cincinnati, was born in Sligo, Ireland, in 1787 and brought to the United States at the age of six. When her father and siblings died, Margaret accompanied her mother to Baltimore, where, at age twenty, she married Lucas George, a professor at St. Mary's College. After losing her husband in an accident and her baby to whooping cough, she met Elizabeth Seton, received her emotional support, formed a fast friendship, and joined her in Emmitsburg, Maryland, as one of the founding Sisters of Charity in the United States.

Sister Margaret Cecilia ministered in schools and orphanages in New York City, and in Maryland, Virginia, and Massachusetts. In February 1845, she went to St. Peter's Orphanage in Cincinnati, where six Sisters of Charity cared for over two hundred children. This experience and the wisdom gained from it she shares with Mother Catherine on request in 1849.

In 1850, Father Louis Deluol, Sulpician superior of the U.S. Sisters of Charity, without consultation or their consent, ordered them to don the French habit and renew their vows on March 25 to the Vincentian Superior in Paris, and thus to unite with the Daughters of Charity in France. The Sisters in Cincinnati, led by

Sister Margaret George, protested this as a grave injustice; they were supported by Archbishop John Purcell, who offered to sponsor them as a separate community in the tradition and practices inherited from Mother Seton. This change was effected March 25, 1852; Margaret George was elected first Mother in 1853. After suffering a stroke and enduring six years as an invalid, she died November 11, 1868.

Sister Helena is thought to be Sister Helena Elder, who was not an SCN but was related to many in that community. Her relatives lived in Bardstown.

3-N

OLB 1, p. 23

Patrick Cavanaugh to G. H. Otto, Dr.
For building one stable for St. Vincent's Orphan Asylum, Louisville, Kentucky, 1849

Brick and laying—1700 at $6.25 per thousand . . .
$105.25
Total amount paid for lumber. 55.80
Carpenter Work. 33.00
$195.50
Nails and hinges. 4.00
$199.05

November 16, 1849
Received payment in full G. H. Otto

I have voluntarily built and paid for the stable above mentioned for the benefit of St. Vincent's Orphan Asylum, and I freely make to the said Asylum a donation of the same.

Patrick Cavanaugh
Witness: Catharine Spalding
November 16, 1849
Louisville, Kentucky

In 1846, an arsonist struck at the orphanage and infirmary, burning down the stable and destroying two cows and a pony, creating a severe hardship and loss of milk for the children. If the name or motive of the arsonist ever became known, it is not recorded for history.

G. H. Otto is listed in the 1860 census as born in Prussia, a brewer and owner of real estate worth $35,000 and a personal estate of $5,000. No mention is made of a building trade; he would have been young in the 1840s and was perhaps versatile in his skills or acquainted with others who might collaborate with him as contractor. Cavanaugh's charity is not recorded in any other document. The rebuilding of the stable may have been done well before he could pay for it and make his charitable donation. One can imagine Catherine's pleasure as witness of his donation.

"I Was Sick and You . . ."

Not every letter that reached Catherine at Jefferson and Wenzel concerned care of the orphans. When the former tavern was purchased for the girls' orphanage, more space was available than was needed for the orphans and some rooms became St. Vincent Infirmary for the sick. Catherine had oversight; wise collaborator that she was, she gave overall direction of nursing service to Sister Appolonia McGill, working with the physicians and families of the sick. Catherine herself, however, had to make some decisions about the kind and extent of care that could be given and the measures to be used. She had legal and financial supervision of both entities, ultimate responsibility for moneys and family properties that might be left for an orphan's later use, as well as for the effects of those who ended their lives in the infirmary—all circumstances liable to create misunderstandings or accusations and conflicts. Two extant letters display the administrative headaches; others reveal Catherine as a pioneer for care of the mentally ill.

3-O

Letter to Mother Catherine Spalding from John Quinn
DLB 14, p. 7

Louisville
June 17, 1849
Dear Mother Catherine,

I regret that anything would be said by any person to you which would be any way calculated to wound your feelings. I am more than conscious that you would do nothing wrong under any circumstance. My advice to you is to keep the trunk and everything pertaining to the dead man, until we hear from his wife at New Orleans. I said the same to the men who came yesterday. They requested me to take it, but I told them that when it was with you I would guarantee its safety. Do this and I know you will be doing what is right. In the meantime pardon them for the fault they have committed, in doing or saying anything to one who deserves every mark of affection and gratitude from their hands.

With the utmost respect and esteem, I am your humble servant.

John Quinn

No known circumstance accounts for this letter, identifies the "dead man," or specifies the accusation against Mother Catherine. Father Quinn's comments and advice suggest that one of the many businessmen or merchants who traveled to New Orleans had taken sick and died in Louisville at the infirmary, leaving his possessions for others to send to his wife. Such a circumstance would not be unusual; only the hostile accusation against Catherine and the Sisters. Father Quinn was more than a collaborator; he was a staunch defender when needed.

3-P

Letter to Mother Catherine Spalding from Mr. John Holburn
DLB 1, p. 206

Louisville,
December 24
Mother Catherine Spalding
Jeff. Street
Louisville,
Dear Madam,

At the instance of the late Marin Murphy, I was sued in the Jefferson County Court on a judgment obtained in the American Court of New Orleans, in the name of Hyde and Clarke against me, and judgment has been rendered here against me. The judgment had been assigned by Hyde and Clarke to Mr. M.; but I am informed that he claimed one half, when he assigned to the Catholic Infirmary in his last illness, and that Hyde and Clarke claim the other half.

Now at the time Mr. M. procured the assignment he was my agent and procured it for me but becoming often [word illegible] with me, he determined to use it for his own purpose. I have been advised that by appropriate proceedings in the Court, I can have benefit of the assignment, and by paying one half to Hyde and Clarke, will be relieved of the other. Such a step I do not desire, but have deemed it better to submit the matter to your consideration, and have taken the liberty of enclosing my own affidavit and the statements of Chas. M. Thruston and Hamilton Pope, Esqr., with the hope that your institution will not force from me Mr. Murphy's claim, and compel me to appeal to the courts. I am

Very respectfully,
Your obedient serv't
John Holburn

This letter must have been written in the 1844–1850 period, when Mother Catherine was head of St. Vincent Infirmary. Charles M. Thruston must have been a lawyer or businessman; no further information has been found about him, Marin Murphy, and John

Holburn. Patrick Hamilton Pope was a lawyer and politician in Louisville, a Jacksonian Democrat, and member in 1832 of the U.S. House of Representatives, the youngest member of the 23rd Congress. In 1836 he was elected to the Kentucky House of Representatives as a member from Jefferson County.

No further account of the case is available—no evidence of Mother Catherine's response, further court action, or result.

The letter simply reveals the sort of decisions Catherine had sometimes to make in the effort to balance justice to the orphans and to various supporters or involved citizens.

In 1845, Mother Catherine received a series of letters from a Mr. H. H. Gray, editor of a newspaper in St. Louis. Four of these letters are extant; they may represent others that have not survived, but they are sufficient to reveal a major challenge that Catherine undertook in admitting to St. Vincent Infirmary a patient with mental and emotional disorders. Grouped together, these four letters tell a story that may not have been unusual except for the access to care and compassion which St. Vincent's and its leader provided.

Mrs. Gray is the first known case of a person accepted to the infirmary with mental illness. How Mr. Gray came to send his wife to Louisville is not known. But Catherine was taking a risk with the public who would learn that a person of mental instability was housed in the home of the orphans. The Sisters may have been uneasy, too.

In an era that had little recognition of mental illness as such and even less will and talent to care for the mentally ill, Mr. Gray's letters are significant evidence of Catherine's awareness, sound judgment, and real compassion for both the suffering spouses. Gray's own awareness of his wife's illness seems to have created in him a degree of ambivalence about his role in her care—a lasting affection and desire to express it, determination to do his "duty as a husband," and a dread of the difficult life he would lead if she were to return to him. He is aware that fair compensation for her board and nursing may be more than he can handle, yet he acknowledges the debt and seems to long for her return, not only to alleviate the financial burden but even more in hope that restoration of her mind and affection for him may yet be possible.

For their historical and biographical significance, these letters are given in full.

3-Q

Letter of Mr. H. H. Gray, of St. Louis, to Mother Catherine Spalding in Louisville
DLB 1, pp. 130–131

St. Louis
March 6, 1845
Dear Madam—

By the return of Mr. Harrison, I am gratified to learn that you have taken my wife under your charge. Permit me, Madam, to bespeak for her your sympathy and all those kind offices for which your order is so justly distinguished.

My circumstances are not such as to warrant me in promising to reward such services as they really deserve.—Nevertheless all the usual reasonable charges shall be promptly met, and to this end, please address me a line stating terms, etc.

You will please keep me advised as to the state of my wife's health with such suggestions as you may think necessary to make. Trusting that experience in similar cases will suggest to you the most effectual course to be pursued to usual speedy recovery,

I remain very respectfully,
Your obedient servant,
H. H. Gray

To Mother Catherine
If this address is wrong, please pardon me, as I have not the honor of your acquaintance, and have heard you called by no other name or title.

3-R

Letter of Mr. H. H. Gray to Mother Catherine Spalding, in Louisville
DLB 1, pp. 134–137

St. Louis
March 30, 1845
Dear Madam,

Yours of the 23rd. inst., together with one from my poor wife, were received yesterday and contents read with painful interest—regretting sincerely that my previous letters did not reach you sooner.

Your details in regard to the state of my wife's mind, together with the few wild and disconnected sentences which she herself wrote, have deprived me of the consolation of even hope for the future. When I assure you, Madam, that with the mere sense of my duty as a husband, my affection increases for her, if possible, with her misfortunes, you can imagine how overwhelming is my affliction. The fact that she is so isolated and friendless in this world, and withal possessing a disposition, where not properly understood, so little calculated to enlist the friendship of others—also calls into action all my best feelings, and causes my heart to bleed at the mere thought of her suffering without my having any power to afford her relief. These feelings are rendered doubly poignant by the fear which has taken hold of me that her affections are alienated from me, and that even should she recover, she would reject the protection of one who cherishes her in his heart's core and foolishly throw herself upon the cold mercies of the world, without a single disinterested friend to sympathize or counsel with her or one single qualification which would lighten her lonely path through life. Then too, dear Madam, think of the various temptations which beset even the path of those accustomed to combat with this world, and see how many are daily falling.—Therefore, wonder not at my anxieties for my poor, but erring wife who is so inexperienced in these things—Oh! I beg you, reason with her on these things, and point out the dangers which surround her if she does not return to reason and duty. Think me not selfish in this matter—for, so help me, God, her wayward disposition has caused me so much unhappiness for the last ten or twelve years, that at the expense of my own happiness for life, I would have willingly consented to a separation at any time had she parents, brothers, sisters or relations who would have borne with her, and taken the same interest in her welfare that I have done and shall ever do. But knowing that she has none of these, and fearing that she would never find one so devoted to her as myself, the idea of a separation was terrible, overwhelming and not to be borne.—The suffering which her temper causes when with me, though hard to be put up with at times, sinks into nothing when compared with abandoning her to her own fate.

But, Madam, I fear I am troubling you with this relation of my private affairs and therefore desist. You fear that you can be of but little further service to her. Well, God's will be done. What course do you advise me to pursue? Were my pecuniary circumstances less cramped, I would come immediately and never again part from her until God in His mercy saw fit to restore to her reason. But as it is, had she not better return to me? If you think so, I will send or come for her; or if you think of anything else, write me frankly and let me know all about it. The doctor surely does not think her mind permanently disordered. Is there not still some hope? You think the subject of her parentage has something to do with it.—This is no doubt the case—but I think the prime cause had its origin in feelings rendered ungovernable by long indulgence, together with the attempt on my part to check them when alas it was too late. But in all this I may be mistaken—God only knows; but to turn to another subject. You doubtless think it is time for me to make arrangements about paying for the care of my wife. When she left here, I put into her trunk some fifty or sixty dollars but little of which I think she will want, particularly if you advise her to return; and you can, therefore, suggest to her that it would save the risk of sending it by mail, if she would let you have such portion as she can spare. But should it be advisable, as has been suggested, to send her to Lexington you need say nothing about it, as in that event, I must, at some sacrifices, come myself, when for your kind attentions to my wife, I will return you my grateful thanks in person and make such other returns as my means will permit.

Ardently trusting with you, that in a few days more, you will be enabled to communicate more satisfactorily, also to induce my poor wife to write, I remain

Your grateful friend,
H. H. Gray

3-S

Letter of Mr. H. H. Gray, St. Louis, to Mother Catherine Spalding, Louisville
DLB 1, pp. 134–137

St. Louis
April 27, 1845
Dear Madam,

Yours of the 21st, though postmarked 23rd, by some adverse circumstance did not reach me until yesterday. You may think I have but slight grounds, but somehow or other, I derive great consolation from its contents; believing that the slight change which you notice in my poor wife's condition augers well for her recovery.

Her conduct when I was with you was so foreign to her general character and disposition, that I was filled with the worst apprehensions for the result. The change, however, gives me hopes for the better, and satisfied me that her mind, however confused for the present, is not permanently disordered, and that, after passing from one extreme to the other, it will finally settle down upon its natural balance. Disagreeable circumstances, real as well as imaginary, connected with the proximate cause (hysteria) of her disease, will doubtless retard, but cannot prevent her ultimate recovery.

In this, however, hope may be parent to belief, nevertheless, it is pleasant to indulge in it.

When I left Louisville, I told you I would collect together such articles of my wife's apparel as I thought she might stand in need of, and send them to you. Since my arrival I have overhauled everything and can find but few articles except summer bonnets and shoes that would be serviceable to her at this season of the year. These, together with some other articles to make up, I will send as soon as I hear from you again, and would do so sooner, but for the hope previously expressed that she will be able to rejoin me very soon.

I again remind you of your promise to keep me regularly advised as to her condition, and whenever she seems to be better, or manifest more kindly feelings toward me, and a disposition to return, inform me and I will immediately send or come for her. In the meantime, I bespeak a continuance of your motherly care and advice to her, for which you will ever receive the most heartful gratitude from an afflicted husband.

Very respectfully,
H. H. Gray

I have not written to my poor wife, believing it would be of no service so long as she is estranged, and so adverse to seeing or hearing from me. H. H. Gray

3-T

Letter of Mr. H. H. Gray, St. Louis, to Mother Catherine Spalding, Louisville
DLB 1, pp. 134–137

St. Louis
May 5, 1845
Dear Madam,

When I wrote you last I was so full of hope for the recovery of my wife that I thought it unnecessary to send things for her until I heard from you, but having a good opportunity in a friend going on, I concluded to send a trunk with some articles which she may stand in need of—among them a piece of muslin and four or five dress patterns which may have a beneficial effect in affording her an employment in making them up.

I am anxiously awaiting your next letter, trusting you may have some more favorable intelligence to communicate and that she has intimated a desire to return. In this hope, I have made inquiries in the neighborhood round, to find a suitable place for her board during the summer, but as yet have not succeeded in finding people with whom I would be willing to leave her. On the next Sabbath, for this is the only day I can spare from business, I intend going to the neighborhood of Alton, where they have a fine female seminary, and where I have letters to several respectable families, in the hopes that I may find a suitable place, so as to have all things in readiness in the event of her coming.

Please inform her of this, and do all in your power to reconcile her to me. I ask it on her account, and not on my own, for as things have gone, there is no happiness for me with her, except that which a consciousness of having done my duty toward her would afford. The date of this reminds me that the time for which I have settled for her nursing and board has expired, and that you will expect me to attend to this matter again. This will be done before the month expires (should she remain so long) and sooner if necessary.

Write me as soon as you receive this, and try to induce my poor wife to do so also. With feelings of respect and gratitude I remain yours,

H. H. Gray

News of the Day

Throughout her years of care for the orphan and the sick, Mother Catherine was not left without contacts from other Sisters, friends, and colleagues, and even her otherwise distant family. Most of these letters are lost; the remainder serve well as typical of the bulletins of news, lingering business, and faithful remembrance and affection that followed her all her life. In their variety of writers and dates, these letters may have punctuated her days with other calls for service and some sad news, but even more with bits of memory and happy connection to lighten her concentration on daily, ever-present duties and cares.

3-U

Letter of the Reverend Joseph Haseltine to Mother Catherine Spalding, in Louisville
DLB 1, p. 133

Nazareth
March 26, 1845
Dear Mother Catherine,

I received yours of the __________ inst. I shall reply but have not the time just now. I beg you to write your name on the back of the draft or check and send it to the Bank and get the money, and send it to me by the first safe conveyance.

I send this by Doctor Smith, who will return in a few days and will call at Nazareth on his ret[u]rn. Sister Pelagia is just as she was when she returned to this place. I don't see the least change in her. The other Sisters are now well and not one girl sick.

Poor Charity will die soon. Mrs. Wellington is at the point of death if not dead. She has [a] strangulated hernia, and no surgeon here is willing to perform an operation to save her life. Respects to all. Pray for me.

Yours sincerely in Christ,
J. Haseltine

Father Joseph Hazeltine (Haseltine) was ecclesiastical superior of the SCN congregation and chaplain at Nazareth. He was an excellent and dependable manager of business and a great friend and support to both the community and the academy. He began a registry of all students, some of whom valued and maintained contact with him.

Sister Pelagia Vallee, of Canadian descent, came from Vincennes. She made vows in 1825, was Catherine's Assistant, 1838–1841, and signed the crucial letter to Flaget. From 1842 to 1843, she was superior at the orphanage. She was especially devoted to Mother Catherine, who came from Louisville to spend days with her before she died of tuberculosis in 1846.

As for "Doctor Smith," the title and context suggest a medical identity. Dr. and Mrs. John B. Smith resided in Springfield, Kentucky; their Catholic daughter Catherine E. Smith was enrolled at Nazareth in March 1847 at the age of twelve. Evidently Dr. Smith was serving the several persons sick at Nazareth in 1846.

Since the letter says no student was ill, Charity may have been a servant woman dying where she had lived and worked. A "Charity" is listed in the St. Joseph Baptismal Register as servant of Francis Smith; her daughter Ann was baptized there in 1842.

Mrs. Wellington may be identified as one of the elderly women who resided at Nazareth or as the wife of Thomas Wellington, who is cited in the Nazareth List of Slaves as having the service of Eliza Ann, daughter of Cecilia.

3-V

Letter to Mother Catherine Spalding from Mary Linton
DLB 11b, pp. 299–300 (abridged)

Terre Haute
March 6, 1845
Dear Mother Catherine:

I have just this moment read the account of the conversion and death of Mrs. Slaughter of Wisconsin. . . . You, dear Mother, a Catholic, can in some measure understand the feelings of gratitude to God and to Nazareth with which I have read and rejoiced in her happy conversion another of us whom Nazareth has given to God. . . . I feel now as though she had been a dear friend to me—how happy, how happy she is, may we all have the grace of perseverance to the end given us. It is my duty as well as my pleasure, is it not, I feel that it is—to write to you for surely you are my mother. [The writer questions the address used.] I directed [this letter] to Mother. Should I now direct to Sister? If so, tell me.

I had the pleasure of receiving letters from Mr. Hazeltine, Mr. Spalding and Sister Louisa, by Mr. Lalumiere, our Rev. Pastor. I should have been so glad to hear from you. He said he did not have time to see you. He went to get us an organ and as we had little to send he solicited the charity of the Catholic brethren in Kentucky and he tells me he received some kind contributions, he mentioned particularly Nazareth, how good of them who have so many calls on their charity.

[A lengthy account follows of her parish in rural Indiana: poor persons, “many of them hired servants in Protestant families,” development from “five members” to “about sixty communicants” and a church, parsonage, and resident priest. Description of church furnishings and vestments, organ, and carpet for pastor’s parlor.

> Long report of her daughter at school, St. Mary's, and of difficulties of developing Catholic practice and education amid "much opposition." She adds: "Surely God will turn it all to the good of souls."]
>
> I was so unfortunate as to lose, some weeks since, the scapular you gave and Mr. Hazeltine put on,—. . . it has given me much uneasiness. What shall I do? I continue yet to say the prayers of it just as I do of all the other societies I joined in Kentucky but . . . [proper protocols of replacement] I do not know and have no book to tell me, please write me.
>
> I am still immersed in business, it is not so easy a matter as you would suppose [it leaves her unable to return to Kentucky]. I am sorry also for the knowledge of the world it gives me. I used to think the most of the gentlemen, as we say, were honest, honourable, I am forced to see and know they are not, it makes me feel sad and tired of the world and, I fear, suspicious. . . . I promised my Husband the last night of his life to try to do my duty in all things that he left to my care and as administrator on his estate and Guardian of our daughter. I took an Oath to the same effect. . . . [Feels "culpably ignorant" for delay in seriously taking hold and learning business.] Now I do not depend on myself for strength in any case, I ask it and hope it will be given me sufficient to do my duty. I am not yet sufficiently acquainted with your rules to know whether I can expect letters from you, now that I have no one under your charge.
>
> [Notes about her sister and daughter.] Give my love to all the Sisters at Louisville. How are the little orphans? I hear you have 45.
>
> Your true and sincere friend,
Mary Linton

This extremely long and detailed letter must have consumed ten or more pages in the original script. Apart from Catherine's record, it has historical value as an account of the early Catholic life around

Terre Haute, Indiana, and the origins of St. Mary of the Woods College.

Mary Linton was apparently a former student of Nazareth and a convert devoted to Mother Catherine, who very likely was her sponsor at Baptism. The 1850 Federal Census lists a Mary Linton, aged thirty-three, whose husband, William Y., was a farmer. They had four children, ages one to seven. If this is the same Mary Linton who wrote this letter, she must have remarried after her first husband's death and after the daughter at St. Mary's in 1845 was gone from her care.

Mr. Spalding is either Father Martin John Spalding or Benedict Joseph Spalding (see Appendix A). Both had a period as pastor at St. Joseph Cathedral in Bardstown and so would have had some acquaintance with Nazareth students.

Father Simon Petit Lalumiere was a native of Vincennes, Indiana, and was the first native priest from there to labor in Indiana. He studied at St. Joseph Seminary, Bardstown, and was ordained there in 1830. After the creation of the diocese of Vincennes, he was appointed the first resident pastor of St. Joseph Church in Terre Haute, Indiana, in 1842 and ministered there until his death in 1857.

3-W

Letter of Sister Scholastica Fenwick to Mother Catherine Spalding
DLB 1, p. 148 (abridged)

Nashville, St. Mary's
September 18, 1845
My dear Mother,

I had indeed almost come to the conclusion you had forgotten me when I was so agreeably surprised and undeceived by the reception of your last kind letter, and since I am unwilling to harbor such a thought, particularly in regard to those I love so dearly, I gladly attribute your long silence to more important and worthy duties. I know they must be very great in such a place as the Asylum. . . .

Indeed, dear Mother, it has always seemed to me that to protect, comfort and support . . . those poor little creatures whom Providence may have deprived of that best of earthly friends, is one of the most pleasing actions we could possibly do; how it must . . . draw the smiles of God upon those who are engaged in it.

. . . May God bless and comfort them, especially those under your maternal charge.

Our school is progressing very well indeed. . . . I do sincerely hope, with you, that it will be for the honor and glory of God since it [is] for this alone we should live. I think such a school is capable of doing much good in such a place, but dear Mother, it requires so much humility, self-devotedness and unity of action, such a fund of true Christian piety where there is so much pretention, so much aristocracy and so much indulgence toward the junior part of society—but my trust is all in God whose power is invincible, whose goodness infinite, and whose watchful care over us is unceasing.

I am glad to hear that you are getting along well in your work of charity. May Almighty God prosper you. O dear Mother, how much I wish I was with you once more and particularly at present that I might assist you in preparing for the fair. . . . You know my will is good, but you would tell me that obedience is better than sacrifice. Therefore, I hope my poor prayers for your success will avail more than would my assistance otherwise, at present. I wish you every, all success possible.

My health is not very good, and indeed, dear Mother, I have almost despaired of its getting any better at least as long as I live in Nashville. . . . I endeavor to follow the good advice that you and others give me, of taking all as it comes calmly and without annoyance, but my dearest Mother, I am not always successful. Pray for me most ardently. . . . The Sisters heard me say I was writing to you, and they have loaded me, as it were, with messages of kindness and affection to you, . . . though according to promise, I must mention Sisters Christine and Euphrasia. Your acquaintances have often inquired for you, particularly Mrs. Co. Marshall. She says she is happy that you remember her, sends her best respects and warmest regards.

. . . Mrs. Stevenson seldom comes to see us now-a-days, but I believe that she is well. Her little Puss goes to a French school in town.

Well, goodbye, my dearest Mother, the bell has already rung to call me to class. . . . Pray for your ever affectionate and devoted child in Jesus,
Sister Scholastica

Be sure to write to me very soon, dear Mother

Sister Scholastica Fenwick taught music in the academy before she went to Nashville in 1842 in Mother Catherine's term of office. After several years, she was recalled to Nazareth and later served as superior in several Kentucky missions and as a nurse in the Civil War.

Sister Christine Coomes was in Nashville from 1843 to 1851. Sister Euphrasia Mudd was in Nashville from 1842 to 1848.

Mrs. T. K. Stevenson was a Nazareth graduate, and she entertained the Sisters in her home before a convent was opened.

Mrs. Co. Marshall has not been further identified than her mention in this letter.

3-X

Letter to Mother Catherine Spalding from Sister Columba Carroll
CLMCC, p. 4

Nazareth, Kentucky
October 27, 1845
My beloved Mother,

I had some pens made to send down by the wagon but I was not aware when it started, so you see I was not so forgetful as I may seem to be. I will keep the case you sent me, and fill it for another opportunity. They tell me trying the pens spoils them; therefore, I am not sure those I send are good.

I am greatly rejoiced to hear of the success of the fair; the children's hearts were gladdened by it, no doubt. I was pleased too, that Augusta and Sarah exerted themselves for it. Do you see them often, Mother? When you do, give them my best love, also to Eliza Breckenridge.

Nannie and Bettie are to be baptized on the Feast of All Saints. They send you much love and beg you to pray for them. Anne Egg wrote to me lately telling me of Joseph's death; she says he died in the most edifying sentiments. Anne seems truly pious and devoted to her religion. Poor thing! She has need of strong faith, situated as she is.

We are in usual health, except one of the Sisters who . . . was taken sick on the very day she took the habit, and yesterday she appeared sinking so fast that it was deemed proper to administer to her the Last Sacraments. Today, however, she is much better, but not considered out of danger. . . .

I gave Mother Sister Philippa's stockings to send. . . . Give her and all the Sisters my warmest love.

I intended writing you a long letter, but I must be brief in order not to be disappointed in sending this. I hope, my dear Mother, you have not ascribed my long silence to any other than the true cause. It seems to [me] I have hardly ever been so much occupied as within the last month or two; and it is only now I begin to feel at leisure, be assured my thoughts and affections were often with you.

Ever truly, your devoted,
Sister Columba

At this time Sister Columba Carroll was assistant to Mother Frances Gardiner and was almost certainly still involved with the academic program of the school. This letter reveals the warmth and informal tone of a Sister who enjoyed one of the longest and closest relationships to Catherine. Columba shares news of their common acquaintances and details to be accomplished and reported between them.

Augusta and Sarah were probably former students living in Louisville and helping with the fair for orphans. Eliza Breckenridge was enrolled at Nazareth from 1838 to 1845. She became a Catholic and married William Caldwell, who built Saints Mary and Elizabeth Hospital in her memory in 1874 when Sister Columba had become Mother. Nannie and Bettie Bradford were nieces of Jefferson Davis. Nannie married Mr. E. Miles and lived at New Hope, Kentucky, after her marriage. Anne Egg seems to be the widow of Joseph, herself a convert. Mr. and Mrs. Joseph Egg of Mississippi had several daughters at Nazareth who became Catholics then or later, but his wife is named Catherine in the record. The girl named Ann would be too young to be the Anne of this letter, and she married a Philip Cox.

Sister Philippa Pollock was missioned with Mother Catherine at St. Vincent Orphanage at this time.

3-Y

Letter to Mother Catherine Spalding, Orphan Asylum, Louisville, from Sister Elizabeth Suttle
DLB 1, p. 155

St. Vincent, Kentucky
February 14, 1846
Dear Mother,

I should have written to you immediately after the return of Father Durbin from Louisville, but he requested that when I wrote to you, to write on one of the new prospectus, and the box that contained them remained at the river until a few days ago.

Soon after Mr. Laughlin came here he told me there was $100 due him at Nazareth, and that when he was coming away, Mr. Haseltine gave him a paper which he left with you (I thought it was a balance of his wages). He offered us the use of that amount, saying that when he wanted it, he could get it from us more conveniently than from Nazareth. We did not need it at that time, but when Father Durbin was going to Nazareth, I told him if he could collect the money—the $100, for Mr. L., he might leave it with Mr. McKay, and that we would pay Mr. L. here. The order was given without any hesitation.

When Father Durbin returned and told me about it, I spoke to Mr. L., and the answer he gave me compelled me to believe that he had taken that means to get from you the money left for the support of his child. A few days later, he told me that if I would let him off, he would go to New Orleans. I did not oppose him, but paid him in full, took his receipt. He is gone. I suppose the restraint he was obliged to be under here was too great for him.

We have had a great deal of sickness here, during the fall and winter. Several of the family are sick yet.

Give my love to the Sisters. Please remember me in your prayers.

Sister Elizabeth

Mother Catherine Spalding was the Superior at St. Vincent Orphan Asylum. Sister Elizabeth Suttle was the Superior at St. Vincent Academy in Union County, 1845–1851, apparently a sharp and competent manager in a then fairly remote area. Supervision, maintenance, and support of the distant mission in western Kentucky cannot have been easy for either of the two women; even letters were not readily exchanged.

Father Elisha John Durbin was ordained in 1822 and, as a very young priest, began his ministry all over western Kentucky. A long list of parishes and churches is testimony to his zeal and labor. His connection with the SCN is chiefly through his pastorate of Sacred Heart Church in Union County, adjacent to St. Vincent Academy. There he ministered to Sisters and students, and other letters witness to his willingness to serve, as well as to direct the spiritual life of all personnel there and to give practical assistance and direction. He died in 1887, sixty-five years ordained and still in service in central Kentucky.

Mr. Laughlin was evidently an overseer or laborer on the farm at Nazareth and then at St. Vincent. The story of his child and of his $100 is obscure, but he seems to have obtained the money and taken his leave from SCN employment. Even with the flexible spelling of surnames at the time, it seems a stretch of probability to identify him with either John or James McLaughlin, neither from Kentucky, both married and with daughters at Nazareth in the very early 1840s.

3-Z

Letter to Mother Catherine Spalding from Rev. W. E. Clark
DLB 14, p. 5

Bardstown
Jan. 14, 1847
Mother Catharine
Dear Cousin,

My Brother Edwin wishes to send for Laura this week;
she can come in the omnibus on Thursday, and stop in
Bardstown at Uncle John Horrell's, and see her relations
here till Sunday, when they will send for her to go to
my brothers. I saw her mother yesterday. She asked me,

with tears, to give you her sincere respects and many thanks, as well as to the other sisters, for your kindness to Laura, and for all you have done for her. She wanted to go and see you herself, but we discouraged her, because we thought there was very little prospect for a home in Louisville. I think she will soon find a good place in this neighborhood. We are trying to get one, and I trust we shall succeed. It is painful to witness the old lady's distress, especially knowing she is a saint.

Poor Edwin has very weak health, and all depends on him, father, mother, etc. His best hand, a black boy, has long been unable to do much, being threatened with consumption. But, my dear friend, you hear of afflictions enough, without my reading you another chapter.

My own health is poor, and will be so, unless I can get rid of a little college work or a little church city, or board somewhere else. Cousin John Elder and wife from dear Donalsonville are here. They have put their two daughters at Nazareth and are very much pleased. I believe they are going to Louisville to spend some days; you will likely see them.

Grandma is well and the rest of the family as usual, except Uncle B. Wight, who is very ill, and I think he will hardly recover. I send you a "Bit" for the orphans.

I remain,
Your Affectionate cousin,
W. E. Clark

The Reverend William Elder Clark was the son of Richard and Clementina Elder Clark; Clementina was the daughter of Thomas and Elizabeth Spalding Elder and thus the first cousin of Mother Catherine. Elizabeth S. Elder must be the "Grandma" of this letter; that would be her relationship to Father Clark and his siblings. An Edwin C. Clark appears in St. Joseph Cathedral's baptismal register in 1845 as parent of Ann Elizabeth Clark. If Laura is also daughter to Edwin or his sibling, then Clementina is her grandmother and Elizabeth Elder her great-grandmother.

The names Clark and Elder proliferate in Nelson County; other names must have entered the family scroll through marriages. A Benj. Wight, born in Maryland and a farmer, is listed in the 1850 census of Nelson County. John Horrell of Bardstown was married to Maria Elder Horrell; if he is rightly called uncle to father Clark, Maria must have been sister to his mother, Clementina Elder Clark. Clearly Mother Catherine had many cousins of varying degrees of relationship, many of whom were still around Bardstown or the near rural area. But not all remain in the public record, and the identity of Laura, John Elder, and Uncles John Horrell and B. Wight cannot be given with more detail or precision.

It would seem from this letter that Laura was the ward, if not the daughter, of Edwin Clark and had spent some time in Louisville in Mother Catherine's much-appreciated care. Her unnamed mother evidently was looking for work, discouraged by prospects in Louisville but being encouraged by family members to search in the area of Bardstown. Father William Clark, ordained in 1833, taught at the diocesan seminary and St. Joseph College while also doing pastoral services at the cathedral parish in Bardstown. This strenuous schedule is referenced in his comment about the effect on his health of his "little college work" and "little church city." He served as chaplain at Nazareth for seven years, and when an epidemic swept Bardstown in 1850 and carried him off, he was buried in the Nazareth cemetery.

3-AA

Letter to Mother Catherine Spalding from Mrs. Ann Baxter
DLB 1, pp. 210–211 (abridged)

Tuscumbia, Alabama
Ascension Day, May 9, 1850
My dearly loved Mother,

Knowing and most gratefully appreciating the deep

interest you are pleased to feel for the welfare of myself and family, I have been particularly anxious to write to you during the last month; as I had tidings to communicate which I know would confer pleasure on you and my other dear friends at Nazareth.

Through my letter to Sister Columba, you heard of my happiness on my beloved husband's return to me and to the practice of his religious duties. The next week brought with it a source of ineffable enjoyment, which crowned all I had previously experienced, no less than the united reception of the Author and Finisher of our Faith, "The Holy of Holies." Just one week after Mr. Baxter's return, Father Brown arrived, and as he had given us timely notice of his coming we had endeavored to be ready to approach the Sacraments, and on the morning of the 8th of the lovely month of our Sweet Mother Mary, twelve out of our little congregation of fourteen adults partook of that precious banquet at which pure angels minister. Never since the blissful day on which I first admitted to the divine privilege, have I experienced such happiness as I knelt between my husband and our colored god-daughter "Aunt Kitty." Oh, may I never forget the feelings and favors of that hour, and may all who with me received the Bread of Life persevere until death in the service of Him who had given us all things, even the Adorable Body and Blood.

Especially would I entreat you, my dearest Mother, to pray for my husband that he may never relapse into his customary failings, but prove ever faithful. I feel that he and I owe much of the happiness we have lately enjoyed to your prayers and those of your pious companions, in our behalf. May the Lord reward you and mercifully grant the petitions I everyday crave for you and for all those connected with you, viz., that your labors may be crowned with success in this world, and with celestial glory at God's Right Hand.

[The remainder of this long letter conveys more

> ordinary news of Mrs. Baxter's visiting friends, her extended family's health or illnesses, her wish to visit them, the death of their bishop, and the beauties and vegetation of May in her home area. "I have often wished that you and my other friends at Nazareth could see my altar which I have kept in the parlor from the day it was consecrated. It is decorated every morning with fresh flowers."]
>
> My dear Mother, it has given me so much pleasure to commune with you even in this unsatisfactory manner that I dislike to part from you. . . . Please [thank] Sister Columba for her last gratifying letter and tell her I will write to her. I send my very best love to her and all my friends, both sisters and girls. . . . Remember me affectionately to Fr. H[aseltine], and best wishes of your dearly attached friend,
>
> Anne Baxter

Ann Carroll Martin, daughter of Mr. and Mrs. Owen Martin of Fayetteville, Tennessee, registered at Nazareth on October 10, 1831, at age fourteen. She remained there until she graduated in 1836. Ann later married Mr. John Baxter. The Nazareth baptismal registry for February 23, 1845 lists the baptism by Father De Luyne of Edward Carroll Baxter, son of John Baxter and Ann C. Martin, his lawful wife. Sister Columba Carroll is listed as Sponsor. Ann and John's grandson, also named John Baxter, then living in Brooklyn, New York, visited Nazareth in 1954 and each year thereafter for some years—at Derby time. In June 1957 Nazareth College honored him by conferring the Medal of Merit.

Others mentioned in the letter have not yet been discovered in a public record.

This is the last extant letter before Catherine was again elected Mother and returned to Nazareth in 1850. The enthusiastic and obviously sincere devotion in the letter and the nature of its principal news may indeed have given her great pleasure and renewed her zeal in time for her own call back to service in the motherhouse and academy the following August.

Conclusion

When August 1850 presented that call, Catherine voiced the pain of another long separation from her dear orphans. As she had long been a member of the Board of Trustees of the congregation's legal incorporation, she had to know some of the special needs and challenges that awaited her: the great need of space for Nazareth's growing student body and resident community, issues rising in the Nashville mission, the need to relocate St. Vincent Infirmary as a distinct hospital, and the ongoing need of funds for daily living and learning in the expanding school, novitiate, and professed SCN population. She might have guessed her labors to come; she could hardly have foreseen the legacy she would leave in August 1856.

Catherine Spalding in Kentucky Women Remembered exhibit, State Capitol, Frankfort. (Painting by Paula Jull, Courtesy of the Kentucky Council on Women.)

Mother Catherine Spalding. (Courtesy SCN Archival Center.)

Pleasant Hill, home of Basil Spalding, Catherine's grandfather, in Pomfret, Maryland. (Courtesy SCN Archival Center.)

Howard–Flaget log house at St. Thomas, residence of first Sisters of Charity, 1812–1822. (Courtesy SCN Archival Center.)

Bishop John Baptist David. (Courtesy SCN Archival Center.)

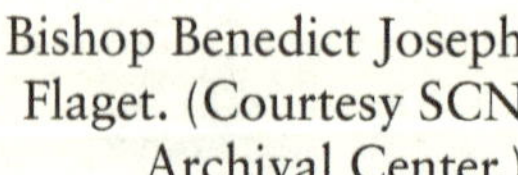

Bishop Benedict Joseph Flaget. (Courtesy SCN Archival Center.)

John Bucklin, mayor of Louisville in 1834. (Archives and Special Collections, University of Louisville, Image No. P00625.)

To the Mayor & Council of the City of Louisville

Gentlemen,

At that gloomy period, when the Cholera threatened to lay our City desolate, & nurses for the sick poor could not be obtained on any terms.— Revd Mr Abell, in the name of the Society of which I have the honor to be a member, proffered the *gratuitous* services of as many of our Sisters as might be necessary in the then existing distress: requiring merely that their expenses should be paid.— This offer was accepted; as the order from your honorable board, inviting the Sisters, will now show.—— But, when the money was ordered from your Treasury to defray those expenses. I had the mortification to remark, that, instead of saying: "the *expenses* of the Sisters of Charity, the word *services* was substituted.— I immediately remonstrated against it,— & even mentioned the circumstance to the Mayor & another Gentleman of the Council.— & upon being promised that the error should be corrected, I remained satisfied that it had been attended to; until a late assertion from one of the pulpits of the city leads me to believe that it stands yet uncorrected on your books; as these same books were referred to, in proof of the assertion. If so, Gentlemen, pardon the liberty I take in refunding you the amt. paid for the above named expenses. Well convinced, that our community for whom I have acted in this case, would far prefer incurring the expense themselves rather than submit to so unjust an odium.—

Gentlemen, be pleased to understand that we are not hirelings.— & if we are, in practice, the servants of the poor, the sick & the orphan;—we are voluntarily so: But we look for our reward, in another & a better World.

With sincere respect Gentlemen,
Your Obt. Servt.

$75.—

Catherine Spalding
Sister of Charity

Feb. 10th 1834—

Letter of Mother Catherine to Mayor of Louisville, 1834. (Courtesy SCN Archival Center.)

1844 July 6.

Right Reverend Father;

Since the reception of your letter, containing your late orders relative to the changes you required in our Community, we have unitedly spent much time in meditation and prayer to God for his light and grace; — we have repeatedly offered up Novenas, supplicating that his holy will might be done in regard to our dear community. And now, most beloved and venerated Father; it is with sentiments of the deepest respect, and true filial regard, together with a profound regret, that we have come to the conclusion to lay before you, our Bishop and Father, our humble and earnest entreaty, that we may be allowed to continue unchanged, in the manner in which we have been established in your Diocess, by your zealous co-laborer, our revered Father and Founder in Kentucky.

We entered the house of Nazareth, and embraced, with our whole hearts, the practices, rules and constitutions given to us by him, being assured that they were dictated by the Blessed Vincent of Paul, solemnly authorized and approved progress of Nazareth, can doubt its being the work of the Most High.

In the presence of our good and merciful God, and kneeling before the sacred image of his crucified Son, we hereto affix our names — earnestly imploring you, our dear and truly revered Father, in the name and for the sake of Him, whose place you hold in our regard, to yield to our entreaties, and once more restore to your children that happiness and quiet of mind they have so long enjoyed at Nazareth — promising you, in all the sincerity of our hearts, that we shall, with the grace of God, redouble our efforts to advance in the virtues of our state of life, and to do good in your Diocese.

Sister Catherine M. Supr.
Sister Pelagia Asst.
Sister Serena Tr.
Sister Cecily Mistress
Sister Frances
Sister Mildred
Sister Clare
Sister Mary.
Sister Angela
Sister Josephine
Sister Claudia
Sister Euphrasia
Sr. Victoria
Sister Agatha

Sister Monica
Sister Dorothea
Sister Veronica
Sister Clementina
Sister Sebastia
Sister Columba
Sister Emily
Sister Petronella
Sister Sophia
Sister Harriet

Sister Mathilda
Sister Bernardine
Sister Mary Vincent
Sister Scholastica
Sister Alice

First and final pages of 1841 letter to Bishop Flaget. (Courtesy SCN Archival Center.)

Mother Catherine's missions in Louisville. Key: 1–3: Cathedral area: locations of first Presentation Academy in basement of St. Louis Church, expansion to street north of church, and first St. Vincent Orphan Asylum on south side of church. 4: Second St. Vincent Orphanage, Jefferson and Wenzel Streets. 5: St. Joseph Infirmary, Fourth Street. 6: St. Patrick School, Thirteenth and Market Streets. (Courtesy SCN Archival Center.)

Richard Pius Miles, Bishop of Nashville, Tennessee. (Courtesy St. Mary's of the Seven Sorrows Parish, Nashville, Tennessee.)

Statue of Mother Catherine with orphans in front of Louisville Cathedral. Artist, Raymond Graf. (Courtesy SCN Archival Center.)

Drawing of Nazareth campus by Sister Hilaria Bamber, ca. 1844–1845. (Courtesy SCN Archival Center.)

Bishop Martin John Spalding of Louisville. (Courtesy SCN Archival Center.)

Print of Louisville street downtown, ca. 1850. (Courtesy SCN Archival Center.)

Print of St. Joseph Infirmary, Fourth Street, Louisville, 1850s. (Courtesy SCN Archival Center.)

Sign for St. Catherine Street, Louisville, 2016. (Courtesy of Diane Curtis, SCN Archival Center.)

Sister Julia Hobbs, SCN, Mother Catherine's helper and for years her replacement at St. Vincent Orphanage. (Courtesy SCN Archival Center.)

New Church, erected 1854, with academy building of 1825–1826. (Courtesy SCN Archival Center.)

Nazareth campus in 1871. Far left building and connecting corridor are from late period. The 1855 academy and the original 1825 building extend right to church of 1854 and rectory. (Courtesy SCN Archival Center.)

Mother Catherine Spalding in the 1850s. (Ambrotype courtesy SCN Archival Center.)

Gravestone of Mother Catherine Spalding, Nazareth Cemetery. (Courtesy Kelly McDaniels, SCN Archival Center.)

4

Development at Nazareth

1850–1856

When Mother Catherine returned to leadership in 1850, she wrote to Sister Claudia, "You know what it has again cost me to be torn away . . . from my poor dear children who need someone to struggle for a living for them" (Letter 4-1 below). She was leaving a loved ministry, heavy, yet light compared to what she would carry in the next six years. These years, nevertheless, would be extraordinarily fruitful, as much as any in her life. She would leave a legacy, both spiritual and material, that still stands.

The community she was to lead had grown by forty-three members. Many of the newcomers were immigrants, introducing a strong Irish strain among the SCN and a cultural challenge to the native-born, of English ancestry. Catherine had the task of unifying all who could "make true Sisters of Charity" (Letter 4-24), urging all, by voice or letter, to the spirit and observance of authentic religious life and placing them in missions suited to their capacities and the existing needs. In governing, she had now to collaborate with a new bishop, her own distant cousin, Martin John Spalding, a man not reluctant to state his views and exert his authority concerning the religious communities of his diocese.

With new members, Catherine and her Council could collaborate in opening new missions. The diocese determined to shelter orphan boys at the old St. Thomas parish, and the SCN would contribute the bricks of the 1818 building as well as the Sisters' labors. St. Patrick Free School at Thirteenth and Market Streets in Louisville could meet the educational needs of the poor Irish immigrants—after Mother Catherine received assurance that the Sisters would be spared the severe hunger and bad housing of their first year. And Bishop George Aloysius Carrell of the new diocese of Covington in northern Kentucky might have SCN Sisters for two schools, once it was clearly agreed that an academy for young ladies would support a Cathedral School for the poor.

St. Vincent Infirmary could at last be separated from St. Vincent Orphanage; it was moved to the former Jesuit college building on Fourth Street and renamed St. Joseph Infirmary. To accomplish this, Catherine had to invest huge amounts of energy, travel, and time in necessary inspections, negotiations, and collaborative decisions. Before the former Jesuit building was purchased from the diocese, inquiries were made about various plots of land in central Louisville. And even after the transfer, investigations were made about the purchase of some property from James Guthrie, in light of possible later construction. No new hospital or mission ever was raised there, but Guthrie gave the area permanent significance in its name, St. Catherine Street.

All these missions, and those longer established, had to be visited. Evidence suggests strongly that the second oldest branch house, St. Vincent Academy in Union County, was a source of ongoing concern. It shared land with Sacred Heart Parish and the oversight of a strong-minded pastor, Elijah Durbin, who was only too eager to have Nazareth share parish expenses. And the "troubles" of the 1830s, which had sadly infected the local community there, seem not to have been fully healed.

Nor was Catherine herself fully healed of the aftereffects of the drastic treatment of her malaria in the late 1830s. Through most of this last administration she had to endure severe headaches and neuralgia, and for the first time she refers in letters to her own poor health and her need to resign herself to "never be fully well again" (Letter 4-22). Her poor health elicited sympathy and serious concern expressed in the letters of her assistant, Columba Carroll. Catherine's own concerns were more for the other Sisters, dying of the demon "consumption"—seventeen in this period, most of them fewer than ten years in vows. Her letters lament them and urge care of health on the living.

No loss of Sisters could strike her with as much grief as that suffered in the separation of the local community of Nashville, St. Mary's Academy and St. John's Hospital, from the SCN community. The long-simmering tension with Bishop Pius Miles over his requests and his challenge to the authority of the Nazareth motherhouse reached its boiling point in 1850, when he and his clerical assistant, Father Ivo Schacht, insisted that the Nashville community separate from Nazareth and become diocesan. The separation took from Catherine one of her most cherished friends and collaborators, Sister Xavier Ross, and five other SCN Sisters, who became the Sisters of Charity of Nashville. Eight Sisters returned to Nazareth, including Sister Claudia Elliott. Various letters of the period illumine this crisis and Catherine's pain. She herself never refers to it. She died shortly before further crisis with the bishop sent the Nashville Sisters to Kansas to form the Sisters of Charity of Leavenworth.

Amid all expansions and contractions of membership and mission, Catherine remained headmistress of the school and hostess for all its events. She still had the leading responsibility to house and feed the growing numbers of Sisters and students, dependent chiefly on payments received from the labors of the academy. And she still had troubles over tuition and still received numerous self-excusing letters of nonpayment. But the students still needed dormitory space; providing it would preoccupy much of this administration.

The need for space at Nazareth especially pressed on the community. In addition to crowding in the school and church, there was no designated convent, and the Sisters took their sleeping quarters wherever they could, even over workplaces such as the laundry. The general need to build again demanded action, requiring Catherine's leadership and collaboration in time-consuming meetings of the Council and the legal Board of Trustees about construction of new buildings.

Expansion began in 1850 with an exchange, acre for acre, with a Mr. Aud for his land adjoining Nazareth farm. Nazareth was also to pay $25 an acre for any of his land in excess of theirs. Planning for extensive construction began with a letter to architect

William Keely in March 1851 and a Council decision in 1852 that Keely be commissioned to build a convent and academy as soon as money was available. Keely and Mother Catherine would go to St. Louis to examine institutions there and, if necessary, to the convent of the Sacred Heart "on the coast."

Bishop David's counsel to build first a house for God prevailed as a community tradition. In later letters, Catherine reports the gradual rise of a church (1854) and a new academy (1855), and the remodeling of the 1825 academy building into a suitable motherhouse. She anticipates joyfully seeing the old school transformed into a newly arranged convent "where we may live as a regular community should live." Then, she says, "I may lay me down in peace" (Letter 4-22).

Catherine's final letters from this period suggest that her last year in office may indeed have been less stressful, or at least allowed her more time to write to Sisters in the branch houses. Loving letters release her tender feelings and concern for their happiness and spiritual growth. In August 1856, her term completed, she could write that she neither knew nor cared where she would go next. "If I can save my soul, all will be well" (Letter 4-25).

Letters by Mother Catherine Spalding, 1850–1856

4-1

Nazareth
August 29th, 1850

Well, my dear good old friend & Sister, here I am again
seated at the old place writing to your own dear self.—
But you know what it has again cost me to be torn away,
as it were from my poor dear children who need some
one to struggle for a living for them. May their Father
in Heaven protect & provide for them as he has ever
done.—I received your long, kind letter in due time; but
we have been so engaged & oppressed with sickness &
trouble this summer that I had neither time nor spirit

to write to any one.—Our poor orphans had measles, scarlet fever whooping cough & cholera at the same time. Several of them went to join the angels in Heaven & I trust to pray for those they left.—The health is much better there now, & that of the city is good. How glad I would be to see you once more—but we must wait the disposition of divine providence, if we live, all things will come around.—Pray often for me as I know you do.—Mother F. & Sister Gabriella will give you all the news.—& I will always be glad to hear from you.—

Ever & sincerely yours,

Tone and specific references suffice to determine that this letter is from Mother Catherine to her dear Sister Claudia Elliott in Nashville. Neither would require the written names in the letter.

Mother Frances Gardiner ("Mother F.") was the Sisters' consistent choice as alternate of Mother Catherine. The two women were elected every six years, each when the other's term expired. At this time, Catherine was resuming office at Nazareth, and Mother Frances had been assigned to Nashville to try to resolve the tensions there with the bishop's requirements and Sister Xavier Ross's leadership.

Sister Gabriella Todd was the daughter of Judge Thomas Todd, a prominent citizen of Frankfort. She was professed in 1845 and missioned to Nashville in 1846, probably returning with Mother Frances after a summer break at Nazareth. When the separation of Nashville from Nazareth became official in July 1851, Gabriella was one of those who returned to Nazareth. She appears later in a letter of Catherine to Bishop Martin John Spalding.

4-2

Nazareth Nov. 18th/50
Mr. Keely

I write this by Isaac Bell, who goes now, according to your last direction, "after two weeks," to live with you.—

We sincerely hope he may prove to be all that you wish him, & that his friends, who feel so much interest in his well-doing, may not be disappointed. Mr. Byrne will write you other particulars.—

With best wishes & sincere regard
Your obt. Sert.
Sr. Catharine Spalding

William Keely was a nationally known architect, chiefly renowned for his church buildings (see Appendix A). He had recently designed the cathedral in Louisville, replacing the old St. Louis Church on Fifth Street. At Nazareth, he was designing and supervising construction of a new church and academy.

Isaac Bell (Ike) was a slave, purchased, according to Council minutes of August 27, 1844, with his wife and two children from a Mr. Linth for $825. Apparently he was considered likable, competent, and trustworthy. In this instance he was sent to work with and for William Keely, very likely as partial compensation for Nazareth's debt to Keely (see Doyle, *Pioneer Spirit,* pp. 122–123, 195).

Mr. Byrne might be either the overseer involved in the construction at Nazareth or a local priest advising in the project (priests then were addressed as "Mr."). Council minutes record the employment of a James Byrne in 1847 for one year at $100, but no record exists of his continuing employment three years later. If a priest, he would have to be the Reverend Robert Byrne, then in his later years and engaged in light missionary work around New Hope, Kentucky. He died in 1856. The Reverend William Byrne, known for building and managing the local colleges and a likely advisor for Nazareth, had died in the 1833 cholera outbreak.

4-3

Nazareth March 8th 1851
Mr. William Keely,
Dear Sir,

Rev. Father Hazeltine directs me to inform you, that the

Base course of stone for our Church, is now all ready to put on; & Mr. Brown is anxious to have it on so soon as the weather will admit of it. They say, also, your presence here will be necessary before anything can be done. I am also desired to request you will not forget the Blocks &c. that you spoke of bringing or sending, for the purpose of carrying the stones to their places.

Now, please, don't think me importunate in saying I would be very glad to see the general plan you have made for carrying out our own buildings here—as I would prefer to have nothing done or commenced, nor even decided on; but in view of, & in accordance with that plan.—Still we are greatly in want of some little arrangements & even of more room.—I write this expecting to find you in Louisville, where, I hope you are returned safe & in good health.—With best respect to Mrs. Keely,

I am very respectfully etc.
—Your obedient servant & friend
Sr. Catharine Spalding

P.S. Your friends here, are all very glad to learn that you have declined undertaking the Cathedral of Pittsburgh, as it will save you much labor & exposure during the coming summer season, particularly should it prove unhealthy. Best wishes & kind remembrance for Ike.

In addition to building the new church and school, the community hoped to gain urgently needed space by remodeling the 1825 building into a suitable motherhouse-convent. Mother Catherine's own competence and sense of responsibility in such matters is evidenced by her forthright but respectful assertion of her need and right to be informed and involved in the specific plans.

Father Joseph Haseltine was ecclesiastical superior of the SCN congregation and chaplain at Nazareth. As this letter indicates, he was an excellent and dependable manager of business and a great friend and support to both the community and the academy.

Of all the Browns resident in Nelson and Jefferson Counties, the likeliest match to this letter's Mr. Brown is Colonel James Marshall Brown, who is credited in Ben Webb's history for doing the brick masonry work on St. Joseph Cathedral, Holy Cross Church, and other sites in Bardstown. He was a veteran of the War of 1812 and was related to the Marshall family of Virginia and Kentucky, and to Browns in California and Texas. He might well have been a contractor or advisor on so significant a project as the Gothic church going up at Nazareth.

4-4

Nazareth, June 17th/'51
My ever dear & good Sister,

I hope you do not think hard of me, for my long silence.—As you know it does not proceed from indifference or forgetfulness.—No, my dear Claudia, I can never forget you.—The longer we are separate, the more I think of you, & your persevering kindness to me while we were to-gether & the more I value it.—I have this evening, while I write, a severe head-ache, which brings you to my mind more forcibly.—Still I have to thank God that I have had so little of it since I came back to Nazareth.—We have such a large, noisy Family that it would be hard to have much head-ache—& at this time all are very busy both in doors & out doors; blacks & all.—But Jane had to take time to have another young boy, her tenth child. & Emily whom you left a little girl, will soon have her 2nd.

Well, I had to stop writing till my head got better & now I return to finish.—Your brother visits us every few weeks, & looks very well, seems in good spirits, he complains that you do not write to him.—Now Sister don't neglect that, & still less must you neglect writing to me your old & true friend.—Your letters are always a great satisfaction to me.—We have two girls baptized this evening & 3 others will be soon, all, except one, have come to school this year.—The school numbers about one hundred & fifty.—Thanks be to God, all are well. Remember me to Mr. & Mrs. Mateer, My love to Sister Christine & all the Sisters.—Respects to the Bishop & clergy.—

Ever yours devotedly
Catharine

This letter to Sister Claudia was written in the final weeks before the Nashville separation was finalized in July 1851. Catherine must have had a foreboding that she could not prevent some Sisters choosing to stay in Nashville, so there is a poignancy in her praise of her "dear Claudia" for her fidelity and "persevering kindness" in their personal friendship. Catherine's writing at all in this time of extra labors and severe headaches witnesses her depth of affection and dread of separation from Claudia.

The girls baptized can be traced with reasonable surety in the archival record of baptisms and confirmations. On June 18, 1851, Elizabeth Gallagher and Lucy Moss were baptized, with Mother Catherine and Sister Harriet Emerson as sponsors; Elizabeth Wilson and Sarah Bradford were baptized, also with SCN sponsors, on July 2. No third student is listed all that summer, though several infants received the sacrament, one the son of Nazareth servants. Sarah (or Sallie) Bradford was the niece of Jefferson Davis and the youngest of four sisters, all Nazareth students; several were converts to Catholicism.

For information on Sister Christine Coomes, see Letters 2-8 and 3-5. She had been in Nashville since August of 1843, so Catherine might have assumed she would be in a struggle of choice about separating. She did return to Nazareth with Claudia and the others and was missioned at the Fifth Street School in Louisville, later at Bethlehem in Bardstown, serving twice as local superior. She died in 1868.

4-5

Nazareth May 20th/52
Dear Rev. Sir,

I have received your enclosing one from Sister Gabriella to which I have replied.—As to her visiting her Father in vacation, I don't think there will be any difficulty made.—The manner of her doing so can then be decided on;—I don't see that she need be any longer restless on that subject.

Our school, thank God, is quite healthy—some of the Sisters indisposed—poor Sister Hillaria's health is very bad. There is a great stir around us with workmen, etc.—When shall we expect you up? I sometimes think I would be glad to have a conversation with you; and then I fear it would be presumption and I hesitate. At least. It might appear so, tho' I don't mean it. I suppose you are much engaged with the weight of the Diocese on your shoulders.

Well, I most heartily wish you success for the glory of God and the good of religion.
Pray for me. Yours truly in our Lord,
Sr. Catharine Spalding

My love to your Sister Susan when you see her. Best respects to Mr. Bruyere and to Dr. Hagan & family.

(Copy of a letter found in a trunk in the basement of the cathedral, Louisville, Kentucky, in 1967. Courtesy of Mr. Francis P. Clark.)

The recipient of this letter has to be Bishop Martin John Spalding, coadjutor and successor to Bishop Benedict Joseph Flaget. Evidently he had received a letter from Sister Gabriella Todd expressing her desire to visit her father, the prominent Judge Todd in Frankfort, also some other matters for which the bishop is sending her letter to Catherine. Gabriella may have been one who never could quite let go of her family and its status, nor of her judgment of Catherine's administration. Catherine tells what the bishop would want to know about Gabriella's request; the rest she reserves to herself to handle with her young Sister. An opinion may be implied in her remark that she sometimes thinks she "would be glad to have a conversation with you."

The situation cannot have been a welcome addition to all else that was pressing on Catherine's mind in 1852. Sister Hilaria Bamber was one of the Bamber Sisters who nursed in the cholera outbreak of 1832; she served as a teacher, but was mainly a nurse in Louisville and Nazareth. She drew pictures of Nazareth as it was in 1844. Now she was dying, and did die in August 1852, during the height of the building era.

Mr. Bruyere is almost certainly the Reverend John Bruyere, a French priest who volunteered for the Kentucky mission in 1841. By 1852 he had taught in the seminary and college, assisted Father Haseltine at Nazareth, and become assistant at the cathedral in Louisville. In 1853 he transferred to diocesan ministries in Canada, where he earned honors and died in 1888.

It is uncertain whether "your Sister Susan" is Susan Hagan, SCN, or some other person known or related to the bishop or to Dr. Hagan. Dr. Hagan may possibly be the John Hagan, who is listed as a student of medicine in the Louisville Directory of 1832. By 1852 he could have an established practice in the city.

4-6

Sr. Genevieve McGinnis
St. Catherine, Lexington
Nazareth May 22nd/'52
My dear Sister,

I ought to give you a long answer to your very kind & interesting letter; it is just such a one as I like because it gives so many little details of such little incidents & common place things as always interest me.—True we have some very heavy undertakings on hand which give us a good deal of trouble, & we are surrounded by work & workmen, besides our very large family.—But we look a good deal for help & assistance from the prayers & efforts of all our dear absent Sisters & as all is for the glory of God, I trust he will bring us thro' & give us grace to save our souls.—We have also just finished our Jubilee, & had the happiness to see all the blacks approach the holy sacraments. They edified us all by their pious attention to all the exercises.—Ed. & Teresa made their first communion.—I hope Sister Francis Xavier's health is quite restored, give her my love, as also Sister Marcella, Sis. Aloysia & all the Sisters.—Tell Sister Humbeline she must not neglect her cough—we have buried Sisters enough now.—I am glad Sister Benedicta's health improves. May God bless you all, & make you true Sisters of Charity, as I doubt not but you are trying to be.—Sister Louisa is now able to sit in the parlor & walk about with her cane. Poor Sister Hillaria is no better, & two or three others are not well.—Perhaps I am too anxious for the Sisters to be well. & God may not will it should be so.—Still I do think everyone is bound to be prudent about her health, for without it the work of God & the neighbor could not be carried on. exercise & duty will never hurt us it [if] we are prudent.—Once more my best love to all.—& respects to Father M'Guire.—I was pleased to see the improvement in you[r] writing & spelling. Your sincere friend & mother

Catharine

A Jubilee was a special period of religious services and celebration, usually related to a particular event or time period, and encouraging renewed faith and spiritual practice. (See Doyle, *Pioneer Spirit,* p. 83 for the Holy Year Jubilee of 1826.) Ed and Teresa were slaves; participation in the sacraments was a recognized right of the servants and encouraged by instruction.

For information on Sister Genevieve McGinnis, see Appendix

A. Recognition of various Sisters is a characteristic of Catherine's letters to any Sister or house. Sr. Francis Xavier Nolan was Irish born, an immigrant at ten with her parents, at twenty, an SCN. She was Nazareth treasurer four times, was elected for three-year terms between her other missions, and was described as a "woman of remarkable business ability—truly Christian woman, greatly loved by all." Sister Marcella Alvey was one of the returnees from Nashville in 1851, sent to St. Catherine Academy in Lexington. In 1858, she became local superior in Newport; in 1863 Mother Columba brought her home to Nazareth, very ill; she died soon after, just short of her twentieth anniversary of vows. Sister Aloysia Pryor also was a veteran of the academies at Nashville and Union County, then Lexington, and later Nazareth and Owensboro; she would be a Civil War nurse and live to 1889. Sister Humbeline Fagan was another Irish SCN. She spent seven years in Lexington and nursed in a U.S. military hospital during the Civil War; she survived to 1886. Sister Benedicta Drury and her sister, Sister Blandina Drury, grew up in Union County, where their father and uncle built a schoolhouse at St. Vincent's. Sister Louisa Dorsey (see Appendix A) had several episodes of broken bones; she is clearly recovering at Nazareth at this time. Sister Hilaria would die in the coming August. With the frequency of illnesses—coughs, canes, consumption—Catherine's concern for the health of her Sisters is not remarkable, only very consistent in her letters. Her respectful greetings to the local pastor are also consistent.

4-7

Nazareth June 3rd/52
My dear Sisters, all,

I have just been away from you long enough, to make me think a great deal about you all, & feel great solicitude both spiritually & temporally, tho' I doubt not but you are all far, better disposed than I am.—Still I hope you may in the sight of God, repair some of my blunders.—We are going on here with a very large building & the new church also; & all getting on very well—& hope, too, before very long, to begin an hospital for the service of the poor & suffering members of Christ.—But dear Sisters what will all that profit us, if we should neglect the spiritual building of our own perfection, by a faithful observance of rules & the true spirit of religion.—Poor human nature is so apt to let every little thing interfere with regular attendance at our religious exercises & other observances; where-as, with a little management & forethought, we might nearly always be able to attend them—& it is a sad thing to contract a habit of neglecting them, as it is merit for us when duty obliges us to postpone or omit them. Oh! Let us then be watchful on ourselves in this as much as with every part of our rules & vows to God.—It is the only way to secure the blessings of God on our labors for his glory & secure to ourselves an eternal crown in Heaven.—You are particularly blest in that house.—as all your labors are for those immediate works of charity. Then have courage—& still strive more & more to make spiritual & corporal works go together & remember St. Vincent says if you keep your rules, they will keep you.—Pray for me while I never shall forget any of you.

Catharine

Nothing identifies the recipients of this letter; the safest assumption is that they are the Sisters Catherine had left at the orphans' asylum less than two years before, whose youthful charges indeed called for immediate works of charity. The letter stands as a main testament to Catherine's love for works of charity and her sense of the need to keep such work balanced with the requirements of a solidly spiritual and communal way of life. It is one of her most frequently quoted letters.

4-8

Rev. Mr. Quinn is respectfully invited to attend the

examination at Nazareth which will commence on the 12th and end on the 15th of July. The exercises will begin each day at 8 o'clock a.m.

C. Spalding
Nazareth June 29th, 1852

(The letter in the archives is not in Mother Catherine's writing. It is a copy of a note found by Mr. Francis P. Clark in 1967 in a trunk in the basement of the cathedral in Louisville.)

Rev. John Quinn was an Irish immigrant ordained for the diocese in 1838. From 1839 to his death in 1852, he was assistant at the cathedral in Louisville; he died just before the consecration of the new structure and is buried beneath it. He would have known Catherine and the other Sisters very well from their presence on Fifth Street and was very supportive of the mission to the orphans.

4-9

Nazareth Nov 13th/'52
My very dear Sister,

I have only time to write you a very little letter. But don't judge of the sentiments by the size of the letter, for I assure you it conveys the warmest, deepest & most sincere love & wishes for your present & eternal happiness. But of this you are sure, because you are daily striving to be a true & devoted Sister of Charity, in the full observance of the rules & the fulfillment of all duties. & such as do that are sure of happiness both here & here-after—altho' they must daily carry a portion of their Savior's cross & often deny themselves & practice humility in spirit & in actions.—For such is the way the Saints followed to Heaven—& the only way left for you & one & all, all of to get there;—let us struggle then for that crown in store for us.—Oh! what a grace the gift of steady perseverance is. St. Ligouri was right when he said we should at every hour implore God to grant us the grace of prayer & perseverance to the end!—My best love to dear Sister Benedicta, I will write to her very soon.—May God bless you all! It is my daily prayer.—

Yours Catharine

I send you this handkerchief—tho' it has my name on it. I hope you will not object to that little blemish; it was marked before I knew it.—Well I am sorry your postulants of last August have been so unsteady or knew their own minds so little.—I am more surprised at Kate Hughes than any. She surely is not sincere or else has no mind of her own as she changed like the weather & spoke so many different ways.—Poor Caroline's health improves, & with it her spirits are better.—Your friend & Mother Catharine

The recipient of this letter is probably Sister Genevieve McGinnis, also the recipient of Letter 4-6, which also mentions Sister Benedicta Drury as present at St. Catherine's in Lexington. Genevieve seems to have been a devoted and frequent correspondent of Catherine.

The postulants mentioned were evidently former students at St. Catherine's Academy, whose entry to the SCN had been guided by Sister Genevieve and others in the Lexington school. Kate Hughes entered on August 19, 1852, and left after less than two months, on October 6, 1852. Caroline Emerson entered on the same day, received the habit and the name Sister Gertrude on March 25, 1853, and made vows on August 25, 1854. So Mother Catherine was able to affirm her in her own last term of office; she did not live to know that Caroline did not finally persevere, but withdrew on July 4, 1859.

The register of the SCN shows that seventeen postulants entered in 1852, six of them in August. Of the seventeen, twelve withdrew, nine in less than a year; two made vows but withdrew in less than five years. Only five persevered in vows until death, three to forty-five years. Such were the exigencies of discernment and choice to develop the community's life. This makes the context for the reference to St. Alphonsus Ligouri, a son of Italian nobles who became a Doctor of Law at age sixteen but who, after losing an important case, determined to labor only for the glory of God, entered the priesthood, vowed never to lose time, spent his life in prayer, ministry, writing, and charity, and died in 1787 at age ninety-one. Catherine may well have felt an affinity to his spirituality and vocational labors.

4-10

Well, my dear Sister Genevieve; All are busy here trying to make April Fools & begging for recreation, but I am so hard-hearted that I won't grant it, so they have to pursue their studies as they have just finished [their] Easter Holy days.—We renewed our Vows on Good Friday. & altho' we were sorry to have no Mass for the occasion still I think it was very solemn and the Sisters seemed impressed with it.—Several of the old Sisters remarked that they had never seen Good Friday pass off more solemnly & devotionally.—In the morning after reciting the prayers to the five wounds of our Lord we pronounced our vows & then said the act of Oblation to the Blessed Virgin, found in the Rules of St. Vincent.—to suit M. Lavial's convenience. We had the sermon & adoration of the Cross at 3 o'clock & the Sisters made the Stations all together.—When we renewed our Vows there were but few in the church except the Sisters & Father Hazeltine & it seemed almost filled with the sisters, the church in black with the Sisters in black, gave a very solemn appearance.—Pray for us dear Sisters all of you that we may advance more & more in our the spirit of our holy vocation, as God pleases to open further & further the ways & means of carrying out its works of usefulness & charity & first of all the sanctification of our own souls.—I suppose you have heard that your dear little Mary Genevieve, at the Asylum, has taken her flight to heaven. I learned it from a letter from one of the Sisters.—Poor child; her bliss for eternity commenced. I hope you have an intercessor in her before God.—My best love to the Sisters Benedicta, Gabriella, Aloysia, Humbeline, &c.—if I can I will write to some of them by this occasion. Did you ever get the handkerchiefs I sent you in little bundle with some other trifles, which that wild Mary left on [F]ifth Street on her way to home?—

Pray for me Yours ever & truly
Catharine

Catherine seems to have welcomed and responded freely to letters from Sister Genevieve McGinnis, connecting through her to the other Sisters with her greetings and affection. For information on Sisters Benedicta, Aloysia, and Humbeline, see Letter 4-6 above. Sister Gabriella Todd, after returning from Nashville, spent some years at Lexington. The identity of "wild Mary" remains an interesting puzzle. "M. Lavial" must be the priest who became the third bishop of Louisville. At this time he was professor of philosophy at St. Thomas Seminary near Bardstown and could easily have done liturgical ministry at Nazareth.

Archival records of the orphan asylum do not list a Mary Genevieve, but three little girls named Mary died there in 1852: Mary Buckman, received in 1851 at four years old after her mother's death; Mary McIntosh, placed there by a Mrs. McCarty; and Mary Fry, received at two years old, baptized, and dead the same year. This scenario may have been all too frequent, trying the emotional stamina of the Sisters who cared for these little girls.

4-11

Nazareth June 8th 1853
Dear Eliza,

We have had the pleasure of welcoming to your old home

your little sister.—She is in perfect health, and I hope will be perfectly contented. She seems very cheerful. It would have greatly added to our pleasure, could you have accompanied her.

You are far from being forgotten; on the contrary, all retain a most affectionate remembrance of you. Medora has commenced her classes today.

Say to your Mother that every possible care shall be taken of her dear child.—

I shall write soon.—Yours with much affection—
Catherine Spalding

Eliza Cook (see Appendix A) was an alumna and the older sister of Medora Cook, recently enrolled. They were among the numerous students from the Deep South in these years.

4-12

Nazareth Dec. 29th/53
Very Rev. dear Sir,

Yours of the 27th inst. was received last evening. & in reply I have to say—the Council are willing to receive Miss Brooks on your recommendation—& she will meet a welcome reception at Naz. whenever it suits her convenience to come. Should she wish any information with regard to her preparation for coming that you could not give her, you might if you choose introduce her to Sister Serena, who can tell her any thing that she might wish to know.

Please accept my cordial good wishes of the holy season, for your self, the good Bishop, & all the clergy. Thank God we are enjoying good health at Nazareth. I am sorry to learn Wm. Keely is ill; all things here stand pretty much as when you last saw them—only we have had the rubbish & dirt cleared out of the Academy & the cross-walls to support the floors are made.—Please

> remember us at the holy Altar & believe me with much respect & esteem
>
> Your obt. sert. in +
> Sr. Catharine Spalding
>
> What day may we expect the honor of a visit from his excellency, the Nuncio?

Since the Council needed to affirm Miss Brooks's reception, it is likely she was to become a postulant. Recommendation by a priest was also usual, as was a Sister's help for the necessary preparations in clothing or other goods. Sister Serena Carney, one of the four founders of Presentation Academy in Louisville, was there again 1847–1860. In fact, a Mary V. Brooks did enter the SCN January 4, 1854, and made vows in August 1855. Her missions included Bethlehem Day School in Bardstown, Covington, Nazareth, and the opening of Newport. In 1862 she was assigned to the U.S. Army Hospital in Louisville but went instead to the Confederate Hospital in Lexington. She died in February 1863.

The actual recipient of this letter was not "the good Bishop" Martin Spalding, as greetings are sent to him; Father John Quinn, pastor of St. Louis Church, had died in 1852. The probable recipient, then, is Father Benedict Spalding, assistant pastor of the cathedral since 1847 and supervisor of the erection of the new structure. The cathedral priests would have been aware of the health of William Keely, architect for that edifice.

The Apostolic Nuncio to the United States was Cajetan Bedini, an Italian cleric who had held various diplomatic posts and was now commissioned by Pope Pius IX to visit the United States, examine the state of the Church there, and visit the President, bearing the good wishes and compliments of the Pope. In June 1853 he paid a courtesy visit to President Franklin Pierce and was well received. His presence, however, roused anti-Catholic demonstrations and even a conspiracy to assassinate him, from which he was saved by the warning of a plotter. The hostility of the Know-Nothings was vehement in Louisville and caused bloodshed in riots in Cincinnati. In January 1854, Bedini left New York by secret transfer to Staten Island to a steamer. Back in Italy, he was elevated to Cardinal and to the see of Viterbo. No evidence exists to suggest he ever visited Nazareth.

4-13

Nazareth Jan. 15th 1854
M Webb
Sir—

The wagon will be in Louisville tomorrow about the middle of the day. Please to send both the statues, if convenient; if not, send one. But please be certain to send all the trunks & boxes, as things are often spoiled by lying so long in Louisville. Guitars also.—

Yours respectfully
Catherine Spalding

This message serves as a good example of the way Catherine had to do business over the miles with the agent in Louisville, the one responsible for filling Nazareth's wagon with purchased goods of all sorts as well as the personal luggage and other perishable goods sent to students from their homes in the South. The date of this memo suggests that statues had been purchased for the new church, now nearing its completion and consecration. The change of agency from Francis McKay to Ben Webb (see Appendix A) and his partner—Messrs. Peters and Webb of Louisville—was made by the Council in March 1849. No reason for the change is recorded; it could have been a matter of convenience or practical costs, not necessarily of dissatisfaction with McKay or his with Nazareth. Webb became well acquainted with Nazareth and an admirer and friend of Catherine.

4-14

Nazareth Feb. 8th 1854
Dear Eliza,

> Sister Columba writes to you very recently, informing you of Medora's excellent health, which I am happy to say, still continues.
>
> Within the past week there have been some cases of Typhoid fever in the family which however we trust will prove manageable. Yet in order to prevent its spread we have deemed it advisable to give a short vacation, anticipating that which is usually given at Easter. The young ladies whose parents are near will spend this vacation with them; those whose parents are remote, we have taken to pass it in one of our establishments in town; having been earnestly solicited to permit Medora to spend her holiday at Mrs. Slaughters, we have consented. The measure adopted by us on this occasion, is, on our part, entirely a precautionary one, but knowing the tendency any disease of a Typhoid character has to spread through a family, we thought it advisable to pursue it.
>
> Be not at all uneasy about Medora as she is perfectly well and will be taken care of, and we hope this precaution, which our extreme anxiety for the children committed to our care had induced us to take, will meet your approval and that of your Mother. Yours affectionately,
>
> Catherine Spalding

As the story of the community's growth carries so many instances of the struggle to keep the Sisters healthy or restored from serious illness, it cannot surprise that a similar effort was required to maintain health in a boarding school for young women, all sharing the same quarters, food, and youthful behavior. The challenge was to impress them with their vulnerability yet not have them communicate terror to parents at a great distance. Accommodation in "one of our establishments" in town might have been in the infirmary area of the asylum, a few spare rooms at Presentation or Bethlehem Academies, or the convent quarters in either Louisville or Bardstown.

Eliza Cook from Mississippi was an alumna of Nazareth; her

younger sister Medora was now in attendance. Mrs. Anna Eliza Slaughter is listed in the 1850 Federal Census for Nelson County as age thirty, wife of Daniel S. Slaughter, a lawyer; they had eight children. They must have resided in Bardstown or vicinity and been known to students, who wanted to visit them and stay with them in the period of illness at Nazareth.

4-15

Nazareth March 6th 1854
My dear Eliza,

Your very kind letter of the 22nd ult. has Just been received, and tho' I wrote to you but a few days ago, I again do myself that pleasure.

Medora is in perfect health, and is busily engaged with her studies. You will hardly recognize her, she has grown so much. She has also become very fond of study, and is improving much. At first she did not know how to study regularly.—There have [been] no further symptoms of the fever, as I told you in my last, and our pupils are in usual health.—Poor Mrs. Campbell! Soon after the date of your letter, she must have rec'd the tidings of the change for the worse in our beloved Lelia. For upwards of a week she had been entirely free from fever, had a perfectly natural pulse, and was visibly improving. On the 22nd and the day previous she manifested an irritability of the stomach, which, however, was attended with no other symptoms to cause uneasiness, but at that period when she seemed convalescent, it made us anxious.—On the morning of the 23rd, she was taken with a spasm, and very soon after followed another. From that moment she sank rapidly. The morning before she was so gay and cheerful, making plans for studies, little thinking that soon she was to be called from us.—I cannot express to you, my dear Eliza, the shock and grief it was to us to behold this sudden and great change in her. Deeply and truly do we sympathize with her bereaved mother, for we know as no others can, how great her Mother's loss. But when God claims his own, we must resign the dearest and best.

Medora sends much love to you and her Ma, and says she intends studying now very hard to atone for her vacation. With kind regards to your Ma, I am, my dear Eliza,

Yours with respect—
Catherine Spalding

Susan Lelia Campbell, daughter of Mr. and Mrs. William R. Campbell of Greenville, Washington County, Mississippi, entered Nazareth Academy in September 1850 at the age of fourteen. Her sisters Caroline, Martha, and Margaret were also in attendance there. As the family was Protestant, the parents must have been appreciative of the education and warm atmosphere their girls were receiving. Lelia died presumably of the typhoid referred to in Letter 4-14. She was baptized before she died on February 2, 1854. The record does not indicate her parents' reaction to her baptism, but it must have been at the wish of the girl herself. She was buried at Nazareth.

Eliza and Medora Cook were from the same area of Mississippi and must have been friends of the Campbell girls and have felt Lelia's death keenly, so to elicit Mother Catherine's consolation.

4-16

Nazareth April 30th

Well my dear good Sr. Genevieve, what are you doing sitting there & I can't hear a word from you?—If you could only see how fast the walls of the new church are running up.—The tops of the window frames are already above the roof of the Sister's house—& where will it be when all is finished?—The Sisters will surely be retired then.—But I trust, if you will all pray for us & help us all you can—that the finishing & fixing that & other things will add much to completing all as a real Community establishment.—I often think of you all up there. & feel so thankful that your school is getting on well.—Oh! strive hard, all of you, that God may be honored by it—& his holy religion well served.—Give my kindest love to all the sisters—& to the girls of my acquaintance particularly the dear orphan girls.—How is Sister Antonia's health? & Sister Eulalia's lips are not quite so white I hope.—I saw Sister Anastatia in Owenboro.—She looks very well & is very active. They think her quite a treasure there.—Our invalid Sisters here, are, I think rather on the mend—& thank God the general health of the Family is good.—My best respects to Father Abraham whose prayers I beg. The Lexington girls are all well.—Excuse this scribbling & blame the old pen—you are young & can write more neatly.

—Ever yours most truly—
Catharine

Pray for those who are gone before you in that school.—

Catherine is clearly writing from Nazareth to Sr. Genevieve McGinnis in Lexington. This letter reflects the interchanges that often occurred among the missions: the orphan girls who were sent to an academy for a finished education, and the girls from the branch school who went on as students at Nazareth or as novices in the community. Catherine's letters at this time begin to reflect a deepening concern for the branch missions and the younger Sisters who served on them; she deeply desired that they maintain both a spiritual bond of interest and the health required to continue those missions and that of Nazareth. The church under construction at Nazareth and the 1825 building to be renovated as a real community motherhouse had a more than practical significance, therefore, as she looked toward the future.

Sisters Antonia Gibbons and Eulalia Gaynor were both on first missions in Lexington; their dates of moving on in mission indicate that this undated letter was written before 1853. Both served in other schools and in the orphanage; Eulalia was twice Mother's assistant; Antonia nursed in the Louisville Pest House and in St. Joseph College. Both lived until the late 1880s. Of the three Sisters named, Anastasia Luckett was the eldest, having served since her vows in 1824 at the orphanage, St. Vincent's in Union County, and then Lexington. She was at the Owensboro Academy from 1850 to 1853 and was obviously valued as a mature and experienced member of the community and staff.

For information on Father Abraham McMahon, see Letter 3-C.

4-17

Naz. Academy Sept. 12. 1854
My dear Godchild,

I received with pleasure and read with satisfaction your kind little letter; and believe me, my dear child, you do not regret more than I do the necessity which compels you to stay from school. For your own sake, my dear, I regret it; as another year would have been of great advantage to you. But as you are disappointed make good use of what you have already acquired.

I fully appreciate your Pa's good qualities, and as for that affair with regard to the road and stream of water, I say nothing about it. We pray to Almighty God for every one.

Not altogether in imagination does your God mother hover around you for often is she present in spirit with you.

I send this picture of our sweet Mother to you, my dear Kate, and St. Vincent of Paul, our holy founder to your Mother, I should like and do promise myself the happiness of seeing you and your Ma at your own house, And in the meantime you must come and see your friends at Naz.—Every one, both Sisters and girls will be delighted to see you who have made herself a favorite of all.

When you see your Grandmother, give my best love to her and tell her from me, to pray for Mother Catherine.

Farewell, for the present, my very dear child, My very best love to Ma. Tell her we will all be pleased to see her whenever she can make it convenient to come and see us. My best respects to Ma & Pa.

Pray for your devoted Godmother
M. Catherine

This letter is one of those that most reveals issues in Mother Catherine's relations and administration, yet conceals the essential information a later reader would most want. Here, a researcher digs in vain for positive identification of "Kate" and her relation to Catherine as godmother, for the reasons she could not return to school at Nazareth, for the trouble over "the road and stream of water," for the qualities, good or troublesome, of her father. Whoever Kate was, she had to have had a short stay at the school, and come from a home in the vicinity; a Catherine Gorman, five years in attendance, Catholic graduate, from Tuscumbia, Alabama, may be eliminated on these grounds. The best probable candidate as the recipient of this letter is Mary Catherine Smith, a Catholic and the adopted daughter of Mr. and Mrs. F. Robert Smith of Louisville. She entered school on March 18, 1853, and left June 29, 1854. These dates would fit with Catherine's lament in September 1854 that the girl could not return for another year. She could have been instructed and received into the Catholic Church during her tenure at the academy; it is conceivable that her parents objected to her conversion, though it would have been forbidden at Nazareth without their consent if she was underage. Her mother and grandmother seem to be among the numerous ladies who became friendly with Mother Catherine; her father must have engaged in a dispute over property boundaries and resources. Catherine's letter is as affectionate as any she wrote a student or godchild, and prudently worded to avoid creating or aggravating a disagreement or hostility or possible legal case for the community.

4-18

Nazareth October 20th/54
Rt. Rev. Dr. Bishop & Father,

It is with a sad heart & much hesitancy that I attempt to express my self to you on the present subject; & in the presence of my dear Redeemer, I wish to do it with due respect, reverence, sincerity & humble submission.—A few days since, my Revd. Superior, as was of course his duty, told me of some things that, it seem had been reported to you, relative to certain things of which they (the informers) accused your unworthy Ser[van]t.—I well know that my faults are great & many—& were I not now speaking to my Bishop, who has a right to know things as they are: I would not offer a word of explanation; but leave all to speak & think of me as they please.—One thing I was accused of was: of having given a Sister a tremendous scolding for having spoken to you, disapprovingly of the Novitiate.—Now, in truth & candor, I have studied & examined. & as far as my poor memory serves, I positively deny having ever done such a thing—& I think even common sense & policy would keep me from it—for if I were opposed to a Sister's going to you to complain of my administration; finding that she had been once, I would surely guard against giving her such an occasion to go a second time.—& if I have done so unknown to myself I would be truly thankful to be made sensible of it.—As regards the Novitiate: I can only say that, if I knew of anything that I could do & have not done, I would surely do it, & if you, dear Rev. Bishop, will give us a better & more efficacious plan, I promise most faithfully to exert myself to have it carried out. We have tried to carry out all that we can learn from our Rules, Constitutions, &c.—to which we add some exercises of Devotion, &c. Admonitions advice & instructions are not omitted. The one who has charge of the Novices, stays with them & devotes her whole time to them, is, I do believe, far more capable both in word & example than I am. & now Father, I leave that in your own hand.

Next.—Some time, not long since, a clergyman observed to me.—that you had, when speaking with him & some other priests about Nazareth, you observed that you believe there was a falling off in Nazareth—Of course I felt sad because I could not see what I could do. & yet I felt responsible.—I could only reproach myself that I had labored harder for this diocese & for my Community, for spiritual & temporal, than I had done for my own sanctification. But farther my conscience does not reproach me, as to temporalities only as a means to do good. & that in your own diocese.—Now my only resolve is, to labor for my own sanctification, & leave all in the hand of my God, trusting in his infinite mercy.—& I think I can say further: You are perfectly welcome to know whatever I may have said, provided it be understood just as I said & meant.—For I have made it a rule through life to say nothing to others, that I cared for being repeated, though I might not wish it; & few, in this world have ever had my confidence in that respect.—I have some recollection that once on an occasion that, I felt perplexed, embarrassed & unhappy, & it was in confidence & for a remedy, that I spoke with one who was my spiritual adviser,—& afterwards I had reason to think that I had not been understood.—Still I believed all was meant well—& this I think, dear Father & Bishop is at the bottom of your feelings toward me.—But I complain not; knowing that if you could see my many faults as God sees them that they would be much greater. I know I have felt very desirous to follow some rule as marked down from our constitutions & rules—believing it was necessary for permanency, peace, & good understanding of the Society. But now dear Father I willingly resign it all into your hands & the Hands

> of my God, intending never to touch upon that subject again. I will only add that if sometimes I have appeared to contend for that point, it was never meant with a view to curtail our contributions to good works, but I now leave the subject & hope God may be better pleased & served.—& now, Rt. Rev. dear Bishop, I come to the point that weighs heaviest on my simple heart.—If I am the cause of so great evil as you believe to exist—as the falling off in our Community—deficiency in the Novitiate, &c.—I most humbly beg of you, to devise some plan for having me removed & my place filled by some one more competent & better deserving your confidence; & I assure you I will most cheerfully take any corner & in any kitchen there, to concentrate all my poor energies for redeeming lost time in the salvation & sanctification of my own soul.— Perhaps no-one in your Diocese felt more real pleasure & confidence at your nomination to your high & sacred office than I did; & I have now only to regret my ill success in giving you pleasure or deserving your approbation, for which, I most sincerely implore your forgiveness & beg your blessing
>
> Catharine—

This painful letter rouses more questions than it can answer about Catherine's situation and feelings as she neared the end of her final term of office. By October 1854, the consecration of the new St. Vincent Church had occurred, and the construction of the new academy was under way. In the coming January she would write that the seats were to be put in the church and the academy would be used the following summer (Letter 4-22). The remodeling of the original academy into a suitable community house would then begin, and despite her own ill health, she could expect to see "all fixed as a community should be" and "to lay me down in peace." What then, in the midst of this hopeful period, had so disturbed the peace and necessitated a defensive letter to the bishop of Louisville?

The bishop is certainly Martin John Spalding, who had succeeded Bishop Benedict Joseph Flaget, who had died in 1850. That he was Catherine's relative, however distant, and that she could truthfully cite her "real pleasure and confidence" in his elevation to office, must have made his doubts of her all the more galling. She has heard from Father Haseltine, Nazareth's ecclesiastical superior, of accusations made against her and her administration by "informers." The bishop had apparently taken their accounts at their word and concluded that Nazareth had indeed fallen off its due religious fervor and observances. Catherine's primary objection and challenge is implied throughout her letter: why had she not heard all this directly from Bishop Spalding himself?

The nature of the complaints indicates they must have been made by one or more discontented Sisters. Catherine either does not know their identity or dismisses it—and them—from the current discussion. The initial accusation of her scolding a Sister for speaking to the bishop she disposes of by rapid denial and appeal to her (and his?) common sense. The novitiate practice she defends in due detail; if he can propose an improvement, let him give it.

A "falling off" in Nazareth is just the sort of vague charge that no administrator can readily dismiss or explain. And clearly it has cut Catherine to the heart. If she has failed in spiritual leadership, she has failed utterly; but she boldly denies that she has been remiss in her efforts for the diocese as well as her community, "for spiritual and temporal." Here the letter suggests that she had had to resist some changes in the Sisters' rule and perhaps in the "contributions to good works" that the bishop had desired. These matters, too, seem to have been topics of clerical discussion and displeasure, including some misrepresentations of what she had said, some violation of her confidence in spiritual direction. Catherine was a woman who wanted what she said to be understood as it was meant by the person to whom she directed it. She as much as says that the bishop is not one of the "few" who have had or will have her "confidence in that respect." She is able, however, with sincerity to entrust into the hands of God her own future and the community's, as they may be shaped through the command of the bishop.

Perhaps no part of the message is more sincere than her offer to resign her office if he can name a suitable replacement and allow her to devote herself to service and her own soul. It is also a bold challenge, as she must have known Spalding was too astute to rouse a furor by taking such action. To assess what this letter represents of Catherine's character, the stresses of her last years of leadership, and her management of relationships, it is useful to compare the tone, content, and style of this letter to those written in earlier crises to Bishop Flaget (Letters 2-3, 2-4).

4-19

Nazareth Nov. 4th
My dear Kate,

Your very kind and welcome letter was received some days since, but owing to my ill health I have been deprived of the pleasure of answering it sooner.

You have indeed my sincere sympathy in your late afflictions by the loss of your dear interesting little [niece]. You ask me, Dear Kate, to write an Epitaph to go on her tomb;—for such things I have no talent. But what I think most expressive would be, to have carved on the tombstone a small stem of Rose Buds—with three broken off—"To bloom in Heaven." The Stone Cutter would know how to arrange it. Yes Dear Kate, let them Bloom and Flourish in the Paradise of God.

I send accompanying this the pretty little present I promised you. It is without alloy and pure as the love I bear you.

With kind regards and respects to your parents,
I am as ever
Your Godmother—C. Spalding

The Kate of this letter may be presumed to be the same former student to whom Catherine addressed Letter 4-17. This message shows the same affection for the recipient, the same sense of an abiding relationship, and the same concern to show respect for her parents. Sympathy for the loss of the little niece is expressed with ample feeling and appropriate reserve born of faith. It is not possible to identify the deceased child nor the present sent to the well-loved godchild, Kate.

4-20

Louisville Nov. 11th/54
Dear Sister:

I am here safe thank God, Now I want you to manage the work just as you think best while I am gone, without minding what I said to big Louise. Can't you make little Louise help to carry the dishes to the mens' table & other places, & help also more in the kitchen if necessary. I only want things to go on quietly.—I will come home as soon as I can, & will get as many things as I can, 'tho I have no money. Tell Louise I will bring her something nice.

I am toler[a]bly well.—
Your Catharine—

Although Catherine does not indicate her reason for being absent in Louisville, she may well have been visiting the missions there—Presentation, the orphan asylum and infirmary—and also businesspeople and other donors. In the early 1850s, however, she had to make numerous trips to Louisville (forty miles by wagon) to enable and direct the expansion of the Louisville missions, especially the transfer of St. Vincent Infirmary from the building shared with the asylum to a former Jesuit College building on Fourth Street north of Prather (now Broadway). There it became a separate institution, St. Joseph Infirmary.

Land was also purchased south of Prather with a view to possible later hospital construction. Catherine was on site for numerous negotiations, which had to include the bishop as well as important members of the laity, and which had to be reported to the Council. And in November 1854, SCNs had only recently collaborated with the Xaverian Brothers to open St. Patrick Free School at Thirteenth and Market Streets for the Irish immigrants. The following summer, the Nazareth Council had to insist on essential living conditions for the Sisters if they were to serve another winter.

The recipient of the brief note above was probably Sister Claudia Elliott or another Sister who was managing the kitchen and meals for the servants. Catherine may have been asked to settle a dispute about labor or simply needed to encourage her deputy's power to manage by her own judgment. The note displays her typical balance of delegated authority and helpful suggestion.

4-21

You must excuse me, my very dear Sister, for detaining Sister Theodora's letter so long to slip in my few hasty lines; but it will at least prove to you that I do not forget you.—No, indeed, I forget none of my dear absent Sisters & if they are only as good & happy as I wish them to be, nothing will be wanting to them neither in this world nor in the next.—Ah, dear Sister, why can't we all be generous & make the little sacrifices & crosses we meet with cheerfully as coming from our merciful Father & God? Then we would always be happy & content, in all places & every situation in which he is pleased to put us.—I thank you dear Sister, for the kind sympathy you express for me, in the heavy crosses you so justly think I have to bear, for it seems one succeeds another; still there is always some consolation with them, I see some good that comes out of them. I have many sins to atone for, & yet it seems I always have to from [*sic*] on account of others; but may not my sins be the chief cause. & what can I say, but Oh! God, be merciful. Continue then, Dearest Sister, to pray for me & for all—& let us strive to be truly what God & our holy vocation require of us.—Kindest love to all the dear Sisters,—& kiss little Julia Maria for her poor Mother. Tell Sister Dear Aloyisia I think she is mighty lazy with her pen.—Adieu, pray for me & believe I will not forget you.—

Your Mother
Catharine
Nazareth Dec. 9th—

The recipient of this letter and its context must be ascertained by references to persons named in the letter. It was customary to save on postage and make delivery more secure by sending several letters in the same packet. Here Catherine is forwarding a letter from Sister Theodora Crowe and including her own with it. Sister Theodora was a music teacher at Nazareth in these years, and Sister Aloysia Pryor, to whom a message is sent for oral delivery, was at St. Catherine's in Lexington. Thus it seems likely that the recipient of Catherine's letter of counsel here is Sister Genevieve McGinnis (see Letters 4-10 and 4-16). The affection expressed for "little Julia Maria" from "her poor Mother" suggests an orphan; this could be true if such a little girl had been sent to the academy in Lexington for further education. Two orphans named Julia had been received in Louisville in May and June 1854, but they were only six and seven years old. Although children that young were sometimes sent to the academies and kept through years of education, their transfer to Lexington by December of 1854 seems unlikely and is undocumented.

The value of this letter is chiefly in its evidence of Catherine's situation at this time and her felt emotional and spiritual response to it. Her "little sacrifices and crosses" included not only daily frustrations and contradictions of administration and community life, but also the major constructions at Nazareth, the expansion of mission and buildings in Louisville and Covington, property transfers in the aftermath of the separation of Nashville, and the decline of her own health into severe chronic neuralgia and headaches. However much Catherine tried to apply the traditional theology of atonement for sins, it is evident that she was beyond pretense or denial of her pain and only too happy to feel the divine mercy for suffering and the sympathy of Sisters who intuited her experience. Her strength was sustained by faith in God and the meaning of the cross, by that "kindest love" consistently exchanged with her Sisters, and by the effort exhorted in her much quoted line, "let us strive to be truly what God and our holy vocation require of us."

4-22

Nazareth Jan. 9/55

No, my very dear Sister, I am not displeased with you,
nor with any one on the place. My heart yearns for you
all with Maternal interest.—Oh, If you all have hearts
as devoted to all the interests of the Community as mine
is, there would truly be but one common interest, & self
would be laid aside,—no one should be anxious to appear
as having done more, nor others less.—Our Community
must be the centre from which all our good works must
emanate, & in the name of the Community all must be
done.—Then let none of us be ambitious, as to who does
more or who less.—God will judge it all hereafter.—
Let us strive hard daily to secure our eternal union in
the bosom of our blessed Lord in Heaven. our church is
finished we are just preparing to put the seats in it.—Then
there will be an edifice to the honor of God, not indeed,
as fine & rich as the one built by Solom[o]n, but as fine as
His poor Daughters of Nazareth could build to his honor
for future generations. We hope to use the new academy
next summer.—Then when that is done & the grounds
fences &c. are finished all round us—we may begin to
fix & arrange this house for the Community where they
may live as a regular Community should live. As it is
we are still scattered, & sleeping about where we may
find most convenient.—Oh! how I long to see all fixed
as a community should be. & then I may lay me down
in peace.—Pray for me, my dear child, that God, in his
own good mercy, may give rest to my dear soul in a better
world—for in this life there has been little rest for us—&
indeed we should not seek rest here—for here is the time

for labor & sorrow.—Now, my good Sister, don't be too particular with your poor mother. You know it is rather hard for me to write since I have suffered so much severe pain & I never expect to be entirely well again. The general health of the family, thank God, is very good.—Poor Sister Stephena does not improve much if any.—My kindest love to all the dear Sisters—& best respects to Father Durbin. Write to me whenever you can. I am always your sincere friend & Mother

Catharine

The greeting sent to Father Elisha Durbin, pastor at Sacred Heart parish in Union County, indicates that the recipient of this letter is one of the Sisters at St. Vincent Academy. The tone, cordial yet serious and concerned for the well-being of the local community, suggests that the recipient is the local superior, who at that time was Sister Elizabeth Suttle.

This letter is one of the few in which Catherine lets herself go to some length in expressing her concerns and giving important spiritual counsel for the Sisters' life in community and mission. Repetition of the phrase "who does more or who less" implies both the nature of the problem and the degree of Catherine's concern about its effects. No detailed account can be gleaned from records of St. Vincent's, but its history and circumstances might well invite difficulties in relationships, despite the finest motivation for the mission. It was one of the earliest establishments (1820), made in dire physical hardship and at great distance from the motherhouse. During the 1830s, the divisions among the Sisters about Bishop John Baptist David, Sister Ellen O'Connell, and Mother Angela Spink seem to have spilled over to this western house, where Sister Elizabeth Suttle received long letters from Bishop David, delineating his intense pain and disappointment in the community, as well as his loneliness and spiritual crisis. After a few years away (1839–1845), Elizabeth returned as superior at St. Vincent Academy (1845–1851) and would hold the office twice more between 1854 and 1863. She spent most of her years as SCN in this mission.

This rural academy was the sort of situation that needed and could nourish mutual support and society in a fairly isolated area, a truly human and spiritual bond among Sisters who were each other's strong friends and colleagues. But it might also promote an unhealthy habit of comparison, or rivalry about influence, leadership, recognition, and achievements. Whatever Catherine had been told or knew as fact, she hastened to reassure the Sisters of her maternal and loving feelings for them all and to plead for a common devotion of all to each other, to the community goals, to the selfless spirit that could unite them in labor for the honor of God.

This plea for a bond of love and zeal led easily into her account of the great community project of the church at Nazareth, consecrated the previous summer and whose interior was now nearly finished. Like the united community for which she pleaded, it was an edifice "for future generations."

Mention of the next project, the remodeling of the former academy into a house for "a regular Community" led her to share her own feelings about it, her need of rest for body and spirit, and finally, to a very rare admission of her own severe pain, her failing health, and her expectation that she would never be "entirely well again." That in turn would lead to news of another Sister all would know, Sister Stephania McCoy, who had served at St. Vincent for two of her early years in vows. Now she was seriously ill and did die at Nazareth several months after this letter.

The month before writing this letter Catherine had turned sixty-one; these bits of information from her late letters and those of Sister Columba Carroll from the same era prepare for the death that would come sooner perhaps than even she had expected. But she would leave behind this letter, one of her most quoted letters, a most powerful expression of her matured understanding of religious life and her spiritual wisdom.

4-23

Nazareth Jan. 15th/55
My dear Sister,

You will find enclosed a letter received by mail this

> evening for you & hope it brings good tidings of your friends. I humbly trust, my dear child, that you are getting on in your holy duties as a true religious & pious docile Sister of Charity. If so God will surely bless you.—But for that you must always be humble & very retiring. take no step without the knowledge & consent of your Sister Superior otherwise you would be sure to get in trouble & perhaps give disedification which would spoil all.—Sometimes I have feared your singing class might get you in some trouble. But if you be prudent & do nothing without consulting your Sister Superior, as she is the only one to decide for you, there will be no danger. Then too you have such a good experienced Sister in school with you to decide every thing there—so that I think you are particularly blessed—& if you attend to all this I have no fears about but that you may do much good.—God will ever bless the humble & obedient Sister.—So good night & pray for
>
> Your poor Mother
> Catharine

The recipient and her location escape positive identification. The message, however, makes this letter an early example of those Catherine would write in her last years to young Sisters. To modern sensibilities, her counsel and some of her diction may seem too maternal, too inclined to relate to a teaching Sister as a child rather than as a maturing individual learning to take responsibilities. Clearly, the Sister addressed is young and inexperienced, possibly bent on doing good deeds in her own way without prudent forethought or advice or at the instigation of others manipulating her weaknesses or her pride. Catherine's wisdom offered the most practical advice: supplement your own limited experience with the plenty of it in others around you, and guarantee the blessings available in a good relationship with authority.

4-24

Genevieve Nazareth Jan 4th/56

Then sure enough, my own dear Sister, you do hold me indebted.—I admit your "claim" & own that my indebtedness is much greater than I wish it to be if I had as much time as good will. Still I will try by degrees, to pay up all.—Rest assured I am always glad to hear you are well & happy.—But if you have sorrows I am also most willing to share them & lighten your Burden.—God will ever "temper the wind to the shorne lamb."—We have about 16 or 18 Novices & Postulants & have still room for more, if they be only good subjects to make true Sisters of Charity.—We have so far had excellent health this year.—But poor Sister Pulcheria has finished her earthly course; & I have just got warm after returning from her funeral. Commence your prayers all of you at once, for the repose of her dear soul. She suffered greatly, tho' as a Christian. Tell Sister Elizabeth to have Masses said for her. I have not time to write to her now.—It afflicts me to see so many of our dear Sisters thus dropping off in the prime of life. But God knows best. The Sisters should all be very prudent about their health, for once the lungs become diseased there is no stopping it.—Tell Sister Julian I received her letter & will write her as soon as I can. I am truly glad you have a prospect of soon getting more room as I am sure you greatly need it.—It has been so intensely cold here that it took all hands to keep fires and feed the stock.—Give my love & best wishes to each Sister I know they all pray for me. I will send dear old Sister Susan a Christmas gift in the true Christmas Carol. She must sing it for you all. Tell Sister Modesta, Lucina & Lucy that I feel indebted to them all & hope ere long to pay the debt.—How is Sister Rose? assure her of my best wishes of the New Year for her health, happiness, & usefulness.—Last tho' not least, my

New Year's respects to Fathers Durbin & Bouchet. Say to Father D. his children at Nazareth are well & doing well. With much love & wishing you every blessing

I am as ever your friend & Mother
Catharine

References to Sr. Elizabeth (Suttle) and Fathers Durbin and Bouchet indicate that this letter was directed to St. Vincent Academy. Father Elijah Durbin was the strong-minded pastor of that parish; the strength of his administration was sometimes extended to SCNs in their school and community life. Father Michael Bouchet was a young priest who had been recruited from Europe as a deacon in 1853. He lived and served devotedly long enough to be prominent in the later history of the archdiocese.

Sister Genevieve McGinnis, the recipient of this letter, had evidently experienced some continuing trouble at St. Vincent Academy and shared her sorrow with Mother Catherine, who responded with typical assurance of her own sympathy and faith in divine care. The few facts known about Sister Pulcharia Corr more than explain Catherine's lamentation about deaths in the prime of life. This young Sister entered in 1851, made vows in February 1853, and was sent briefly to St. Joseph Infirmary, then back to Nazareth, where she died of consumption in 1856.

In SCN lore and tradition, this letter is often cited for its message of concern about the health and too-short lives of many Sisters who were still dying of "consumption" (tuberculosis), which attended the damp and often erratic weather in central Kentucky; it could not be arrested by any known or regularly used form of treatment, let alone by transfers to warmer climates in states that were not yet incorporated in the Union. Louisville's well-known TB sanitarium was yet in the future. Catherine's counsel was in fact the best she could give: simple prudence in self-care, for the sake of community and the mission.

In another vein, "dear old Sister Susan" Hagan was a pioneer whose influence was to be noted and encouraged. She had served on the ill-fated brief mission at Long Lick, Breckinridge County, and had gone to Nazareth in March 1822 to prepare for the move of all in June; she served many years at St. Vincent, Union County, where she died and is buried. Little is known about Sister Rose Read; she made vows in 1842 and was missioned to the Louisville Asylum, where Catherine would have been her local superior. After a brief period at St. Vincent, Union County, she withdrew from the SCN in 1859.

Sisters Julian Carney (also Creany, Kearney), Modesta Graham, Lucina Gowdy, and Lucy Lampton had also written to Mother Catherine; they were all in vows less than ten years. Sister Julian had made vows as Sister Baptista in 1846, stayed in Nashville at the separation in 1851, then returned to Nazareth and made a second novitiate in 1853 with the name Sister Julian. All served several years at St. Vincent Academy and far outlived Mother Catherine. Sister Lucina at her death was seventy years in vows and the oldest in the community.

Letters from Catherine's final years indicate that she felt a special debt of gratitude for the communications of young Sisters as indications of their attachment to community as well as to their reliance on her interest and care. Maintaining this correspondence was surely one of Catherine's ways to contribute the counsel the younger Sisters might need and also to continue imparting the SCN spirit she wished to leave as her prime legacy.

4-25

Nazareth August 18th/56

It is raining & so dark that I can hardly see what I am doing. Yet I must write a few lines to my dear Baptista the promptings of my own heart will not permit me to wait longer.—Well my dear Sister I suppose you begin to think of resuming your old duties at St. Patrick's at least I hope you will go back & that you will have agreeable & efficient help. Rest assured if a few hints from me will do any good, they will be given. Continue to gather up all the little knowledge you can, especially for the branches you will have to teach. Don't be thinking of dying too soon, you have some time to labor yet, & content with the contrarieties of this life.—I often think of you my dear child & hope I shall always find you a true devoted friend & Sister—& be assured whatever may be my situation you will ever find in me a mother's heart & as far as I can ready to render you every possible service.—I am still here neither one thing nor another nor have I any idea what is to be my future destiny. Nor do I much care, God's holy will be done. If I can save my soul, all will be well. Pray much for me my dear Sister.

Give my best respects to Father Joyce & beg him to pray for me sometimes at holy Mass.—My love to Sister Amelia, tell her Margaret is well, & getting on very cheerfully. I hope she will do well.—I enclose here a little note for Sister Julia, which please give to her.—All here in usual health.—Sister Mary George seems rather threatened with bad health, but hope it will pass.

ever your devoted friend & Mother
Catherine

It is not surprising that the last known letter from Catherine's last term of office was directed to one of her well-loved very young Sisters. Baptista Walls had entered in January 1852 and made vows in August 1853; she had thus been affirmed for progress through the novitiate and for her first vows by Mother Catherine, perhaps with enough personal interaction to cause Catherine's urgent wish to write to "my dear child." Baptista would receive five letters from Catherine at two missions: St. Patrick's or the Thirteenth Street School, Louisville, and St. Frances Academy in Owensboro. At the time of this letter, Baptista must have been in temporary summer service at the orphanage, where she was requested to deliver a letter to Sister Julia Hobbs, Catherine's alternate in leading the orphanage mission.

Sister Mary George McCloskey, professed in 1846, seems to have remained at Nazareth her entire mission life; she is cited as school infirmarian in an 1854 letter of Sister Columba and in a document entitled "Reminiscences 1853–58." She died in 1861.

Several Sisters carry the surname Craney: Sisters Amelia, Julian, and Cecilia Craney. Julian (Elizabeth) and Cecilia (Margaret) were sisters from Pittsburgh; Julian, already in vows since 1846, far outlived her sister. Amelia may have been related to them; she was at St. Patrick's with Baptista at the time of this letter, hence the message to her that Margaret was doing well.

Catherine would have been recently relieved from office by the election of 1856 but not yet reassigned to her final period in Louisville. The very affectionate freedom of her tone and messages, the assurances of any possible future help, the specific counsel about continuing education "especially [but not exclusively] for the branches you will have to teach" and about contented devotion to life and mission—all these are casual yet powerful indicators of Catherine's relaxed spirit, her readiness to move into her own final mission in full trust in the Providence that led her. As usual, she finishes her letter with personal greetings, respects, and affectionate remembrances.

The letters by Mother Catherine and those written to her in her final term of office reveal one significant difference. Of extant letters, most of hers are directed to Sisters, giving personal affection, counsel, and general news. Only a few are directed to the two Spalding clergymen, to former students, and to architect William Keely and business agent Ben Webb. The extant letters written to her, by contrast, are mostly from parents or guardians, many indicating that they are responding to a communication from her and asking her for some further response. Only the letters from the bishop and the vicar of the new Covington diocese constitute a rival bundle, and they, too, speak of her letters to them. Of the many letters thus cited by persons who wrote to her, none remain. She either did not make copies or they were eventually destroyed. None of the letters from Catherine printed here prompted the letters to her in this period, yet they make clear her preference for sisters over debtors, and community life over tuition payments, as topics for correspondence. It may well be that Nazareth Academy and other missions endured mainly thanks to her persistence and her patient zeal to read and write what was necessary.

Letters to Mother Catherine Spalding, 1850–1856

The extant letters written to Mother Catherine during her final term as leader of congregation and academy are clearly replies to a letter from her; these letters of Catherine's no longer exist. Unsatisfying as that fact is to one searching her correspondence for clues to her personality and the manner of her relationships with others, still the letters to her do suggest what issues Catherine could or needed to think about and decide, and do imply a great deal about her character and mode of dealing with persons and serious issues. Catherine Spalding was an able and heavily occupied administrator, kind and understanding, but realistic and firm in the management required to accomplish both huge building projects and the daily sustenance of students, servants, and Sisters. She could see the Nazareth mission as a whole with parts to be cared for thoroughly. She could recruit and inspire followers, deal with large projects and their details, and handle problematic circumstances and people, their complaints and demands; she could pursue solutions even while waiting in what patience she had. Letters to her indicate that her leadership and management style were the vital support of the community and the present and future of the missions.

A first cluster of letters records the varied motivations of parents for sending their daughters to Nazareth and their expectations for their education. Some recruitment publicity did appear in Catholic papers or general publications, but none of it is cited in the extant letters about admissions. Word of mouth was evidently the major force of recruitment, generating enrollment both from within Kentucky and from places far south and north of the state. Parents' wishes for an accomplished young lady generated numerous requests (or demands) for particular curricula, and in the beginning, at least, assurances of payment.

Some letters to Catherine during this period are extremely long or tediously repetitive or detailed. These have been excerpted or summarized below, in part or whole. As with earlier such letters, they are so marked at their headings and by brackets or ellipsis in the text.

4-A

Letter to Mother Catherine Spalding from William G. Beall
DLB 11b, p. 157 (abridged)

Brandenburg, March 1, 1856
Mother Catherine,
Dear Madam,

I have just this moment had a conversation with a friend of mine, Mr. Jesse Gaylor, a young lawyer of this place, who is very anxious in relation to the education of a sister of his, being a warm advocate for the advantages gained by an education in the Institution under your charge near Bardstown, I at once represented to him, its surpassing excellencies in my opinion, and he is anxious to embrace the opportunity of entering her at once in your school. His mother, a widow lady, has a farm and well enough off, but has not the money to advance at present, could pay all, when Mr. Gaylor, her brother comes up after her at the end of the session. I will willingly endorse any obligations of his to do so. . . . [Five gentlemen of Bardstown and Brandenburg are named as references for Mr. Gaylor's integrity and secure payment.] Miss Gaylor would wish to learn music, (piano) and the English branches, together with drawing and painting. Should you wish Miss Gaylor to enter your school, please state your terms for balance of session, and direct to Mr. Jessee Gaylor, Brandenburg, Ky.

Your friend,
William G. Beall

Beall is listed as father of Frances Ann Beall, who attended Nazareth from October 1853 to January 1854, about three months. Despite his daughter's brevity of experience at the academy, Beall was willing to wax eloquent about the "advantages" and "surpassing excellencies" of a Nazareth education. A Miss Gaylor has not yet been found in the academy register, nor are any Gaylors from Brandenburg listed.

4-B

Letter to Mother Catherine Spalding from John H. Gay
DLB 11b, p. 173

Oktibbiha City, Miss.
Sept. 7, 1855
Mother Catherine Spalding,
Dear Madam,

Permit me to introduce to your acquaintance my friend Wm. Gordon who visits Nazareth for the purpose of leaving his daughter with you. I take great pleasure in saying that Mr. Gordon is a gentleman in every way worthy of confidence, and I am in hopes he will leave his daughter with you. Remember me kindly to my nieces Eugenia and Sarah. Say to them we have been expecting a letter from them for some time since.

Very respectfully,
John H. Gay

No Eugenia or Sarah Gay are listed in the register of 1855, but the family names of Mr. Gay's nieces may not have been his. Mr. John Gay does not mention a daughter of his own, and the only Gay in the register of 1855 was Martha Louisa, daughter of David Gay of Williamsport, Louisiana. John H. Gay may be the father of Mary Gay, a student from 1851 to 1855, or of Emily, 1851–1854.

4-C

Letter to Mother Catherine Spalding from Wm. J. Napier
DLB 11b, p. 174 (abridged)

124 Washington St.,
Chicago, Ill.
Tuesday Sept. 25, 1855.
Mother Catherine Spalding,

This will be handed to you by my daughter, Clementine, who her mother and I commit to your charge and beg your earnest attention to the formation of her young mind as regards her religious duties. . . .

We wish her taught all the branches of a thorough English education, French, music, and singing, and whatever books are necessary, if you will have the goodness to furnish us with, by your transmitting me the account thereof, I shall send you a check for the amount. I have paid into R. K. Swift & Co., Bank, fifty dollars and send you by Clementine a check for same which she will sign or endorse when you can have it checked. When you send the account of the books etc., if any further sum is required, please say so.

[A full account is given of the immigrant mother's lack of "leisure" to give enough time to her daughter's "improvement" and the recommendation of a priest that Clementine be placed "under your care." Mrs. Napier earnestly hopes the girl will use her opportunity to acquire "all the advantages of education and amiable manners so desirable in a young lady and to be attained in your excellent academy." The letter also reports that a Mr. Sollitt, on Mr. Napier's recommendation, is sending his two daughters to Nazareth. Though a Protestant, he is unlikely to control his daughters' possible desire to convert.]

On that account my wife feels a two fold responsibility, but bids me assure you she confides in your superior judgment and discretion regarding the two young ladies. I am respectfully,

Your obedient servant,
Wm. J. Napier

Clementine Napier, age fifteen, enrolled two days after the date of this letter and remained until June 26, 1856. She married and died young.

4-D

Letter to Mother Catherine Spalding from John Sollitt
DLB 11b, p. 165

Chicago
June 20, 1856
Dear Madam,

I received your letter and bill which was very satisfactory and I am truly grateful for the interest you have taken in my daughters. I will try to send Jane and a younger sister back again. Enclosed you will find $250.00 a draft on New York your account against me is $221.96, the balance $28.04 you will please give to my daughters to enable them to come home with, as I shall not be able to come after them. Their mother is very sick, else I should have been much pleased to have seen your beautiful place. You will please be so kind and forward my girls home in the best way you can.

I remain yours respectfully,
John Sollitt

Jane Sollitt, fifteen, attended Nazareth Academy from September 1855 to June 1857. Her sister Hannah, eighteen, attended during the same dates. It is not clear who a "younger sister" to Jane might be, unless the father was mistakenly referring to Hannah.

4-E

Letter to Mother Catherine Spalding from A. Perrault
DLB 11b, p. 162

Natchez
June 10, 1856
To Mother Catherine,
Nazareth,
Madam,

Mrs. Perrault, one of your ancient pupils, under the name of Elizabeth Owens, comes today to put under your particular protection her only daughter. The faith she has in your institution induces me to consent to let her go so far away from us. It is only yesterday I gave my consent though I knew the plot. You will excuse them if everything is not according to your rule. It is our wish she should be taught all the branches necessary to a woman. Besides the French, I insist upon that being a Frenchman, piano and vocal music. A quarter or two dancing if she wishes it. Thanking you in advance for the kindness we know you will show our daughter.

I remain yours with respect,
A. Perrault

This letter registers an apparent conspiracy of mother and daughter to get the father's consent for another girl of the Deep South to attend Nazareth—provided she will be taught all the customary feminine "branches": French, music, dancing. In fact, Adelaide I. Perrault, sixteen, Catholic daughter of Mr. and Mrs. Arnaud L. Perrault of Natchez, Mississippi, attended less than a month, June 17–July 10, 1856. Perhaps the registrar did not record her return for the following term.

For unknown reasons, the extant parental letters recording the problems of payment for a Nazareth education are nearly all dated 1855. (Just one survives from 1851 and two from 1856.) One may suppose, however, that Catherine received letters in similar abundance, with a similar variety of problems and excuses, in all the intervening years of her final term. With a minor deviation, the 1855 letters are given in chronological order.

4-F

Letter to Mother Catherine Spalding from Fannie Geohagan
DLB 11, p. 96 (abridged)

Lexington
Dec., 15, 1851
My dear Mother Catherine,

I have many reproaches for not writing to you before this. However, late as it is, friendship and business urge me to write.
[The writer then comments on her daughter's writing and her weight.]

Dear Mother, you remember the contract for Ann's going to Nazareth was made by our dear lamented mother, with you. You are aware we have had some trouble with our brother-in-laws. We prefer stopping our legal dispute about the property and giving those gentlemen what was first offered them. My cousin, who is a lawyer, says you can make out your bill as finishing the year that was begun in mother's life time, then it will be recognized as an estate account. You will please do this as soon as our lawyer wished to finish this business. . . .

[Details follow of which men will or will not relinquish a claim, and the writer's distress.] I hope, dear Mother, you will remember me in your good prayers. Ask our Heavenly Father to give me grace to bear all the crosses He will send me, and to make me persevere in my Faith, as my saintly mother did. I need not ask your prayers for her, I feel assured she is already remembered in your prayers, and if she stands not in need of them, they will be returned tenfold to you. She loved you on earth and surely in heaven, you will not be forgotten.

Please remember me to all the good Sisters whom I know. Love to Ann. [News of the weather and the health of various members of the SCN in Lexington.] All my sisters join in love to you. May our Lady and St. Joseph protect you is the sincere prayer of

Your devoted friend,
Fannie Geohagan

Fannie (Frances) Geohagan, a Catholic graduate, had attended Nazareth Academy 1839–1841, ages fifteen–seventeen. Here she refers to her sister Ann, who attended 1850–1852, from age sixteen to around eighteen. They were the daughters of Mr. and Mrs. Patrick Geohagan of Lexington. The letter reflects the concerns for tuition that arose due to the death of the girls' parents and the rights to estate funds claimed by male heirs or the husbands of daughters.

4-G

Letter to Mother Catherine Spalding from Wm. M. Crosky
OLB 17, p. 60 (abridged)

Salem, Ky.
March 2, 1855
Miss C. Spalding, (Mother)

My health continues bad, but I think better than when you saw me. I intend taking a trip South in a few days with a hope of benefit and will be absent about 4 or 5 weeks. As I wrote to you last summer, think it is, should again, as accidents sometimes happen with boats etc. let you know that if anything should happen with me, . . . I have amply provided for Mary in that event. I expect to be up next summer again as usual. Let me hear from Mary in about 5 weeks.

Very respectfully,
Wm. M. Crosky

Give my love to Mary and tell her to learn fast.

As will be seen from this letter and Letters 4-H, I, and J, through the summer of 1855, William Crosky wrote often to Catherine, recording his persistent concern with his health and efforts to improve it, and promising, when that goal was achieved, to come to Nazareth and to pay up his daughter's account. The academy register lists no Crosky, but does mention a Mary McCrosky, who entered in 1853 at age six, became a Catholic, then graduated and left in June 1865. She was daughter of Mr. and Mrs. William McCrosky of Salem, Livingston County, Kentucky. The four letters here detail the writer's situation and his state of mind about it and about his daughter and his debts.

4-H

Letter to Mother Catherine Spalding from Wm. M. Crosky
OLB 17, p. 69 (abridged)

Salem, Ky.
June 17th. 1855
Miss C. Spalding,

I wrote to you some time in February stating I would start to New Orleans in a short time and requested you to write to me about 5 or 6 weeks as I wished to hear from Mary when I returned. If you wrote, it miscarried, as I have received nothing since I started for N. Orleans, and returned 6th. April. . . . [The writer then gives an account of his suffering from asthma, fever, noise, and cold on the riverboat, which confined him to bed for five weeks.] It is my calculation now to be at your place in August some time, if my health will permit me and the river does not get too low. . . . You will please to have my bill made out up to the end of the session and inclose it to me. . . . I cannot help thinking there was some mistake in the summer part of my bill. The first year it was $19.35. Let me hear from Mary. Hoping yourself and all your large family are well,

Very respectfully,
Wm. M. Crosky

4-I

Letter to Mother Catherine Spalding from Wm. M. Crosky
OLB 17, p. 51 (abridged)

Salem, Ky.
July 9, 1855.
Mother C. Spalding,

I wrote to you a short time since for my bill for the last year. Your treasurer enclosed the within which is not as full and as satisfactory as I wish which is here returned for one commencing from the date of the first bill rendered up to June 1854 to the end of your last session, . . . [specifies dates and amounts for outstanding bills, encloses $150.00, requests bill up to final session] and if I should not visit you this summer, will enclose you the amt. immediately. I want a full account rendered at the end of every annual session so that I can settle fully once a year. . . . [There follows a further account of his asthma, other ailments, and travels to find a cure.] I will make the little draft payable to yourself not knowing who is the proper one. Let me know respecting this so I may know hereafter, there was a little debt coming to me from Scott County. Hoping you and your large family are all well,

Very respectfully,
Wm. M. Crosky

4-J

Letter to Mother Catherine Spalding from Wm. M. Crosky
OLB 17, p. 66 (abridged)

Salem, Ky.
July 27, 1855.
Mother C. Spalding,

Your very kind favor of 10th. inst. duly at hand which was very satisfactory to me to hear that my little Mary was well learned the last session and gave satisfaction. I hope she will continue [the] same, and not give you any more trouble than little girls of her age. By this days mail I received from your treasurer a statement of my account up to the 1st. inst., showing a balance due Nazareth from me of $44.78 which you will please say to her is entirely satisfactory. I have enclosed $45.00 which you will have placed to my credit. If I should fail to visit you this summer will send you about the first of September about $75.00. . . . [There follows an account of the writer's asthma and his travels for a cure.] I want to see Mary very much. Give her my love and say to her I will be to see her if I can next Spring or summer. . . . Write to me soon and as often as you conveniently can.

Very respectfully yours,
Wm. M. Crosky

P.S. Please acknowledge the receipt of the account with first mail.

4-K

Letter to Mother Catherine Spalding from Margaret Campbell
DLB 41, p. 78a (abridged)

Greenville, [Miss.]
February 16th, 1855
Dear Mother Catharine,

A short time since I received a letter from your agent in New Orleans requesting my immediate payment of the expenses of my daughters. I sent immediately a draft for four hundred dollars, and wrote your agent I thought there was a mistake in the bills. . . . I understand that my poor dear Lelia was taken sick on the 22 of Jany. And Carrie before or about the close of the session; they are both charged with all the extras generally attending a spell of sickness all of which appear to be fully charged. I do not think I am asking anything more than is just and right, when I ask to have the whole of the session deducted upon which neither entered—[The writer notes that she has employed a woman of New Orleans and "of your Church" as tutor for her children.] Carrie is applying herself to study much better than I expected. As soon as you change the bills and deduct the remainder of the tuition for the second session, I will send a draft for whatever balance there may be. Carrie, Em, and Mattie join me in kind regards to yourself and the Sisters.

I am as ever very truly yours,
Margaret Campbell

You will please keep the spot where my dear Lelia lies well marked, if I do not remove her I shall ere long have a neat monument put up over her—

Margaret (Mrs. William R.) Campbell was the mother of Susan Lelia Campbell, who died while a student at Nazareth Academy, February 23, 1854. She was buried in Nazareth Cemetery; her remains were not removed. Her mother's letter follows that event by nearly a year.

4-L

Letter to Mother Catherine Spalding from L. M. Gordon
DLB 11b, p. 203 (abridged)

Alexandria
Feb. 22, 1855
Miss Catherine Spalding,
Madam,

I received your account through your agents at New Orleans T. S. Elder & Co., amounting to $123.50 which has been paid. But I was astonished at the amount, because I had been led to believe that yours was not only a scholl [*sic*] favorable to the attainment of knowledge, but a cheap and economical one in all respects. In the latter I have been disappointed, . . . I think exorbitant, a music book to cost $10. . . . I fully expected that $350 or $400 would have been entirely sufficient to cover all her expenses at Nazareth, but it seems from a reference to your account the last session cost $260 this would amount to $522 per year, besides her board during vacation. I did not suppose that I should have so much reason to complain of your charges. Our love to our dear child,

Yours respectfully,
L. M. Gordon

Janette Gordon, from Alexandria, Louisiana, entered Nazareth Academy in July 1854 and remained two years. Her father's name is given as Smith W. Gordon, not as L. M. No other Gordons have been found. The letter represents bluntly one parental complaint: price.

4-M

Letter to Mother Catherine Spalding from Mr. W. Montgomery
DLB 11b, p. 197

Locut
March 2, 1855
Miss Catherine Spalding, (Mother)
Madam,

I have received both of your letters open and never was sealed, the first was a demand, the second a request to pay you what I do not owe, what I never had anything to do with. Mrs. S. K. Montgomery is entirely able to pay the amount. She has no family, on her hands, you must have very intimate correspondence as you send your letter open, and slip them into my house during my absence from home.

I have all along thought I would pay the princip[al], If I could see the items charged to her, and if they were correct, but a few more open letters from you inspected by everyone and slipped into my house in my absence, will prevent my even thinking about it. Send your account, all the items charged and prices, and perhaps I may pay you what I think right. It will depend on circumstances entirely, I disapprove of the matter in which your open letters sent by private conveyance and underhand[ed]ly conveyed to me, and unless you make some explanation about things better and inform me who the polite person is that sends your letters to me, you must expect nothing from me. I have nothing now to say about the matter. I know nothing, and if I do pay you, it will be when I please, and that shall be mainly a donation only I acknowledge no debt on her part or mine. Her guardians are the ones responsible and able to pay. I remain

Yours,
W. Montgomery

The circumstances of this letter—a second reminder of delinquent debt, an agent's mode of delivery, the ruptured relationships of the girl's parents or guardians—all remain a puzzle. Mr. Montgomery does not acknowledge the student as his daughter, nor Mrs. S. K. as his wife. Three girls named Montgomery are registered at Nazareth: Malvina and Martha, both of whom had left two years prior to this letter of 1855; and Emma, who was enrolled from 1852 to 1857. Malvina's father was Mr. John Montgomery; Martha's and Emma's parents, from Louisville, were Dr. and Mrs. J. R. Montgomery. The location of "Locut" is unknown, and so is of no help in identifying Mr. Montgomery. If Mrs. S. K. Montgomery is wife to the letter writer or mother to any of the girls or another relationship altogether, no record of her or her possible payments can be found. This letter must stand simply as the choicest example of any insulting letters Catherine may have received. As such, it is given in full.

4-N

Letter to Mother Catherine Spalding from C. B. Rice
DLB 11b, p. 192 (abridged)

Mount Hope, Cobiah Co. Miss.
March 2, 1855
Dear Mother Catherine,

I owe you an apology for not sooner replying to your kind and welcome letter long since received in which was conveyed the pleasing intelligence of the progress and general good conduct of my children under your charge. I may say particularly pleasing was that portion in relation to Mary . . . more especially in her that being the eldest the force of example might have the effect to lead her younger sisters, and brother on in the path of duty and virtue. The reason why I have not sooner replied is that I waited to see my merchant who . . . did not come until last week. [The writer then offers explanation of delayed payment due to a banking issue of a draft that "did not come in the shape" he "understood."] Whilst I take pleasure in . . . the progress of my children, it is with regret that in a subsequent letter from your agent in New Orleans, I have received the indubitable evidence of their rapid progress in another line. . . . I mean extravagance. I was much surprised to find the[ir] account over $600.00 for the session passed. I hope not to be presented with such another bill, what is necessary in an economical way for their comfort I wish and no more. [He gives examples of repeated purchases of the same articles and questionable charges for dancing lessons.] My best respects for Sister Columba, Louisa etc., and accept for yourself the assurance of my highest respect,

C. B. Rice

Mr. and Mrs. Charles Benjamin Rice from Gallatin, Mississippi, had three daughters at Nazareth in 1855: Mary Ann, Elizabeth, and Lucie. The two eldest left in June 1855, Lucie in 1856. It may be understandable that girlish extravagance was a parental issue; whether Catherine could be held to control it entirely is another issue. A second letter below, written in April, details more of Rice's problems in making payments in due time and amount.

4-O

Letter to Mother Catherine Spalding from C. B. Rice
DLB 11b, p. 193 (summary)

Mount Hope, Copiah Co. Miss.
April 23, 1855
Dear Mother Catherine,

[The letter begins with pleasure at Catherine's "glowing account of the good and meritorious conduct of my children" and continues with an apology for the writer's hasty and inaccurate reading of their accounts and his "unwonted censure" of the charges. He cannot "liquidate the account" due to a "very short" crop and sale price, heavy expenses, lack of money, and inability to borrow any. He will try to send clothing for the children, but "I hope you will not let them suffer." Hard times may compel their return home for the summer, but wants them not told yet, "as it might have a bad effect on them."]

Very truly your friend in Christ,
C. B. Rice

P.S. In writing to me it is not necessary to pay postage direct to me as P. Master M. Hope.

4-P

Letter to Mother Catherine Spalding from Michael Gorman
DLB 11b, p. 175 (abridged)

Greenwood, Miss., Carroll City
March 29th, 1855
Mother Catherine Spalding
Dear Madam,

Today I have wrote [*sic*] to Catherine and gave her a severe scolding and putting a stop to her extravagances and expenditure of money. I told her she should be entirely directed and controlled by you in everything. I am not able to indulge her in foolish and extravagant habits. Her mother has written me . . . she states she had received Kate's account for $147.00 and a dentist bill for $22. This I don't understand as she never consulted me about it. Her mother speaks of her dancing lessons, and vocal music . . . all of which must take up much of her time from her more solid studies and add to her expenses which I cannot well afford. [He forbids the lessons.] You will please to control Kate and not suffer her to have her own way in anything. . . . With much respect,

Your obedient servant,
Michael Gorman

Catherine Gorman attended Nazareth from 1852 to 1857; she was the daughter of Mr. and Mrs. Michael Gorman of Tuscumbia, Alabama. They seem to have had variant opinions about their daughter's studies and feminine accomplishment. That the letter was written from Mississippi suggests that, if Mr. and Mrs. Gorman were not separated, the father must have traveled on business, but kept control over the expenses he would willingly incur.

4-Q

Letter to Mother Catherine Spalding from E. C. Wilkinson
DLB 11b, p. 202 (abridged)

Yazoo City
April 14, 1855
Dear Mother Catherine,

Although my health is much impaired, I am yet able to give some attention to business, and in this matter of Mr. O'Reilly procured his bill of exchange payable at New Orleans in the fall, with interest added. . . . [The rest of the letter concerns getting bills of exchange honored in New Orleans and Louisville, "preferable to suing. . . . I have little doubt that I can arrange the affair in this way."] The Messrs. O'Reilly who are passing some time in our house, are much mortified at their brother's neglect. They . . . would doubtless have kind regards for you. Eliza sends you many. Grateful for the interest you express about my health, I am

Yours most gratefully,
E. [Eliza] C. Wilkinson

Lizzie V. Wilkinson, daughter of Mr. and Mrs. John Wilkinson of Bolivar County, Mississippi, attended Nazareth only during the years 1858–1860 as a young teenager. The letter here must have been signed by her mother, for whom Lizzie is named. The O'Reilly brothers are unknown, as is their financial connection to the Wilkinson family.

4-R

Letter to Mother Catherine Spalding from R. Miller
DLB 11b, p. 153 (abridged)

Democratic Hill
April 21, 1855
Miss C. Spalding,
Dear Madam,

I received a few days since from you a few lines directing my attention to a balance due by me to your institution on account of my daughter, Irene. I am sorry it is not convenient for me to send you the whole amount, please find enclosed a draft . . . for two hundred dollars which I hope will suffice for the present as money matters with us at this moment are harder than usual. . . . . [The writer goes on with his planned time to pay, and says he hopes she will not be inconvenienced and that she will ask only 1 percent interest.] We are all in good health, and hope your institution is prospering. Irene writes often, appears satisfied and [is] I hope learning. We would be very glad to hear from you often. Mrs. Miller joins me in respects to yourself and the ladies of your place generally.

I remain yours truly,
R. Miller

Irene Miller, daughter of Mr. and Mrs. Robert Miller of Burton-ton, Mississippi, attended Nazareth from 1853 to 1856, in her later teen years.

4-S

Letter to Mother Catherine Spalding from W. H. Morgan
OLB 17, p. 55

R. M. I.
April 13, 1856.
Mother Catherine,

I have been expecting for some months past a remittance from home with which I could settle the accounts of little Sallie and myself, but yesterday I received a letter from home requesting me to obtain the amount of Sallie's account or what it will be at the end of the session, and to send it home with my own and the necessary amount would be forwarded immediately. Please, therefore, let me know the amount of the account and at the end of the session, a traveling outfit included and other clothing necessary, also a word if you please about Sallie's health, which I rejoice to hear is improving.

Yours respectfully in trust,
W. H. Morgan

4-T

Letter to Mother Catherine Spalding from W. H. Morgan
OLB 17, p. 55

R. M. I.
Apr. 23, 1856
Mother Catherine,

I wrote to you about a week since, respecting Sallie's account, but not receiving any answer I suppose that you did not get my letter. About the time that I wrote to you, I received a letter from my Guardian requesting me to obtain the amount of Sallie's account at present and also what you think it will be at the end of this session. . . . I have been trying all winter to get the amount from home. . . . It will be forwarded now though, as soon as I can send the amount of her indebtedness home, simply the amount.

Yours respectfully,
W. H. Morgan

Letters 4-S and 4-T relate to Sallie Morgan, daughter of Mr. and Mrs. Jacob B. Morgan, of Vicksburg, Mississippi. She attended Nazareth from 1854 to 1856, so her account evidently was paid up. W. H. Morgan seems to have been a male relative attending school in the area, perhaps St. Joseph College in Bardstown. See also Letter 4-Y below, from H. H. Southworth, who identifies Sallie as his ward; evidently he was responsible for her tuition and other needs.

While most parental letters concerned payment for tuition and board, another frequent topic was the daughters' clothing. Mother Catherine was, in effect, to be the purchasing agent or dressmaker, arbiter of style and propriety, readily accessible to any and all the young ladies.

4-U

Letter to Mother Catherine Spalding from William Moss
DLB 11b, p. 171 (abridged)

Washington, Hempstead Cty. Ark.
April 25, 1855
Dear Mother Catherine,

We have just received a letter from Lucie giving a list of articles, which she wants for the examination, and which I have just ordered to be sent her from Messrs. Mark Dulaney & Downs of Louisville. Lucie appears to express a great deal of anxiety in looking forward to the time when she anticipates our presence at Nazareth. I doubt at present, whether it will be convenient for us both to be present or not, at the examination. . . . Being at such a great distance, I must enjoin upon you to see that Lucie is suited in all her needs, particularly in the arrangement of her clothing, so that she may have them made up to suit her and in due time. . . . If she lacks anything procure it for her. . . . Please give my respects to Father Haseltine, Sister Louisa, and Sister Columba, and also accept the same for yourself. All well with us.

Respectfully your obedient servant,
William Moss

Please tell Lucie to inform us when the examination comes off. W. M.

4-V

Letter to Mother Catherine Spalding from Thos. Young
DLB 11b, p. 172 (abridged)

Mississippi, Clarborn County,
May 8, 1855
Catherine Spalding, Supr.
Dear Mother,

Your kind favor is at hand and had given us a great deal of pleasure in hearing of the health of our dear children, and the progress they are making and particularly their conduct and satisfaction given by them to their teachers, and I sincerely hope they will . . . justify a similar report at the close of their term, for the kindness and attention shown them by yourself and the sisters, accept our warmest feelings of gratitude. In regard to their clothing etc., we wish you to furnish them at your own discretion for we cannot know at this time what they may really need, nor can we have them made at home with any prospect of fitting them, if we were to attempt it. I presume all would be to alter and fit over. We received a few lines dated March 13th., from Sister Ambrosia Abbott, treasurer, enclosing the children's accounts, making together fifty nine dollars and thirty four cents, then due you. . . . [He encloses $100 on a New Orleans bank to pay his debt and leave a balance up to July 1.] We have hoped . . . to have come up to your examination, but their mother's delicate situation will render it impossible, and her anxiety to see them is such that we will be under the necessity of bringing them home during the vacation. During which time, hope to have them supplied for the ensuing fall and winter.

Thos. Young, and Amelia Young.

Say to the children we are all well.

Esther Amelia Young, ten years old, spent one year at Nazareth. She evidently did not return from the summer vacation in 1855. No other Young daughters are known.

4-W

Letter to Mother Catherine Spalding from S. C. Leland
DLB 11b, p. 191 (abridged)

Panola, Miss.
May 22, 1855
Miss Catherine Spalding,
Madam,

Enclosed please find thirty five dollars which I was advised would be the amount that it would take to furnish Mary with such articles of clothing as she will need previous to the close of the session of your school. I wish her to be furnished with such things as she positively needs and for that purpose I hope this amount sent will be sufficient. I send Tennessee money such as I understand to be current in Memphis which I learn will pass readily in Bardstown.

Be pleased to present our kindest and most affectionate regards to Mary.

Respectfully your servant,
S. C. Leland

P.S. [He explains a shortage of $2 in the last payment, to be made up in the current one.] Please acknowledge the receipt of this.

Mary Louise Leland, fourteen, spent three years at Nazareth, leaving in June 1855, a month after her father's letter above. It is recorded that she lost her mind in 1859; no explanation is given.

4-X

Letter to Mother Catherine Spalding from R. Miller
DLB 11b, p. 161 (abridged)

Democratic Hill,
June 9, 1855.
Miss C. Spalding,
Dear Miss,

I received a letter from my daughter, Irene, this day stating that she had been informed a few days since that she must send home for clothing in consequence of the large expenditures of your institution. You could not be able to furnish such things etc., etc., I hope you will be kind enough to furnish her with such clothing as you yourself see she stands in need of, as it would be very inconvenient for me to buy clothing now and send them to her, as I would be compelled to pay about the same rates here and incur the risk of their being lost and it would be impossible for Mrs. Miller to have them made here to fit her anyhow I sent you by mail two or three weeks ago a draft for $200, which I hope reached you by this time. [He continues about paying through delivery by friends, his financial condition, and the need to leave his daughter at school through summer vacation.] I do hope you will during your vacation exercise over my child that parental care that will be necessary indeed. I feel assured that you will so, or I should certainly not feel easy for one moment. Mrs. Miller joins me in love to you.

I remain your. friend,
R. Miller

As mentioned in Letter 4-R above, Irene Miller of Burtonton, Mississippi, attended Nazareth 1853–1856, approximately from ages sixteen to nineteen—a teenaged girl's most clothes-oriented years. It is unknown whether she eventually got clothes made in Kentucky or whether her parents ever paid for any.

4-Y

Letter to Mother Catherine Spalding from H. H. Southworth
OLB 11b, p. 199 (abridged)

Sidon, Carroll Co. Miss.
October 18, 1855
Mother Catherine Spalding,
Dear Madam,

I received a letter from my ward, Miss Sallie Morgan, last mail in which she stated that she wanted some winter clothing. You will be kind enough to let her have such things as she may want. . . . We have not been able to get but little of our cotton out of the Yazoo yet, but hope to do so in short time, and then I will make all things right. The yellow fever has been prevailing our River this fall, though not so bad as last year. . . . .

H. H. Southworth.

See Letters 4-S and 4-T above concerning Sallie Morgan, her needs, and the issues of payment.

4-Z

Letter to Mother Catherine Spalding from S. W. Gordon
DLB 11b, p. 170

Woodlawn Home,
July 13, 1855.
Miss Catherine Spalding,
Dear Madam,

As I have concluded to let my daughter remain with you another year, I wish you would make out your account and send it to your agent in N[ew] O[rleans], and it will be paid immediately on presentation, and also the advance for the next session. I desire my daughter to be as economical as possible in all her expenses. Of this matter you have the control, and I look to you for a compliance of this request.

Yours respectfully,
S. W. Gordon

S. W. Gordon had earlier written to Catherine about expenses for his daughter, Janette (see Letter 4-L). This letter is one among several sounding concern over girls' extravagance in personal expenses and requiring Catherine to exert supervision.

Despite appearances, not all letters of this period to Mother Catherine were from parents, and not all concerned payments due the school. Some concern a miscellany of topics, from girlish extravagance to possible religious vocation (sometimes in the same girl). Other letters concern the practical management of the school and property, including hiring lay faculty, purchase of equipment, and hiring of workers. Finally, a letter from an alumna offers insight on the tender relationship that could and did arise with some of the students who had special care from Catherine during their school days.

4-AA

Letter to Mother Catherine Spalding from R. Clannon
DLB 11b, p. 188 (abridged)

New Orleans,
April 28, 1855.
Respected Mother Catherine,

In a letter received from my dear Kate a few days since and in one written to Father Buteme, she mentions of having a desire or an idea of or that her vocation is to be a sister, and only wishes to return to see me, her sister and brother. Now the purport of this is, Dear Mother, to please to ask the sisters not to influence her in any way, only to leave her to her own free will and our Lord in His goodness and mercy will do the rest. If it should please Our Lord for her to be a Sister, I am certain it is another act of goodness and kindness in Our Lord towards me. I did or was opposed to my dear Julia becoming a sister, her health was much impaired, she was biased and influenced by a sister and the mother, so I thought. . . . I shall do nothing nor say one word to dear Kate for or against, shall fervently pray for her true vocation, and shall return with her if it should please Our Lord so to will it. [A lengthy section follows, concerning the girls' return home in June by "the last trip of our good boats" and the marriage of the writer's daughter Lizzie.] Dear Mother, please answer this at your earliest convenience. My love to my dear children and accept for yourself the humble prayers, and for your dear Sisters and children under your charge also, of

Yours most respectfully,
R. Clannon

The Nazareth Academy register lists two daughters of Mr. and Mrs. Robert Clannon of New Orleans, Ellen and Kate; both were teenagers, with Kate the elder. The girls entered in July 1854 and left in mid-March 1856. Ellen died single at home; no information is given about Kate's settlement in life. Nor are the other daughters mentioned in the Clannon letters listed as Nazareth students.

4-BB

Letter to Mother Catherine Spalding from Robert Clannon
DLB 11b, p. 176

New Orleans,
Dec. 19, 1855
Respected Madam,

Knowing the interests you feel in the welfare of my children, I take the liberty to write you a few lines in relation to them, particularly to Kate. I find she is inclined to be very extravagant, and not easily satisfied; she had nearly forty dollars when she reached Nazareth and a very few days after in a few lines to her little brother, she tells him to ask me to send her some money. Mother, please [do] not allow Kate any money and you will also inform Messrs. Quin Hayden & Co., not to let them have anything unless on order from me. Wenny is a good child and easily satisfied, but Kate is not, and I find it will not answer to indulge her in her extravagances. I send a bill of exchange by Kate to [the] Academy. I hope she has not forgot to deliver it, as I have had no acknowledgement of its receipt. Wishing you and all the inmates of your happy home many happy returns of the holy season, I remain

Most gratefully and respectfully yours,
Robert Clannon

4-CC

Letter to Mother Catherine Spalding from E. Leyraque
DLB 21, p. 18

New York
April 29, 1856
Madam, Superior of Nazareth,

Last April 9th I had the honor of sending you a letter in which I agreed, in accordance with the choice that you permit me to make in your proposal of last March 29th, to the conditions of $500.00 from Next September to July, 1856 [*sic*].

I pray you to acknowledge the reception of my letter as definite proof of this reciprocal engagement. Almost a month has passed and you have not answered. Am I to think that your intentions are no longer the same or that you have not received my letter? Whatever may be the case, please, Madam, be so good as to write me immediately concerning the opportunity for a placement. I do not want to wait for a longer delay than that required for the exchange of our letters in order to know your final decision.

It was with joy that I had the interview with you, Madam; and you should have known that from the prompt[it]ude of my answering you. This prompt[it]ude has been such that I have failed to tell you that I speak very little English. In the house of Madam Chegaroy much French is spoken, and I spent there two years counting from my leaving Paris.

Since I have more knowledge of French, I could accept the position of French Mistress in New York. I should not need very much for Nazareth. I can make all copies of translation of English into French; but I should not know how to translate from French into English. I can, of course, give in English, a simple explanation to beginners, but I could not, in this language hold a conversation. Do not think, Madam, that in this, my confession, I am expressing any desire of not serving you, and, therefore, of remaining with you for a long time. I want to prevent, between us, even the appearance of deception.

If you want me, such as I am, I am entirely at your disposal. I am waiting for your definite answer. There it is now; I will consider myself as engaged face to face with you.

Accept, Madam, my respectful consideration. I am
Yours sincerely,
E. Leyraque

Do not think, however, that I could not correct the translations of French into English. I can do so perfectly; but I could not do, with open book, an oral translation of French into English, at least, a translation that would leave nothing to be desired.

No archival search has revealed either the full name of E. Leyraque or the outcome of her application for employment. Whether she ever taught at Nazareth, with or without sufficient English, remains an interesting puzzle. If no Sister could fill this need, it may not have been easy to find a lay teacher who could.

4-DD

Letter to Mother Catherine Spalding from B. J. Webb
OLB 17, p. 66

Louisville
January 17, 1855
Nazareth Female Academy
Bot. of Webb, Peters & Company

3 No. 1 Hall & Soris Guitars	$1613	$39.00
1 No. 2 Hall & Soris Guitars	$2517	17.00

1 No. 3 Hall & Soris Guitars	$28	21.00
1 French Guitar No. 20	211	16.00
1 French Guitar No. 19	18	14.00
1 French Guitar No. 17	17	13.00
		$120.50
Cr. By defect in two cases	.75	−1.50
		$119.00

Dear Sister,

We could not promptly get the two guitars repaired in time for the wagon. They will be ready tomorrow, and we will try to get them and the three books taken up by the stage.

Most respectfully,
B. J. Webb

Minutes of the Nazareth Council, March 6, 1849, record that the post of agent was taken from Francis McKay and given to Peters and Webb of Louisville. The reason for the change is not recorded; it need not have been any negative performance of McKay. Ben Webb was a known and reputable businessman in the city as well as a historian of his era.

4-EE

Letter to Mother Catherine Spalding from A. H. O'Brien
OLB 1, p. 146

Bedford
February, 1854
My dear Mother Catharine,

I would have written to you some time ago, but I wished to give you the ages of the children, but I could not ascertain them to a certainty and I thought I would [w]rite now and tell you what I could. Ellen, the eldest will be 7 in March. The next, Margaret is between 5 and 6. Cornelia Elizabeth is about 4. I think, I will go to their Aunt's soon and then I will write to you again.

I would have been in Louisville sometime since if Dr. O'Brien had been at home, but he is still in Frankfort and it is uncertain when he will be at home. I have thought about you and your children this cold weather and was fearful that coal was scarce, but I hope you have not suffered. I spent a few days in Frankfort and had the pleasure of seeing Mr. Reynolds a few minutes. I heard severe remarks about the Catholics, but I did not mind them. Sometimes I retorted. I have nothing to write at present. Mary sends her love to you and the Sisters. My love to the Sisters, and accept my best love for yourself.

H. O'Brien

My respects to Mr. Reynolds.

This letter remains a puzzle of identities and situations. The writer appears to be a woman, possibly wife of the Dr. O'Brien named, but hardly the mother of the girls, since she has to investigate their ages. The relationships of the writer, the girls, and their aunt all remain obscure, as is the topic of the letter, which seems to concern the girls' future. They are too young to be prospective students, and Catherine was not, in 1854, directing the orphanage. Annals of St. Vincent Orphan Asylum record an Ellen O'Brien, age nine, who was accepted in 1853. Both of Ellen's parents were dead, and she lived with Judge John E. Newman in Bardstown. If his wife was the "Aunt" of this letter, the discrepancies in ages and relationships still remain unsolved. Mr. Reynolds may be an unknown layman or the Reverend Ignatius Reynolds, long of the Bardstown diocese but in 1854 bishop of Charleston, South Carolina.

4-FF

Letter to Mother Catherine Spalding from Edward L. Miles
DLB 11b, p. 178

New Hope,
January 3, 1855
Mother Catherine,

I will take the boy you offered to hire me at your price for the present year. I did not know of some disappointments when I was at your place yesterday, or I should have taken him without hesitation. I sent the little boys, Jeff and David back to college today; if you conclude to send him, he can ride one of the horses back. I will execute my note the first time I come to town and deposit it with Mr. Smith. It will oblige me very much if you can send the boy.

Yours in Christ,
Edward L. Miles

No known situation or business of the Nazareth campus explains this letter. It is evidence that Nazareth at least on one occasion engaged in the common practice of hiring slaves out to neighbors or other persons in greater need of labor. New Hope, Kentucky, is a rural area near enough to Bardstown that Mr. Miles may have been well known to Mother Catherine and considered trustworthy in his handling of a servant.

4-GG

Letter to Mother Catherine Spalding from Clara Bowen
DLB 1, p. 32

Cincinnati
November 7, 1852
Dearest Mother,

Although I have never before written to you, dear Mother, you must not think that I have not thought of you. Your dear face has always claimed a prominent place among the pictures that memory loves to paint of the dear old home of my happy school days, and I have often wished to write to you, but have always been prevented in some way or other until now.

Do not therefore suppose for an instant that my long silence has risen from any diminution of affection for [you], though my home is very dear and my cherished friends who loved me there, with that depths of tenderness and strength of feeling, which those scenes around which cling the bright memories of kindness is treasured up, and least of all can I forget the one who watched so untiringly by my sick-bed, and rejoiced so truly when the danger was past, and I was restored to life and health once more.

Mother, do you recall one evening when I was just recovering, you were alone in the infirmary with me, and throwing your arms around me, you suddenly knelt down and kissed me? I have never forgotten it, for until then I thought you cold, but after that, I knew you loved me. If I am vain in writing thus, you must excuse for I follow the principle that so much love must need a little return, and therefore, I cannot help being just a bit dear to you.

But I have exhausted my sheet in telling that I have not forgotten you, and am obliged to close, hoping to get a little farther the next time.

Goodbye for the present, Pray for little Clara.

Clara Bowen from Cincinnati, Ohio, came to Nazareth in 1847, aged twelve years five months. She withdrew in 1850 but became a convert while enrolled. The baptismal register gives the data:

> Mar. 19, 1850, I baptized Clara Emily Vincentia, daughter of Mr. Aaron S. Bowen and Martha Augusta Barrett, his lawful wife; born 26, Nov. 1834. Sponsors were, Rev. J. Haseltine and Lucy Barrett. She received Communion and Extreme Unction at the same time.
>
> [Signed] J. Haseltine R.C.P. [Roman Catholic Priest]

The conversion and danger of death seem to have been linked, at least in the timing. The letter to Mother Catherine is written in a beautiful hand on lovely note paper.

Catherine's last new establishment was the mission in Covington, Kentucky, in 1856. It began with the following series of letters, which issued in two distinct schools, La Salette Academy "for pay," and St. Mary's Cathedral School for the poor. These schools would be followed by others in the northern Kentucky region near Cincinnati, making that area prominent in SCN mission history for many years. Because of the importance of the history embedded in the letters below, they are given in full, with needed explanatory context.

4-HH

Letter to Mother Catherine Spalding from Geo. A.
Carrell, Bishop of Covington
DLB 1, p. 276

Covington, KY.,
Sept. 24, 1855
Dear Mother Catharine:

I have requested Very Rev. T. R. Butler to have a conversation with you on the subject of establishing in this city a house of your Sisters. We could begin only in a very humble manner—our children are like ourselves, poor. I know well, that they will never be well taken care of, until they have the members of a Religious Community to train them in virtue and knowledge. You will, I am sure, in the progress of time have so many members, that it will be an object to find a field for labor, and you could not find one more in need of the presence and labors of the Sisters. V. Rev. M. Butler will explain all these matters and whatever he says and does you may consider as coming from myself.

Commending myself to the holy prayers of yourself and
Community, I remain
Yours in our Lord
+ Geo. A. Carrell
Bp. of Covington

The diocese of Covington was created in 1833, an offshoot of the diocese of Louisville. It comprised eastern Kentucky and had seven priests. The new bishop, George Aloysius Carrell, was known for his zeal in building churches; by 1855, the diocese had thirteen. Catholics who had gone by boat to worship in the Cincinnati Cathedral had their own Covington church in 1834, and in 1853 their own St. Mary's Cathedral. The Reverend Thomas Butler was its pastor and Vicar General of the diocese.

4-II

Letter to Mother Catherine Spalding from T. R. Butler
DLB 14, p. 9

Covington, KY.
Nov. 6th 1855
Esteemed Mother:

We have been very patiently looking for some indication of the early fulfillment of your kind promise to send a colony of your good sisters to the aid of our poor people. And we do humbly and prayerfully trust that our patience may but be tried a little longer. A Miss Esther O'Bierne is eagerly preparing for her departure for Nazareth; she has closed her school and will be off in about two weeks. I am obliged daily to visit and encourage the venerable old parents to make the sacrifice. I flatter myself with the idea that they are perfectly resigned to give their all—their only earthly treasure for the duties of charity, and the more perfect fulfillment of the Divine Will, by their excellent child and themselves. Father B. Maria's advice has determined the intentions of Miss Laura Knapp, also, to seek the community of your good sisters, the more sure way of salvation and perfection. She says she will be ready to go to Nazareth to enter the novitiate with Miss O'Bierne. But of all this you have probably been more regularly informed by the good children themselves. Our Bishop has desired me to visit the family of Dr. Anderson at Flemingsburg, I shall be happy to do so. I am much interested in the admirable character of his amiable daughter Caroline. I have little doubt of her being called to religious life. Am inclined to direct her towards Nazareth. There was a probability of her visiting you in bringing her younger sister to your school. Will you kindly inform me if she has done so? Or if you have any certainty of her intentions in that regard.

The forsaken condition of our poor children, especially after the close of Miss O'Bierne's school, renders us exceedingly anxious to know when the Sisters may be looked for. The renting of a house may be a great difficulty if we give up the one in which Miss O'B. taught—her school next to our residence—This we must do if you do not make us more sure of the time of the coming of the Colony. This property is now as they say Marked—it is the property of heirs, and cannot be sold for anything like the amount of the debt of the estate; therefore the heirs expect to get nothing from it, and the creditors have obtained a decree for its sale. It is worth, I was told yesterday by the lawyer who has the business of the estate in his hands, seven thousand dollars, its cash value, $5000, but he thinks it will not bring that much. It will be sold by the sheriff within a month or two. Lawyer Spillman tells me the credits on it may be made easy, as the principal debt on it, will not be due for some years. Our own poverty and the debt of the Cathedral alone prevents us from purchasing it. It will be a great bargain and no other place of this size can be found either to buy or rent in any central part of the city.

It is eminently suitable for the sisters—with [this] single objection, of being rather too near our residence. Yet this may be obviated by building a close wall, and by making hereafter new buildings on the front of Scott Street. I will make an enclosed platt [plan] of the position of the lot and the building, with the cathedral and our house so that you may understand all about it, so your Mother Superior, Father Haseltine, and the Council can form an idea of it. If you would buy it, I will at once transfer to you a very safe note of a responsible person for—$500. It has an indefinite time to run, but could be paid in small sums on the interest or your purchase, or would be paid at the last payment on the house. This is my individual offering towards the property. By fairs and other means you could doubtless, easily obtain the rest of the means. I think the payment of this purchase money, which will make you the owner of the property, can be made after the first payment, with as much ease as you would pay the necessary rent of any other property which could be used for the residence or school for the Sisters. If you do not entertain this proposition to purchase so convenient a place, at so fair a bargain, we shall offer you the old brick church as a school house and will have to look out for a house to rent for you near to it. But in the name of charity and zeal for the great work which your holy community is invited daily more widely to engage in, do let me entreat you, kindly, promptly, and favorably to act upon our requests and reply as early as you can.

I send you the bill for the lamp, which you perceive I have paid $104.75.—The $10.25 is my offering for your sanctuary lamp. If I were richer, I would give something more worthy of your beautiful church, and more expressive of my desire to honor our loving and merciful God, and of my wish to enlighten all hearts with the knowledge of His ways and enkindle in all hearts the fire of His love. May I ask of yourself and your pious community an occasional prayer before that solitary lamp, which so touchingly expresses by its perpetual light and constant watching in God's holy service, the untiring faith and charity of your devoted lives.

Someone, Mr. O'Bierne, Dr. Knapp or myself will accompany the young ladies—Miss O'B. and Miss K. when they go down to Nazareth to be subject to you as their new parents, and we fervently hope that you will have the colony in readiness to return with the persons who may accompany the young ladies. I must request an early reply to this letter, that we may have time to make some humble efforts to prepare a roof and shelter for the young colony. Begging to be especially remembered to Father Haseltine and the Community, to whose sacred prayers I again solicit, I remain very truly & respectfully.

Your friend & humble servant in our Lord,
T. R. Butler, V.G.

Mother Catherine may have responded to Bishop Carrell's invitation with interest and encouragement, interpreted by him and his Vicar General as a "kind promise." The Council, however, did not make a definite decision until December 27, 1855, and its choice of Sisters for the "colony" was altered on February 29, 1856. Meantime, Father Butler repeatedly urged a commitment and a date for their coming.

Esther O'Bierne and Laura Knapp both entered Nazareth on December 6, 1855.

4-JJ

Letter to Mother Catherine Spalding from T. R. Butler
DLB 1, p. 277

Covington, Ky.,
Nov. 6th, 1855.
Esteemed Mother,

I have written to you at some length this morning about

several matters and omitted to mention anything about our print of Nazareth—I send you a copy of the Proposals for both the smaller print to head letters and Bills and for the large colored print for framing and preserving as a picture.

For making the drawing on stone for letter sized print	$20.00
For printing a ream (480 sheets)	5.00
Paper to be selected by yourself and paid separately for	4.00
	$29.00

By having three reams printed on different qualities of paper—some gilt edged and on common bill paper and—the price would be reduced and even this expense could be regained by the sale of the paper for the correspondence of such older pupils as might wish to [use] it. But the actual payment of such an outlay is by the extended knowledge and usefulness of the Institution—.

For lithographing the view rather large[r] than my drawing and printing in seven colors—which will make a finely colored print—for the first hundred $88.00, for each following hundred, including paper, $28.00. If you would have three additional hundred printed after the first hundred, the whole four hundred prints would come to $172.00 or 43 cents each. They would be worth each $1.00 and by the sale of 200 copies which would hardly more than supply your present school with one apiece, you would clear the whole expense and have two hundred copies for your own distribution or for charitable purposes. Charging 75 cents for the print would repay you and widen and hasten its circulation—and it will be your best mode of advertising.

I have ordered the small print and it will be done in about two weeks—I hope to send or bring it when Miss O. B. goes home to you. Please write and direct me as to the number of copies or reams of paper and the quality of the latter, also say what I shall order about the large print.

I enclose a copy of the bill of lading and it may be of no further use, but as I have no news of the lamps since they left here it may be well for you to have it.

The Sanctuary lamp requires only a stout tumbler and good oil with a taper and cork float—this is the most sure and lasting light you can use in it.

Again begging your kind remembrance and prayers,
I beg to remain,
Very respectfully your friend in our Lord,
T. R. Butler, V.G.

This letter seems to be an immediate follow-up on the previous and to be based on the same assumption that Sisters were definitely coming to Covington. Only the lost letters of Mother Catherine might explain the purchases and financial responsibilities discussed here. But inquiry to the Diocese of Covington has yielded assurance that they have no letters by her.

What does seem clear is that the two clergymen expected the Sisters to pay for most or all the furnishings of the school and that Father Butler had invested freely in what he deemed necessary or appropriate. Catherine may have heard echoes of some of the financial dealings preliminary to the new mission in Nashville; in 1855, that memory could hardly be encouraging.

4-KK

Letter to Mother Catherine Spalding from T. R. Butler
DLB 14, p. 11

Covington, Ky.
Dec. 19th. 1855
Mother Catharine Spalding:

No doubt, kind Mother, but you have given me up long ere this, as an uncivil correspondent. In fact, I felt quite disappointed by the great uncertainty in which your letter left the matter of the colony of the Sisters for Covington. Again I deferred writing, as I expected to accompany your young novices to Nazareth. Finally, I have for some weeks been quite ill of a cold—cough, in fact inflammation of the lungs, nor am I yet quite well. I hope and pray that you and all are pleased with our young friends, Esther and Laura. I hope and pray that they are pleased and happy with you. Give them my love and blessing and that of our good Bishop, who has a very high regard for them. Tell Esther her venerable Mother is much consoled every day by looking at the nicely framed picture of Nazareth which I gave her last week. She is well and daily more pleased with her good child's offering and her own. Laura's Mother is also delighted by the possession of her copy of the picture, which takes Laura's place among, and keeps them hourly in mind of her.

I have sent a framed one to Father Haseltine and another to yourself. I enclose the offer of the artist about the larger print, which I strongly advise you to have done. You will see how much cheaper they will do it than the men who wrote offer No. 1. And yet the last are not half so good artists as those who make the low offer. If you have any fault to find or wishes of change express them and the picture can be much improved. I see several defects which should the buyer order done, shall be corrected. I have forwarded today to Webb-Peter's and Col. Music Dealers, a bundle by express, containing three reams of paper, with the small print of Nazareth. Two reams are of letter paper, one of bill foolscap. The cost has been as follows:

Lithograph	$20.00
Express	1.00
Paper	8.50

The enclosed bill shows the particulars. This amt. may

be added to the bill for the chandeliers, taking out the $10.25. I think it is the cost of my little offering of the sanctuary lamp. A check can be sent to me for the amt. Now what about our colony? We are trying to get a dwelling for them next to the old church on 5th St. three squares from the Cathedral, where the Bishop thinks it better to commence the school. But please, say when they are coming. We want to have not only a house for them but also something to furnish it. Give us then, as early a notice as you can, as to the time of their coming. I said something about paying the travelling expenses if you would send the colony at once with me when I was at Nazareth. I will not be entirely forgetful of that word—though your part of the condition was not fulfilled. If I knew what day the colony would be ready to leave Louisville, I think I could obtain a free passage on the Steamer. Pardon these hasty lines, they are written with pain at a very late hour of the night. Humbly asking your prayers, and a remembrance from the Sisters I am,

Most Respectfully, your friend,
T. R. Butler, V.G.

This letter is still prior to the date of the Council meeting that determined to send a "colony" to Covington (December 17, 1855). The importance Father Butler attached to the picture of Nazareth is not explained, except as consolation for the mothers of the two women who had entered the SCN and an incentive to hasten the arrival of the Sisters in Covington. It is not known whether Catherine did order that any more be made and, if she did, what became of them.

4-LL

Letter to Mother Catherine Spalding from Rev. T. R. Butler
DLB 14, p. 12

Covington, Ky.
Jan. 23rd 1856
Dear Mother Catharine,

Your letter covering the check for $150.75 was received yesterday. Half of that amount I shall return to you as my personal contribution for the travelling expenses of our Colony. I hesitated about asking for any of the sum I had paid for the Prints and chandeliers, but I find several claims for sums of money which I was not aware of being responsible for and am thus constrained to be less generous of my small means than I had intended. I sent you by mail a newspaper containing a notice of the coming of the Colony of Nazareth, and an advertisement of our intended Fair and concert and supper for the purpose of furnishing a house and school for the Sisters. In these hard times we must make use of mixed motives to obtain the means of carrying out our benevolent undertaking, as a direct appeal to charity or generosity can meet with but little success. We shall be able to put a house in going order next week and shall be ready any time after the first of February to welcome your good Children of St. Vincent.

Our people as far as I can hear, the whole community are greatly pleased with the prospect opening now for the education of their children, and many are eager to send their children to the pay school. I have looked about Cinn [Cinncinati] for bedsteads, and shall have eight or ten very nice ones, mattress and pillows, feathers are too high for our beginning. We must request of you notice of one or two days before the arrival of the Sisters here. It will be better for them to pass through Lexington, if the ice continues to obstruct the river, as the steamer cannot run; it is quite dangerous to cross on the ice, as they would have to do twice, at Louisville and Cinn [Cinncinati]. I shall remit the travelling expenses of $75.00 in a day or so. I am busy right now day and night in arranging and managing affairs as Chief Butler of the Fair so that I cannot get to Cinn [Cinncinati] for banking purposes.

I have a particular request to make—that is—that you return me the bill of Ulanpech & Menzel for the engraving and printing of the small picture of Nazareth, by the next mail. I am very certain I paid the bill and sent it to you, because I thought you should have the receipt from them please send it directly, or I may have to pay it a second time.

I find it impossible to make a visit to Nazareth; my duties are so pressing at home, besides it would be better perhaps if the Sisters would have the protection of some secular gentleman on the journey. Dr. Knapp, it seems, will visit you in a few days. It might be well to make use of the occasion of his return to forward the Sisters' luggage to Lexington. Anything larger than ordinary baggage must [go] on the freight train of cars, and for that reason bedding should be put in boxes and sent several days in advance of the Sisters to Covington via Lexington R.R.

I have besides your letter, one from my good child Esther. I am saddened by the evidences of discontent it contains, and regret the turmoil of my present occupations prevents me from writing as I wish to do, to her and yourself on this important matter. I think as you do of the signs of her vocation, and feel assured that she will find no peace in the world. May God guide this good child through the darkness of this trial. I will write to her as soon as possible. In great haste, I remain most respectfully,

Your humble servant & friend in God,
(Rev.) T. R. Butler

By the late January date of this letter, Father Butler must have been made aware of the Council's decision to begin the mission in Covington. The *Cincinnati Commercial* in late January notified the public of the coming of the Sisters of Charity and of a "Concert,

Fair, and Supper" to support the new school. Father Butler was not aware, it seems, or ignored here one major negotiation about the SCN school that was still to be decided: the socioeconomic clientele it was meant to serve.

4-MM

Letter to Mother Catherine Spalding from Rev. T. R. Butler
DLB 14, p. 13

Covington, Ky.
March—1856
Dear Mother:

Where shall I find a fitting apology to offer our esteemed and kind Mother Catherine for my long and uncivil silence. Surely you will have reason to believe I think that "your charity beareth all things" if you really are not displeased with me after such treatment of your letters. Now in explanation there is much to say. Our Fair busied me night and day for some time. We have made by it, some seven hundred dollars, which I have put at interest. We still find it impossible to get any other house than the frame one near the Cathedral. It has been sold, meanwhile, and the deal is disputed. The question will be decided in the March term of Court, which sits in two weeks. If this house cannot be secured, we have but a poor chance for any other, except our old shanty home attached to the old brick church which has been used since the building of the Cathedral as a boy's school, and is now vacant. This would answer for the poor school and was intended for the service of the Sisters in that way. Yet that alone would not answer the necessities of our people, for though most of them are poor, still there are many able to pay for the schooling of their children, and also many protestants are asking for a good school, and have promised to send their children, if we have such a school established. In fact, Esteemed Mother, if the school should be only a plain and simple poor school, we shall not be able to carry out our good intentions, as our poor cannot support such a school, and our better off people will not help us, unless we get them a proper school, as a pay school for their children. The Bishop has no manner of resources on which he could draw for support of a simple poor school; and it has been the hope of all that you would send as you promised a good colony. This would enable us to have such a school as would compare with our neighbors, and enable parents here to educate their daughters under their own eyes. We do not yet hope to have a boarding school, but your last letter alarms us, when you say "Don't forget that it is to be only a common school, common branches."—Our Bishop was about starting to make a retreat when he read your letter, some days afterwards he wrote to me—"You had better write to Mother Catherine about the pay school, music, embroidery, etc., without a good school the Sisters will not make money to buy bread, much less to pay the rent of a house, etc." I do trust your good Councillors will reconsider our colony and grant us such members as will form an inviting school, calculated to help us develop the resources of our City and to be a religious comfort to all classes of our people.

Thank you kind Mother for the papers you returned to me. They were just what I wanted. I have settled with the engravers, and have spread abroad a good number of the prints [of] your beautiful home. I hope it may prove a benefit, and that yourself and our good Sisters may enjoy all the comforts of it for long years to come. I will send you the large drawing which you can have copied altered if you should want it printed. I am in some sense sorry for the return of our good Esther, yet I am convinced that the excellent child has been well directed and that no reasonable ground to doubt the uprightness of her intentions which are as sound in leaving, as they were in going to Nazareth. The very instability of mind she has exhibited is a proof of want [of] sound vocation, such a trait is not voluntary, but a constitutional weakness, which would make her ways make her uneasy if not unhappy. Such a mind when soundly religious as Esther's requires more room change and variety, than a religious house affords. Then too I am pleased to see her at the side of her parents, indeed I am quite easy about her return, she is, I think the first of my many postulants, who has not persevered. And decided as I was of her religious vocation, I am now as decidedly of the opinion that she had not. Laura—to whom I beg you, give my assurance of my prayers and blessing. Her family are all well. Also do I pray for my new postulant Carrie Anderson. I received a letter from her an hour ago. I am delighted to find her with you, and happy as I thought she would be. May God bless her with the grace of constancy in her holy duties of a life of perfection. Tell her now the embargo on my writing is removed, that she may expect a letter from her old friend, yet, I am of the opinion that outside influences are by no means needed by the pious children of Nazareth. If I do not write much or often, it is because I feel assured prayers and sacrifices will be better from me, than any small effort at wise direction, I may otherwise make.

Hoping soon to hear something more cheering about our colony, and begging a kind remembrance in your pious prayers. I beg to remain,

Very Respectfully & Truly,
Your friend and humble servant in Our Lord,
(Rev.) T. R. Butler, V.G.

Esther O'Bierne left the novitiate on February 23, 1856. Laura Knapp would leave on July 4, 1856. Nothing further is known of either woman. Carrie Anderson persevered and became Sister Xavier. She died in 1875.

The central issue of the school's purpose was finally resolved by a decision to open two schools, "pay" and "poor." La Salette Academy offered the "finished" accomplishments demanded by the parents able to pay for a full curriculum. Tuition was $1.00 per month, sometimes paid in goods. In 1855, the city had a boys' school of three rooms staffed by Franciscan Sisters and laymen teachers. In 1856, the SCN opened a girls' school for the poor in a two-story, four-room house on Scott Street: St. Mary's Cathedral School. Tuition was 50 cents per month, but most parents could not pay it. About $10.00 per month was realized from this school. Some parents gave a contribution. According to the LaSalette Annals, Sisters at both schools relied on donations of food and other goods: coffee, "milk and butter and eggs all month," the cost of a day's labor.

The contract made with the Nazareth Council and Father Haseltine stipulated a yearly clothing allowance of $50 per Sister. The house was to be furnished from the proceeds of the school; any surplus was to be given to the bishop. If the school did not support the Sisters, the bishop or Vicar General were to do so. "So related to Sister Clare Gardiner by Mother Catherine Spalding," according to the La Salette Annals.

The Council minutes record that on February 29, 1856, Sister Clare Gardiner was to go to Covington as "Sister Servant" (superior of a local house). She kept close records of early payments, donations, and purchases: "April 23, 1857 . . . 5 pairs of shoes . . . $5.50; sugar, flour, lard, tea" (Annals of La Salette). The fair must have been an annual fundraiser for some time; the annals of La Salette record the net of one fair as $2,252.51 and two pairs of donated boots: "fine" and "garden." Music was introduced into the curriculum in August 1856, and a piano was purchased in August 1858 for monthly payments of $50.

A year after the opening of the Covington schools, in 1857 the Council would vote to open a school in Newport, Kentucky, for girls, "pay and gratis." Sister Helena Tormey, later to be Mother, and Sister Mary Catherine Tully are recorded in the annals as walking each day to Newport poor school with their lunch of bread and prunes.

Conclusion

The schools opened in the Covington diocese may have been felt as a sort of final achievement for Catherine Spalding as she wound up her responsibilities in August 1856 and prepared to leave office for what she certainly knew would be the last time. If she visited branch houses in that year, and if she walked around Nazareth in that last month, she could have had a powerful sense of what had been built, spiritually, physically, and organizationally. She could, if she thought of it, pray her own "Nunc dimittis" (Luke 2:29) as she reflected on all she saw and prepared to return with full and grateful heart to her orphans.

5

Final Years

1856–1858

Twelve letters or notes remain from Catherine Spalding's last eighteen months of life, all but two of them written to Sisters, the beloved Claudia and the young Sisters whose vows she had approved and received. In the two other letters, Catherine is again engaged in the business of the orphanage, seeking and safeguarding the welfare of God's most vulnerable children.

The priceless value of this small gathering of letters is their deeper revelation of the matured heart and hopes of Catherine in her final years. Though she must have written more than two letters on orphanage business, the proportion of extant letters suggests that she was giving more than usual thought and time to support the spiritual and general well-being of the Sisters, especially the newer members. To them she writes with little or no formality, out of her long and loving, frank and humorous friendship for Claudia and other old friends, and out of her genuine interest and deep maternal concern for the younger Sisters. In them, she clearly sees the future of the congregation and her own mission to give herself to them with whatever loving guidance and encouragement she can offer in the time she has left.

Catherine could not have known how very near she really was to her final day, although she was past sixty years old, a "good old age" in that era, and her health was not good. She had severe neuralgia and frequent severe headaches. She certainly knew she could not hold office as Mother again, and would refuse the position if nominated. The Council had sent her back to the orphanage to care for the children and maintain contact with her many supporters in Louisville. She was leaning more than before on the increased staff of the orphanage, especially on Sister Julia Hobbs, her most valued assistant. But she had stopped neither her primary responsibility there nor her visits to the sick poor; she would serve as long as her Lord called and gave strength.

Letters by Mother Catherine Spalding, 1856–1858

5-1

Louisville Sept. 22nd/56
Or. Asylum
My very dear Sister Cleophas,

This morning the Bishop left for Lexington & I fear you think me very negligent not to have answered your kind & welcome letter by him, as I fully intended to do.—How truly glad I was to know you were happy & getting along well, as I believed you would. Knowing you would cheerfully exert yourself to fill the duties of your situation. Nothing contributes more to content, than to be well occupied & have no time left for sad thoughts.—I have had one letter from Sister Ann. She seems inclined to be a little sad; & says she don't know what would become of her, were she not so closely occupied.—& poor little Dominica! They have made her prefect in school & she has several hours to preside either in recreation or study; & has cried a plenty. But all that will pass; & I have no doubt that she will exert herself & succeed well;—& will conduct herself with dignity & propriety.—I am here again, taking my chance with the orphans; may we deserve to have God for our Father.—We have hardly got all things regulated as the girls made their retreat last week & the Sisters made theirs the week before.—so we have just got thro.'—How many letters have you received from Nazareth yet—& have you written.—Whether you write there or not, at least you know you have to write to me often & I will not be forgetful of you. I suppose you have the same cold, fall weather that we have; & we must suffer a little here, as they have not burnt out the chimney we are afraid to make fires.—Sister, I think there are some of the finest voices among these orphan girls that I have heard in a long time & one of them is going up in a few days to join the noviciate at Nazareth.—Give my best love to Sister Gabriella & all the Sisters & ask them to commence the Litany of the Immaculate Conception & say it daily in common till November to obtain a just & peaceable election. Tell Sister Gabriella to be sure to do it—& we poor orphans will join.—Now good-bye my precious Sister: & that Almighty God may bless you is the sincere & humble prayer of your poor Mother.

Catharine

My love to all who inquire for me.—How is Sister Laurentia's health? I hope improving. The health of the children here is very good, but several of the Sisters seem quite frail.—

For information on Sister Cleophas Mills, see Appendix A. Sister Cleophas had been on her first mission at St. Patrick's in Louisville, and was now in Lexington. She would serve as local superior in several schools and hospitals, and would be elected twice to a three-year term as treasurer at Nazareth before election as Mother and member of the Board of Trustees for two terms. She died in 1905.

Sister Laurentia Harrison, after taking vows in March 1851, served at St. Catherine's in Lexington. She went to St. Vincent's in Union County in 1858 some months after Catherine's death. In a letter of 1862, Mother Columba called her home to be Directress of Studies at Nazareth Academy, from which she had graduated in 1849. In 1871, Laurentia went to the academy in Paducah, Kentucky, then in 1877 to Bethlehem Academy in Holy Springs, Mississippi, as superior. There she became one of the "Yellow Fever

Martyrs," dying in care of the sick and buried among them. Archbishop William Henry Elder of Cincinnati noted in an 1895 letter that he had been told Sr. Laurentia Harrison had offered her life for him when he was stricken in the epidemic.

Two Sisters Ann were in the community in early 1858: Ann Lawler, of whom there is no record but her brief membership from 1857 to 1858; and Sister Ann McIntyre, who remained at Nazareth after her vows in August 1851 to study and to teach.

Sister Dominica Greaney made vows in 1854 and was assigned in 1856 to Nazareth Academy as a prefect. Aside from the stress of her duties, she must have had some health issues; she died on Christmas Day 1858, less than a year after Catherine.

Catherine's urgent request for prayer for a peaceable election was prompted by the uproar of Nativism in Kentucky and riots in Louisville on Bloody Monday, August 6, 1855, during the election of a governor and representatives. Another election in 1856 created no small fear of repeated violence. Sister Gabriella Todd was the superior in Lexington, so she would be the one to organize the community prayer for peace.

5-2

> Do you think my dear good old Sister that I can ever forget you? No, no, never whether I write or not, you are always the same to me.—I send you the coffee pot, tho' not exactly such as I would have preferred. It is however of a good quality & I hope it will suit you.—Next time I will try & send you better coffee.—Sister Ida can give you all the news. Don't you think poor Sister Matilda breathes fast.—She seems to me very frail.—Tell Mary Frances I will send her something nice soon.—She must be a good girl. Pray for your old & sincere friend
>
> Catharine—Oct. 19th

The content and style of this friendly letter make it probable that Sister Claudia at Nazareth was the recipient; with her Catherine would banter lightly about a coffee pot and recent news as well as offer assurance of faithful remembrance.

Sister Ida Brophy, professed in 1856 and sent to the orphanage, returned to Nazareth in October, apparently carrying the promised news of others. She seems to have served in nursing care and did so in the Civil War. Sister Matilda McIntyre, professed in 1839, had served at Presentation and at St. Vincent and St. Thomas orphanages in Louisville and Bardstown. In October 1856, the month of this letter, Sister Matilda had returned to Nazareth, evidently showing signs of the lung illness that so concerned Catherine for the Sisters. Mary Frances could have been a student at Nazareth (see Letter 5-5), an orphan sent there for schooling or training, or one of the servants under Claudia's supervision.

5-3

Dear Sister Claudia,

I send you here a pair of soft gloves for your poor chapped hands; I expect they are pretty sore by this time. I send you also a bar of Rosin soap. I know some of the Sisters used to want it. Don't know whether it was you or who.—best love to every body.—how does your table ware come on?—I expected you would send to me before this, to get the vacancies filled.

Yours ever in our dear Lord.
Catharine
Nov. 19th

I can't afford to keep any fire in my room at all, not even to sleep by. We only keep fire in the Sisters' room thro the day, & in the school rooms & nursery.

5-4
Now dear Claudia,

Did you ever get a pair of strong kid gloves I sent you? I

fear that package went astray with several other things, as I can't hear of it.

New years gift and a happy New Year for you!

Truly yours,
Catharine
Orphan Asylum

What has become of the Muly cow? Milk is mighty scarce for so many babies.—

Several elements have made these two letters favorites among the SCN: the casual yet intimate diction and tone of Catherine to such a friend as Claudia, and her interest in and care of details for the comfort of all the Sisters. It seems that Claudia could make Catherine a sort of purchasing agent for her needs in her domestic service of the community at Nazareth; Catherine, however, wanted accountability of the goods' arrival. Claudia must have inquired about Catherine's self-care against the cold. The letters, by their frankness, are valuable evidence of Catherine's spirit and of the poverty and physical hardships endured at the orphanage during the often bitter winter weather in Louisville.

The exact meaning of "muly" cow has been debated among later Sisters; a cattle farmer's daughter has noted that the term signifies a polled cow, one without horns, especially if so born. It can breed, usually has a calf or two before being called a cow, and can be valuable for production of milk. That is clearly the value Catherine, mother of orphans, placed on the cow in question.

5-5

Or. Asylum Jan. 14th/57
My dear Sister Claudia,

What is the matter with you? I have sent you several messages & I never get a word from you.—I thought at least Madame Blaique would bring some kind news from you but you are as dry as ever.—Why don't you tell me whether you got your kid gloves or not.—I told you I always feared that bundle went astray. Well, have you heard any thing about the muly cow.—or have you seen Mr. Wathen.—Well never mind, I won't tea[s]e you any more about muly. Pray for me daily.—& I shall never forget your kindnesses past. Do jog Sister Margaret's memory about sending back those beer barrels, as they are not worth paying for.—Lizzie Wathen wrote me that her brother Thomas talked of moving near Owenboro. Is it so?—I should be sorry for him to leave.—Pray for me—

Yours as ever—Catharine

This letter completes a little group in the Catherine-Claudia letters. It is now Catherine's turn to complain of scarcity and delay of letters. Madame Blaique had an undated contract at Nazareth to teach dancing with "elegance of carriage and deportment" at $10.00 per student per quarter, but with a 10 percent cut for loss of payment by the parents. She had arrived with a Mary Frances (see letter 5-2). She must have been a fairly regular courier of news and letters between Nazareth and Louisville. The Wathens may have been one family if the father worked at Nazareth. An archival item says that Thomas moved near Owensboro in January 1857; the letter to Catherine it cites has not been found.

5-6

St. Vincent's Orphan Asylum, Lou., KY
March 18th/57
Mrs. Harbison
Dear Madam,

Having seen your letters both to Bishop Spalding & Dr. Johnson—I now write you, to inform you, as to the condition on which your children are received & kept in this institution.

When we receive orphans, destitute, we raise them, give them a plain education, & teach them to sew &

> do all kinds of domestic work that a female should know; to enable them when grown, to gain their own livelihood respectably, & be good members of society. We claim the full control of the children to the age of 15 or 16 years; no one can take them from the asylum before that time without our consent, & then pay their board & expenses at the rate of $75 per annum for the time they have remained.—If placed here by a surviving parent or friend & the board paid—they can then be taken out by the same authority at any time; the expenses being paid up to the time of their being taken out.—If you wish your children to remain here, you can simply write to me, obligating yourself to comply with those conditions & specifying the same.—& you may rest assured that we will, if we have charge of them, do all in our power according to the means of the house, for their improvement & real good.—The little girls are in good health, & progressing pretty well in their studies.—They seem to be cheerful & happy & both desire their best love to you.—I shall now await your answer; & shall assuredly not give them up to any one with out your authority. If you wish to send them any thing you can direct to them to the care of Dr. Johnson & Clarke.
>
> Very respectfully your obt. sert.
> Supr. of the Or. Asylum Mother Catharine Spalding
>
> Please understand when I say we instruct the children in the asylum, in [This postscript is left incomplete]

This letter, factual and businesslike yet cordial and sympathetic in tone, is valuable for historical evidence of the practices and policies of a home for children in the mid-nineteenth century. St. Vincent's may not have differed in many particulars from other asylums of the time, few as these were in the nation; one distinction probably is to be inferred from the incomplete last sentence—that the children received religious instruction along with "plain education" and domestic work. A few other values and practices in rearing orphans may also be inferred: that the children could claim St. Vincent's as a stable home and place of protection and nurture until they were old enough to be on their own; that the amount spent on them betokened a suitable and sufficient diet as well as warm shelter; that no attempt was made to detach them emotionally from parents; that the ultimate claim and authority of a parent were recognized.

The archival story of Mrs. Harbison and her children is simply that they were being admitted to St. Vincent Asylum at the date of the letter. Apparently she had appealed to a Dr. Johnson (lawyer or physician?) as well as to Bishop Spalding to have her little girls taken in. No mention is made of their father or Mrs. Harbison's husband. All that can be inferred is that the recipient of the letter was alone, genuinely concerned for her children's future, and unable to sustain all their needs.

5-7

Asylum May 25th/'57

Your kind little letter my dear Sister, together with the wrong directed one is received.—Tho' it is no evidence of my going there shortly, but only the direction of a crazy brain.—I now enclose you a letter that has been lying in the drawer here for some time I expect. Still it will no doubt afford you some pleasure—& you will, I hope, pardon the delay on negligence.—A death is always gloomy to poor mortals; still one that you speak of, has too much of consolation in it to make us sad.—There is so much to suffer in this life, & so little to live for, that I can't grieve to see anyone leave this world well prepared.—& then so many dangers & risks for us in this life.—& some so blind as to their real God;—that they are all the time getting into worse & worse troubles. As to you, my own dear child, I trust God will guide & keep you faithful in his service & enable you to do much good in the path of your holy vocation. Yet we must suffer &

meet with some trials.—We should not be followers of Christ if we did [not].—Let us be humble, & we can do all things, & bear all things.—Love to dear Sister Aloysia & each of the Sisters. Say to Sister Gabrielle I shall always be glad to get a letter from her.—We have generally good health here.—Sister Martha is about the same as usual.—God bless you

Always your friend & Mother—Catharine

This letter is a conscientious effort to make delayed contact and express sympathy at a death.

The Sister recipient seems to be in Lexington, where Sister Gabriella Todd was local superior in 1857. Sister Aloysia Pryor was in Lexington until September 1856. She then went to Nazareth; her record may be imprecise on the date of her transfer. Sister Martha Drury alternated service at Presentation and the Free School on Fifth Street from 1845 to 1858; Catherine would have seen her often and observed her steady, strong constitution and service to the sick.

5-8

St. Vincent's Orphan Asylum Asylum [*sic*]
Louisville Ky June 13th/57
Dear Sister,

I hope you are all well, tho' I seldom hear from you—& never see you.—Can't you come & stay awhile with us after your examination is over.—Sister please tell Mrs. Dillon I wish to see her & request her to come up & see me as soon as she can—tho' I am sorry to give her the trouble. Give her my love—& also to the Sisters.—God bless you, I hope you are well.—

Always the same
Catharine

This letter may be to Sister Baptista Walls or another SCN at St. Patrick's. Baptista was still in Louisville, where she would remain until August, and could make a visit or communicate a message. A card in the archives notes this letter and mentions Mrs. Dillon, but offers no information about her. There is a vague oral tradition that she may have been a peddler who traveled the city with her goods. She might also have been one of the Lady Managers who volunteered at the orphanage.

5-9

Louisville Orphan Asylum
October 30, 1857
My dear Mother Josephine,

At the request of the Ladies, Managers of our Orphan Asylum; I take the liberty of laying before you the necessitous situation of our numerous dear little orphans, & to solicit your charitable aid & that of your branch establishment in their behalf. They would, as in the preceding years, have recourse to a Fair; did they not think that the present state of public feeling & the general depression in money matters, render it unadvisable to do so. Tho' the actual debt of the Asylum & the laying up of provisions, fuel, &c., &c., for the approaching season make it indispensable for them to raise a collection in some way. This has determined them to apply now to the different clergymen & Catholic Institutions in the diocese to effect this object,—& they do hope that as this is the only Catholic Asylum in the Diocese, that they will not be disappointed in their expectations. Allow us then, in the name of those dear destitute little ones to lay before you their humble petition & to hope soon to receive, with sentiments of the deepest gratitude, your benevolent & charitable offering & thus establish you[r] claim to a large share in the prayer that is daily offered to Him, who deigns to call himself the Orphans' Father.

Allow us also to beg a remembrance in the daily prayers of your dear community, while I remain with every sentiment of cordial & sisterly affection that should ever exist among the communities of our holy religion;—for after all, we should make but one common family to carry on the different works of our common & divine Master.

Wholly yours in our dear Lord
(signed) Sr. Catherine Spalding
By order of the Board of Managers

(Copy of a letter in the archives of the Sisters of Loretto)

Mother Josephine Kelly, SL, was Mother General of her order from 1832 to 1838. She had come to Kentucky from Baltimore in a group of nine women escorted by Father Charles Nerinckx to enter the Sisters of Loretto. Her ministry was education. Little more about her is known; her role at the time of this letter is obscure, but she was evidently at Loretto, and Catherine seems to think she had enough influence for the appeal.

The Lady Managers of the orphan asylum constituted a board of advisors, and they did not take their managerial role lightly. In the past, Catherine had needed to clarify that the ownership and primary management of the orphanage lay with the SCN congregation.

The fair in those days was a very large event, lasting as many as six days, involving the presence and labor of many Sisters and the collaborating ladies of Louisville. Its proceeds were vital to the operation of the orphanage. That so public a Catholic fundraiser was considered inadvisable so soon after Bloody Monday is understandable and a witness to the scarred feelings on all sides inflicted by that event.

5-10

I feel [guilty?], my dear good Sister, for keeping Sister Vincentia's letter so long just to put my scrawl in. I am glad you are pleased with Owenboro, & have no doubt, while you find it a pleasant Sojourn, you will be able to render many services in that school, as you have already learned what it is to carry on a school with so few Sisters.—May you ever prove my dear child to be all that I believe you to be.—St. Patrick's School is quite large, they say larger than it has ever been, so Father Joyce says. The Sisters there seem pleased.—I have been there once.—Sister Rosalia has been up here once, but not the other two.—We have quite a large day school, about 130 on the list. [O]ur orphans still increase.—Sister Mary Magdalen called to see us the other day on her way with Sister Camilla to help Sister Euphrasia in Newport. I believe they are going to housekeep there & live at the school.—Give my kindest love to Sister Gertrude & say I will write to her soon. Also to Sister Constantia.—Love to each Sister there.—We have finished our new wash & bake house & got all the clothes yard paved between that & the other house.—The family here are quite healthy now. We have three babies that can't walk. Pray for me & please write oftener.

Always your the same—Catharine

The date of this letter is very likely 1857, as Mother Catherine returned to the orphanage in 1856. The recipient is almost certainly Sister Baptista Walls, an especially "dear child" to Catherine. She had been at St. Patrick's and been sent to Owensboro in August 1857. She later served on various Kentucky missions and died in 1898.

Catherine seems to have encouraged visits exchanged by Sisters in different missions within the same city or area. Sister Rosalia Huff, a visitor from St. Patrick's, was a seasoned veteran, having made vows in 1826 and served in Vincennes, Lexington, Bardstown, and the Free School on Fifth Street in Louisville before a long period of service at St. Patrick's. She endured seven years of illness before celebrating her Golden Jubilee in 1876 and dying in 1886. The "other two" can be identified as Sisters Bibiana O'Sullivan and Melania Callen (see Letter 5-12).

Catherine delights in reporting the expanding facilities in the orphanage. Its extensive grounds had room for the new buildings; however simple and practical their construction, they greatly improved the lot and the services that could be rendered in a timely way.

Sister Euphrasia Mudd was another seasoned veteran, having made vows in 1824, then been missioned to St. Vincent's in Union County, to Nazareth, to the opening of Nashville, and to Owensboro in 1849. In 1855, she led the group opening Immaculata Academy in Newport, Kentucky. In the group were Sisters Mary Magdalen McMahon and Camilla Weston, both very young in vows. The former had come from Ireland at age five; she would teach small children on all her missions until her death in 1921. Sister Camilla made vows in May 1857, went to Newport in November, and served forty years until her death in 1897.

Catherine's last letters regularly contain greetings for various Sisters in the recipient's local community. Sister Gertrude Emerson had made vows in 1854, was thus one of the young Sisters whom Catherine had approved and sent to Owensboro; she left the community in 1859. Sister Constantia Robinson was a girlhood friend of Sister Xavier Ross and facilitated her conversion and "elopement" to the Nazareth novitiate. (She had no part, however, in the Nashville events.) Just when Xavier was leaving, Constantia was treasurer at Nazareth. In 1856 she became the local superior of St. Frances Academy in Owensboro.

Identifying the often-mentioned Father Joyce is complicated by scattered references to two first names: Patrick Joyce, who opened the church and school for the Irish at Thirteenth and Market; and Thomas Joyce, who had to deal with Nativists searching for munitions in the church prior to Bloody Monday. It is not clear whether one priest or two served St. Patrick's; neither is included in Father John Lyons's book of sketches of priests ordained before 1841, the year of the transfer of the diocese to Louisville.

5-11

Orphan Asylum Jan. 11th/58
My dear good Sister,

You are not mad with your poor Mother, are you?—for
being so late in wishing you & all the dear Sisters there,
a most holy & happy New Year!—Yet do not think for

> a moment you were forgotten, No, no, no,—Well now see how this pen spatters!—Thank God, this leaves all in pretty good health, both Sisters & children, only Sister Martina has been right sick a day or two, from a cold; but is about again. Our poor school here, quite large. The lists number about 150—attending as suits their convenience! tho' mostly they are pretty regular.—I hope this will find you all well; and getting on in good spirits as usual.—You speak of Sister Ann's not writing.—She seldom writes to me, tho' I hear of her writing long letters to other places.—But believe me Sister, I am not jealous in that, I wish all to follow their own inclinations.—I have lived long enough to learn to take all these things just as they come, & whether I write or not the Sisters are always the same to me, dear to my heart. & my best wishes are always for each one of [them]. & rest assured my dear Cleophas is never forgotten but often thought of with pleasure. My kind love to Sister Johana & say that I feel my indebtedness to her & a long letter.—We have a few pay schollars in our school, & among them Sister Cornelia has 5 music schollars & two others from the town.—Now,
>
> God bless you and continue to pray for your Mother
> Catharine

Reference here to "our poor school" records the final efforts in Catherine's lifetime to make education part of her constant outreach to the poor. The separation of the infirmary from the orphanage had left space at Jefferson Street that could become St. Mary's School, one of the "free schools" for those who could pay something or possibly nothing. This letter's mention shows an increase of 20 in attendance over the 130 of the previous letter; it also reveals something of the difficulty of conducting a school of regular procedures and steady instruction.

Sister Cleophas Mills seems to be the well-loved recipient of this letter, as well as of several earlier ones. Sister Martina O'Brien was Cleophas's aunt, also sister to Sister Bernardine O'Brien. She went to St. Vincent Orphanage in 1856, a year before Catherine returned there. Her total service to orphans was thirty years. Sister Ann McIntyre, chiefly a young music teacher, was in Lexington at this time, as was Sister Cleophas. Sister Johana (or Joanna) Lynch came from Ireland in 1850, arrived at the SCN in 1851, and made vows in November 1852. Poor eyesight prevented her teaching, but for fifty years she had charge of the laundry at St. Catherine's in Lexington; prepared children, both black and white, for First Communion; and instructed converts. She would celebrate her Golden Jubilee with Sister Cleophas and live to 1912. Sister Cornelia Paine had been in Nashville in 1850, then returned to Kentucky to several missions and to the orphanage free school in 1856. Catherine's mention of "music schollars" is evidence that the tradition of music students as vital support of a school was a very early practice that made possible the education of many poor students.

5-12

Or. Asylum, Jan. 23rd/'58

And, you want a long letter, do you dear Sis.—& what shall I say in a long letter? just keep repeating that: I love you; wish you every happiness; that I feel the deepest interest in your well-being & well-doing; & finally: that I ardently desire to be eternally united with you in another & a better world in the mansions of our Heavenly Father:—&, all this depends on ourselves.—I am glad you are content & pleased with your new home.—You can ask through your Sister Superior to renew your vows. It was good if you asked that way, it is often done.—I suppose you have a pretty good school, so that your time is filled. All the schools here, continue full.—I suppose you heard of Father Tom Joyce['s] Fair, for the poor children of that part of town. I understand they cleared between 800 & a thousand dollars, which I thought good.—I have not seen Father Tom, for some time. &

> Father O'Calighan did not leave me time to write either a long or short letter. Has Father Coghlin received his flowers, were they safe, & did they please him?—What has become of our Sister Bridget? I never hear from her these days. But perhaps she is too busy teaching French, as you have no other French teacher there. Give her my love, also Sisters Gertrude, Generose & Mary Paul. I went out to see poor Mr. Keely this week. His health is very bad & poor man he seemed so gratified to see us & Mrs. Keely even more so. She is so much confined. I expected them in here today but they have not come. Thank God, we have good health generally here now, but as the scarlet fever is prevalent through town, I am in dread of it. I have had two letters from Sister Euphrasia: She says they are doing well in Newport & are comfortably fixed. We have finished our new house for baking, washing, &c. & it add much to the appearance of the place as well as to the convenience. You must pray for us every day & write me by every opportunity. I [shall] never cease to think of you. I suppose you never hear now from your brother's wife.—Sisters Bibiana & Malania have been to see us once. Sister Rosalia also. They all seem to be in good spirits & have a large school.—You must forget all the last year times & only labor more for the present & leave all the rest to God.—
>
> Always your friend & Mother
> Catharine
>
> Please send the enclosed letter by first opportunity—But my letter is not ready—

Though the identity of this letter's recipient cannot be certain, archival records assume she was the well-loved Baptista Walls, who had moved only the previous August from St. Patrick's, Louisville, to St. Frances in Owensboro. She was there when Catherine died the next March. The tender tone, the loving and maternal counsel in the opening and closing portions, and the news given of other young Sisters, all make this identification plausible and meaningful.

From this letter, it is possible to assert that the pastor of St. Patrick's was indeed a Father Thomas Joyce; he and the chapel had survived the mobs of Bloody Monday and their search for stored munitions. Father Eugene O'Callaghan (1821–1897) was ordained in 1850. Two issues of a Catholic Almanac, from 1856 and 1858, record his position at St. Stephen's in Owensboro, where he would have known the SCN community. He was chaplain at the Loretto motherhouse when he died, and was buried there. In his will, he left money for the erection of the Sisters' Infirmary at Nazareth. Father Michael Coughlin (1819–1877) is listed in the same two almanacs as attending the "station" of Hawesville in Daviess County, also western Kentucky, where he could have met the Sisters in Owensboro. Why flowers were sent to him is not known.

The central section of this letter bears witness to Catherine's abiding interest in the younger members of the community and her will that their peers maintain a similar active interest. Sister Bridget Gormley made vows in March 1852 and was sent to Owensboro that September; she taught music, possibly also French. After a later stretch of mission at St. Vincent's in Union County, she died and is buried there. Sister Gertrude Emerson made vows in 1854 and went to Owensboro, but left the community in 1859. Sr. Mary Paul Brennan, from Sligo, Ireland, was professed in 1855, served in Owensboro until 1859, and later in other Kentucky missions. She survived until 1912. Sister Generose O'Mealy was an elder in Owensboro, having been professed in 1843 and missioned to St. Frances only in 1851. She remained there a long time and was then one of the pioneer group in rural Rhodelia, Kentucky.

Sisters not in either Owensboro or Union County are part of the general exchange of news. Sisters Bibiana O'Sullivan and Melania Callen are the "other two" mentioned in Letter 5-10, along with Sister Rosalia Huff. All were at St. Patrick's on Thirteenth Street. Sister Melania left the community in 1859. Sister Bibiana became mentally ill and was sent to St. Louis for treatment; she died there in 1870 and was buried in a grave marked "Sister Ann Sullivan" (her baptismal and family names). Years later, Mother Ann Sebastian Sullivan arranged for its perpetual care.

William Keely was the architect of the new church and academy, recently completed and put to full use. He and his wife became Catherine's devoted friends and admirers.

It is impossible to know whether this last extant letter was in fact the last Mother Catherine ever wrote. But penned only two months before her death, it serves well as witness to her spirit, her concerns and hopes, and gives voice to her love for both community and individuals and her final counsel to both.

Letters to Mother Catherine Spalding, 1856–1858

Of the mere five extant letters to Catherine in this final period of her life, four were essentially misdirected. They all came from the Deep South and deal with payments due to the academy or services desired for the writer's daughter or charge. As so often, payments were to be received after delays, special timing arrangements, complex banking and third-party transfers, and negotiations. Typical services for students were the purchase or production of clothing, adding uncertainty to the amount and timing of payments. These academy concerns were not Catherine's task since her return to Louisville in August 1856; she probably returned the letters happily enough to the responsible parties at Nazareth.

5-A

Letter to Mother Catherine Spalding from B. F. Edge
OLB 17, p. 56

Lexington
October 30, 1856
Mother Superior,

Eliza Jane Hurley needs a dress and likely some other small articles. Please get them for her and send me the bill and I will send you the money with the balance due on her next session, the first of February next. By complying with the above will very much oblige,

Yours respectfully,
B. F. Edge

5-B

Letter to Mother Catherine Spalding from C. B. Rice
DLB 11b, p. 169 (abridged)

Mount Hope, Miss.
Nov. 22nd, 1856
Dear Madam,

I am in receipt of your favor of the 3rd. inst., in regard to the amount due Nazareth. I have this day included the amount in a draft to Mr. Baker Smith, on my merchants in New Orleans, La., . . . with a request of him to settle with you. In relation to the amount paid by me for Mr. E. R. Brown . . . I have requested him several times to forward a copy of the receipt as requested. He says it shows a want of confidence, but that he will find and send a copy. I am clear in mind that the settlement was made with Sister Constantia in the latter part of June or first of July 1854. . . .

Very respectfully yours,
C. B. Rice

Charles Benjamin Rice had three daughters enrolled at Nazareth in 1854. The last one had left in June 1856.

5-C

Letter to Mother Catherine Spalding from Jas. R. Chalmers
DLB 11, p. 167 (summarized)

Holly Springs Miss.
Dec. 21, 1856.
[Sends $100 for his two sisters; requests receipt from Nazareth's treasurer.]

5-D

Letter to Mother Catherine Spalding from M. L. Burnley
OLB 17, p. 50 (abridged)

Pine Ridge, Copiat Co. Miss.
May 3, 1857.

[Discusses clothes made and sent with daughter; requests dresses be made at Nazareth.] Cousin Taliaferro says they can be made very cheap in the institution. . . . We wish her to learn to be economical. . . . confide her wholly to your care, feeling conscious that she will not be neglected.

5-E

Regulations
OLB 17, p. 48

For the Orphan Asylum of St. Thomas.

Order of the day, Breakfast half after six in the forenoon. Dinner, after 12 o'clock, recreation or work from breakfast to nine o'clock then to study till twelve. Recreation after dinner till 2 o'clock then to study till five in the afternoon, Then recreation or work till supper. Study commence with Catechism.

The evenings of Wednesdays and Saturdays for recreation or work and Sundays and Holy days Catechism twice with beads, Confession once a month, viz., on Saturday preceding the first Sunday of every

> month. The children will be very particular in their respect and submission to their superior, viz., clergy and sisters, as also their teacher. They shall never leave the yard without permission of their superiors even at their recreation.

This document summarizes the regulations of St. Thomas Orphanage for boys at St. Thomas, the location of the first seminary and first SCN convent and school. Someone may have sent it to Catherine on request, or for the information of Sisters appointed to serve in this diocesan institution. It cannot be said, fortunately, that the strict regulations of the boys' institution were the same for the girls' asylum in Louisville, though both must have emphasized study, work, and religious instruction and observances.

Conclusion

The correspondence of Mother Catherine's last term of office and her last months at the orphanage makes clear that she gave herself fully to community life, to education and child care, to relationships of many sorts. Her acknowledged decline in health and energy did not prevent her exertions in the mission of charity to the limit of her strength. Sisters, students, small children, the impoverished and sick, the lonely, unsettled, and undirected of the city—all had a claim on her heart as soon as she knew of their plight. What she could do, she leaned forward to do quickly and well. To no one's surprise, the end of her life began with such an outreach.

On a mission of charity to a destitute family in the late winter of 1858, Catherine was penetrated by cold and thawing snow, and contracted pneumonia. All medical remedies were tried; none could alleviate the sufferer's misery or prevent its fatal effect. She died on March 20, 1858, amid her orphans, as she had hoped. Amid their cries of distress, her remains were taken from the orphanage and transferred to Nazareth for a solemn funeral Mass and rite of burial in the community cemetery. Her grave is marked with a rising sun, symbol of her character and mission in Kentucky and eventually far beyond.

Acknowledgments

Kathy Hertel-Baker, Director of Nazareth Archives, transcriber of Mother Catherine's letters from the originals, consultant and partner in the process all the way, and Anna Powell and Kelly O'Daniel, Assistant Archivists and speed researchers.

Steve Hester, Computer Specialist; and Spalding Hurst, Communications Specialist. At the least request, they contributed technology know-how, fine formatting and design, all the skills I lacked and urgently needed.

Sharon Cecil, SCNA, volunteer research assistant. While I was dealing with fractures and illness, Sharon was in the archives, at the Nelson County library, and on the Web, searching the oldest, most remote newspapers, registries, census records, Nazareth Academy records, indexes, abstracts, books, and lists of all kinds, for persons long deceased and otherwise forgotten. Her incredible finds have given to Mother Catherine a personal and populated history, and to her correspondence an extension and meaning it could never have had otherwise.

Mary Naomi Elder, SCN, for her swift and accurate retyping of the entire collection of letters to Mother Catherine, thus making old and poor copies readable and accessible in the archives and electronically usable for this volume.

Mary Collette Crone, SCN, for a previous collection, putting Catherine's letters in chronological order with many important identifications of persons mentioned or recipients of letters.

Father Clyde Crews and Sister Maria V. Brocato, SCN, historians and friends, who read the manuscript in progress and offered questions, answers, and suggestions that enriched the context of the letters and the accuracy and readability of the editorial text.

All the above gave essential interest and encouragement; they made this volume possible. For the varied effects they had on it, I offer the gratitude they deserve!

Appendix A

Recipients of Letters from Mother Catherine

Bucklin, John Carpenter (1773–1844): First mayor of Louisville, March 3, 1828–1834. He came to Louisville with his family in 1820 and worked in insurance and varied merchandising. He served six one-year terms, and succeeded in persuading the City Council to establish the first public school and to drain the infected ponds that caused flood damage and gave the city the name "Pondtown." He was near the end of his final term when he led in vindicating the good name of the Sister nurses. (Letter 1-5)

Cook, Eliza: Student at Nazareth Academy, July 1834–August 1838. Daughter of Judge and Mrs. William Cook of Washington County, Mississippi; sister of Medora Cook, who followed her to Nazareth as student. (Letters 4-11, 4-14, 4-15)

Crozier, Mrs. Maria: Wife of John Crozier, merchant of Bardstown, and mother of Eliza Crozier Wilkinson, student at Nazareth 1825–1826. In her memoir of Nazareth, Eliza says Mother Catherine was her mother's first Catholic friend. Father Ignatius Reynolds, when bishop of Charleston, wrote to "my respected, venerated, dear friend, Mrs. Crozier." (Letter 3-3)

Dorsey, Louisa, SCN: Entered from Baltimore with Mrs. Ann O'Connor (Sister Scholastica), July 25, 1821. Vows November 21, 1822. Pioneer at Vincennnes, Indiana; there when Harriet Gardiner died. 1834–1838, led transfer of school from White Sulphur to Lexington. Superior of Louisville orphanage, August 1839–1841. Four times elected Assistant, twice each to Mothers Catherine and Frances. A flexible, go-fix-it sort of person. Died June 14, 1868. (Letter 2-1)

Elliott, Claudia, SCN (Ellen): From a large family of Maryland origin. Her parents were Stephen and Mary Dant Elliott. As far as known, her siblings included brothers Raymond, Matthew, James, and probably Stephen Jr; and sisters Anna, Eleanor, Elizabeth, Nancy, and Julietta. Ellen entered the SCN on January 21, 1826; vows August 15, 1827. Missions at St. Catherine, Lexington, and St. Mary's in Nashville, Tennessee; chiefly at Nazareth in charge of farm, servants, general maintenance, and well-being of persons and environment. A warm-hearted "gatherer" in the community, much loved by students and servants as well; devoted friend and collaborator of Catherine. Sixty-seven years in community; considered both a foundation stone and a bridge from pioneers to later Sisters. Died March 9, 1893. (Letters 2-6, 2-7, 2-8, 2-9, 2-10, 3-2, 3-5, 3-6, 3-7, 3-10, 3-15, 4-1, 4-4, 4-20, 5-2, 5-3, 5-4, 5-5)

Flaget, Benedict Joseph, SS (1763–1850): Native of France, priest of the Society of St. Sulpice, and teacher in seminaries in Nantes and Angers. A refugee from the French Revolution, he ministered in Vincennes, Indiana, and taught at Georgetown College in Havana, Cuba, and at the Sulpician seminary in Baltimore until appointed first bishop of Bardstown, Kentucky. He moved the see to Louisville in 1841. (Letters 1-3, 2-3, 2-4)

Harbison, Mrs.: No full name or facts have been found for this lady. The letter indicates she was left alone with children who might be placed permanently at St. Vincent Orphanage. (Letter 5-6)

"Kate": Two letters (4-17, 4-19) are directed to a former student of this name. They indicate that their recipient had a short stay at the school, came from a home in the vicinity, and was a godchild of Mother Catherine. The most probable candidate: Mary Catherine Smith, Catholic, adopted daughter of Mr. and Mrs. F. Robert Smith of Louisville. She entered school on March 18, 1853, and left June 29, 1854. In 4–17, Mother Catherine laments that the girl could not return for another year. She could have been instructed and received into the Catholic Church during her tenure at the academy.

Keely, William: Nationally known architect, designer of the cathedral in Louisville and of St. Vincent Church at Nazareth. He and his wife became good friends of Catherine. (Letters 4-2, 4-3)

Kelly, Mother Josephine, SL: Mother General of the Sisters of Loretto, 1832–1838, having come from Baltimore with eight other women escorted by Father Charles Nerinckx to join that order. Her work was in education; little is known of her later years. (Letter 5-9)

McGinnis, Genevieve, SCN: Came from Ireland with younger brother Peter. Vows January 6, 1847. Cousin of Bishop Andrew Byrne of Little Rock, Arkansas; letter from him a month after her vows commends her for gratitude to all who helped her become SCN. Card notes she was "loved by Mothers Catherine and Frances for her loyalty and fine spirit." Main missions were Lexington and St. Vincent's, Union. Died December 6, 1899 (Letters 4-6, 4-9, 4-10, 4-16, 4-21, 4-24)

Mills, Cleophas, SCN: Vows October 15, 1852; young sister devoted to Mother Catherine. Missions to Thirteenth St. Free School in Louisville, then Lexington. Superior in Covington, Lexington, Saints Mary and Elizabeth Hospital (twice), and Mount Vernon, Ohio. Treasurer at Nazareth twice; elected Mother, 1885–1891, 1897–1903. On Board of Trustees, 1886 to her death, May 28, 1905. (Letters 5-1, 5-11)

Norris, Vincentia, SCN: Convert, baptized by Father Haseltine, 1837. Entered in 1838; vows August 24, 1840. At Nashville 1842, co-addressee of letter to Claudia Elliott. Described as "gifted with no ordinary talent." To St. Vincent, Union, 1852; died and buried there in June 1853. (Letter 2-10)

Quinn, John: Born in Ireland, educated at St. Thomas Seminary, ordained in 1838. Served as pastor of St. Louis Church, then Cathedral of the Assumption in Louisville. Died of cholera just before cathedral consecration; is buried in its crypt. Was collaborator of Mother Catherine in placing orphans with her. (Letter 4-8)

Rosati, Joseph, CM: One of the Vincentian priests recruited by bishop-elect Louis DuBourg for mission in Missouri. En route there, he resided at St. Thomas from November 1816 to September 1818, learning English and helping in mission to local congregations and to the SCN. He then taught at St. Mary's Seminary at the Barrens (later Perryville), about eighty miles from St. Louis; became superior of the Vincentians in the Americas; and, in 1827, was named bishop of St. Louis. He remained a close friend of both Bishops Flaget and David, and was a friend and consultant to Mother Catherine. (Letter 1-1)

Skinner, Juliann Pierce: Niece of Mother Catherine, daughter of her sister Louisa Spalding Pierce (Leonard). Married Harley Skinner; apparently separated or widowed. Seems to have had several children but no success in settling anywhere and finding work to support them. (Letter 3-8)

Smith, Mary Catherine: Student at Nazareth, March 1853–June 1854. Adopted by Mr. and Mrs. F. Robert Smith of Louisville. Internal evidence in two letters suggests strongly that she is the "Kate" to whom the letters are addressed. (Letters 4-17, 4-19)

Spalding, Benedict Joseph (1812–1868): Younger brother of Martin John Spalding and, like him, educated at St. Mary's College, Marion County, St. Joseph Seminary, Bardstown, and College of Propaganda in Rome. Ordained in Rome, 1837. In diocese of Bardstown, he taught at preparatory seminary at St. Thomas and served as administrator and vice-president of St. Joseph College and pastor of St. Joseph Church. In Louisville he was pastor of the cathedral, vicar general of the diocese, supervisor of the construction of the new cathedral, and administrator after Martin John's transfer to Baltimore as archbishop. He died suddenly in 1868. (Letters 3-4, 3-11, 3-12, 4-12)

Spalding, Martin John, Bishop of Louisville, Archbishop of Baltimore (1810–1872): His education was that of his brother. He also was ordained in Rome, 1834. Pastor at St. Joseph Cathedral and teacher at the college, then pastor of cathedral in Louisville and Vicar General of diocese. At age thirty-eight, made coadjutor to Bishop Flaget; began administration of diocese in 1849. As Bishop of Louisville, very active in building new cathedral, in visitation of parishes and supervision of religious communities, introducing Xaverian Brothers and St. Vincent de Paul Society, leading local church through Bloody Monday and Civil War. Also a writer and speaker. Made Archbishop of Baltimore in 1864. The Spalding brothers were distant cousins of Mother Catherine. (Letters 3-1, 4-5, 4-18)

Walls, Baptista, SCN: Entered 1852; vows August 15, 1853. Young Sister dear to Mother Catherine. Missioned at Louisville Free School on Thirteenth Street (St. Patrick's), 1854–1857, then to new St. Frances Academy, Owensboro. Letters to her from Mother Frances as well as Catherine. Later missions in Bardstown, Louisville Cathedral Free School, Paducah, Newport, and Uniontown. Died September 19, 1898. (Letters 4-25, 5-8, 5-10, 5-12)

Webb, Ben J. (1814–1897): Journalist, historian, author, businessman, legislator. Born in Bardstown, educated at St. Joseph College. Married Sarah McGill; father of ten children. Worked for *Louisville Journal*; in 1836 became editor of the *Catholic Advocate*; wrote defenses of Catholic doctrine and practice. In 1847, partner in Peters and Webb, a firm manufacturing pianos. Turned from Whig to Democratic party in 1850s when Whigs became Nativist, Know-Nothings, anti-Catholic. In 1867, elected state senator. Remembered chiefly as author of history, *The Centenary of Catholicity in Kentucky*, 1884. (Letter 4-13)

Appendix B

Cosigners of Letter to Bishop Flaget, July 6, 1841

An account is given here of the Sisters who supported Mother Catherine in her letter of dissent to Bishop Benedict Joseph Flaget of July 6, 1841 (Letter 2-4). All the information is drawn from the Card File in the Nazareth archives (see Sources and Bibliography), which often leaves gaps in mission lists, yet also gives other references for many Sisters. Signers of the letter used only their first, religious names; family names were added in later typed copies of the letter.

The handwritten letter (a copy of the original?) preserved in the Nazareth archives carries handwritten signatures; it and an early typed copy in a collection of Catherine's letters offer two lists of signers: those who were present to sign at Nazareth (twenty-eight) and those who wrote from branch houses affirming their agreement with the petition (twenty-three). A third list was later compiled and added to a copy of the letter; it is not known who compiled that third list; most of the names there are already on the first two lists. Various other discrepancies indicate that Sister Nancy Lynch is the only one on that list who could have signed.

Thus, a total of fifty-one or fifty-two Sisters apparently signed after Mother Catherine—a very substantial, probably unanimous, agreement. The bishop was left with little choice except to grant their wish or dissolve the community outright—a not very likely outcome, given his respect and affection for both Catherine and the community he had helped to establish and certainly still needed in his diocese. In fact, many cosigners outlived both Bishop Flaget and Mother Catherine and served on missions that were opened after her death.

Alvey, Agatha: Vows October 29, 1826. She spent her entire religious life at Nazareth. Letters cite her for making or repairing mattresses "for nearly every bed in the house" and for care of Bishop Chabrat in his illness.

Bamber, Hilaria: Vows August 24, 1831. She nursed cholera in both Louisville and Bardstown, and served as teacher and nurse on missions in Bardstown, Louisville, Nazareth, and Union County.

Bamber, Margaret: Vows August 24, 1831. Sister of Hilaria, also of Patricia Bamber, who died of cholera in Bardstown in 1833. Margaret was superior of the cholera nurses in Louisville, later superior of St. Vincent's in Union County and St. John's Hospital in Nashville, from which she returned to Nazareth at the 1851 separation.

Buckman, Seraphine: Vows May 3, 1825. Sister of Generose Buckman, who died of cholera in Bardstown. Missioned at St. Catherine, Lexington, later at Louisville orphanage.

Buckman, Victoria: Vows March 25, 1835. Was at Vincennes at illness and death of Harriet Gardiner, 1826. At Nazareth thereafter, as infirmarian, disciplinarian, assistant to Mothers Frances and Columba, and mistress of novices.

Carney, Mary Vincent: Vows August 24, 1840. Missions at Nazareth, Day School of St. Vincent Orphanage, and St. Mary's in Nashville. She remained in Nashville at the separation and did remarkable work in the West in her later life.

Carney, Serena: Vows October 18, 1830. Irish born, one of four founders of Presentation Academy in Louisville, later superior there and at St. Mary's Academy, Nashville; treasurer at Nazareth and member of the Nazareth Literary and Benevolent Institution (NLBI) Board.

Carrico, Teresa: Vows February 2, 1816. First member of SCN, in first group making vows. Spent her life at Nazareth in all forms of domestic and maintenance service; considered a model of commitment and spirituality. Died shortly after Catherine.

Carroll, Columba: Vows February 2, 1827. Dublin-born, immigrant with parents to Louisville, then orphaned by illness. First graduate of Nazareth Academy, teacher and directress of the academy after 1832; treasurer after death of Sister Johanna from cholera. Later assistant to Mothers Frances and Catherine, and mistress of novices. Mother, 1862–1868 and 1874 to her death in office, 1878.

Carroll, Sophia: Vows August 23, 1836. Sister of Sister Columba Carroll. Missioned at Lexington and Nazareth Academy. Died of tuberculosis, November 28, 1841.

Chapman, Basilla: Vows January 11, 1826. Was at St. Vincent's, Union County, during crisis of 1833, received message from Bishop David. Also there in 1838 and 1842; died and is buried there.

Coomes, Christine: Vows September 29, 1826. Missions in Lexington, Louisville, Nashville, and Bardstown. One of the Sisters who returned to Nazareth at the time of the Nashville separation.

Dorsey, Louisa: See Appendix A.

Drury, Alice: Vows August 24, 1840. Her missions are not listed until 1846, so she must have been at Nazareth. She served in schools and both girls' and boys' orphanages, once appointed superior. When she signed the letter to Flaget, she was less than a year in vows. Mother Catherine greets her in letters to Nashville in 1844. She returned to Nazareth from Nashville and later was superior at both Bethlehem Academy and St. Vincent Orphanage.

Drury, Isabella: Vows October 15, 1825. First at Nazareth, then at Lexington, Nashville, Union County, Owensboro, and Newport, Kentucky, at short and repeated intervals. Four times a local superior, and treasurer at Nazareth.

Drury, Martha: Vows December 18, 1823. Sister of Isabella. Famous for competence and readiness for many sorts of labors: teaching, nursing, household management, leadership. Infirmarian at Nazareth, first principal of St. Michael's, Fairfield, nurse of cholera in Louisville and Bardstown, teacher in Union county, Presentation, Paducah (first principal and superior), nurse there during Civil War, nurse at St. Joseph Infirmary, Louisville till her death in 1890.

Duffy, Veronica: Vows May 3, 1825. In Union County, 1832, very likely at Nazareth the rest of her life.

Elder, Emily: Vows September 14, 1833. Parents migrated from Maryland. She was Dominican at St. Catherine's; transferred to SCN, apparently at urging of her brother, the Reverend George Elder. Received name and habit on day of entrance. Replaced Sister Johanna Lewis, cholera victim, as music teacher. Spent entire religious life at Nazareth. On Board of Trustees from 1856 until her death in 1886.

Elliott, Claudia: See Appendix A.

Emerson, Harriet: Vows December 25, 1836. From New Orleans, where English father did business. Mother died: son sent to St. Joseph's to school, three daughters to Nazareth. Was music teacher at Nazareth all her life.

Fenwick, Scholastica: Vows June 1, 1841. Music teacher at Nazareth; in Nashville four years, then back to Nazareth. Local superior in St. Vincent's, Union; Holly Springs, Mississippi; Bethlehem, Bardstown. Civil War nurse.

Gardiner, Clare: Vows April 11, 1820. One of four Sisters opening Presentation Academy, Louisville, and nursing cholera. First superior of day school for poor children, Louisville, 1836, also of

La Salette Academy and Cathedral School for poor in Covington, Kentucky, 1856.

Gardiner, Frances: Vows April 11, 1820. Nicknamed "Little Moses" for youth and small stature, but major figure in missions and leadership. Pioneer in opening of St. Vincent Academy, Union County, Kentucky, 1820. Elected treasurer of SCN, then Mother, alternating terms first with Catherine Spalding, then with Columba Carroll. In intervals was missioned in Lexington, Nashville (at time of separation), St. Vincent's, Union County, and Frankfort. Led community during Civil War and opened major schools in Owensboro; Covington; Newport; Paducah; and Yazoo City, Mississippi.

Hagan, Susan: Vows May 1, 1818. One of those sent to new Nazareth to prepare for others coming later. Sent on short-lived mission to Long Lick, Breckinridge County, then to St. Vincent's, Union County, 1821–1832; listed as still there in 1843; died and was buried there.

Harkins, Eugenia: Vows March 25, 1825. Missioned at St. Vincent, Union County, during 1830s; recalled to Nazareth by Bishop David; spent some months at Presentation, Louisville; returned to St. Vincent in 1839; was still there in 1842.

Higdon, Josephine: Vows November 21, 1822. Believed to be sister of Mother Agnes Higdon. Missioned in Vincennes; several intervals in Louisville at Presentation or in charge of the free school in the cathedral basement. Superior in Lexington, 1838–1841, but is listed among signers at Nazareth.

Huff, Rosalia: Vows September 29, 1826. From Virginia, an orphan at St. Thomas, then one of those preparing the move to Nazareth. Served in Vincennes, Lexington, Bardstown, and in Louisville at Presentation, the Free School, St. Patrick's, and St. Vincent Orphanage.

Leake, Mary: Vows August 6, 1822. From a family near Nazareth;

Bishop David instructed her and permitted her First Communion at the age of eight. Missioned at Nazareth for twenty years; taught music, drawing, painting. Later at St. Vincent, Union County, and Bethlehem, Bardstown. Poor health for years.

Luckett, Anastasia: Vows February 5, 1824. Procuratrix at Nazareth twice. At St. Vincent Orphanage, Louisville; St. Vincent, Union County; Lexington, Owensboro, and St. Thomas Orphanage.

Lynch, Nancy: Vows March 25, 1816. One of three opening Bethlehem in Bardstown, 1819. At St. Vincent, Union County, in 1832; rest of her life at Nazareth. Died in 1848.

McDermott, Mary Agnes: Vows August 24, 1839. Missioned at St. Vincent Orphanage and Infirmary and St. Joseph Infirmary, Louisville; also Lexington, Nazareth, Bethlehem, and Rhodelia, Kentucky. One term as procuratrix at Nazareth.

McGill, Appolonia: Vows July 19, 1824. One of founders of Presentation Academy and nurse of cholera; briefly superior at St. Vincent, Union County, 1835–1836; then at St. Vincent Infirmary/St. Joseph Infirmary, 1836–1859. Was first superior at new St. Joseph Infirmary site; best-known and respected nurse in Louisville. Nursed in Army hospital there in Civil War; died in service, 1862.

McIntyre, Matilda: Vows January 1, 1839. Sent to Louisville orphanage in 1839; served later at Presentation, Bardstown, and Nazareth, and St. Thomas boys' orphanage.

Morheiser, Rufina: Vows January 21, 1830. Was first German SCN, from Baltimore. Brought German orphans from Portland area to Presentation; was part of group opening St. Vincent Orphanage on Jefferson Street in 1836. Served in full range of missions, longest in St. Catherine Academy, Lexington, 1839–1851.

Mudd, Euphrasia: Vows February 5, 1824. Wide range of missions; was in first group to go to Nashville and to Owensboro. Superior in Owensboro, Covington, and Newport, Kentucky.

Norris, Vincentia: See Appendix A.

O'Brien, Bernardine: Vows January 1, 1837. Missioned mostly in orphanages, including St. John's in Nashville. Was one of those who returned to Nazareth at time of separation in 1850.

O'Brien, Cecily: Vows November 22, 1820. First pupil of school at St. Thomas; in first group opening St. Vincent, Union County, December 1820. Served at Bethlehem, Presentation, and the orphanage in Louisville, twice as elected procuratrix at Nazareth, and as superior at both the Thirteenth Street Free School (St. Patrick's) in Louisville and St. Thomas Orphanage at St. Thomas. In 1870, she was the fourth SCN Golden Jubilarian.

O'Nan, Petronilla: Vows May 16, 1833. Noted as at Nazareth in 1842–1843; may have been there her entire mission life. Sister of Dafrosa O'Nan (d. 1837).

Paine, Clementia: Vows March 25, 1828. Missions in Lexington, St. Vincent Orphanage and Infirmary in Louisville, Nazareth (twice procuratrix), superior at St. Thomas Orphanage, and St. Joseph College, Bardstown.

Pollock, Philippa: Vows February 2, 1831. At St. Vincent, Union County, during crisis of 1830s; twice procuratrix at Nazareth, known for special talent as cook, making food palatable despite poverty of time. At Fifth Street School and Orphanage in Louisville, mistress of novices for ten years, and Army nurse in Louisville and Lexington in Civil War.

Price, Monica: Vows October 19, 1826. At entry, a widow with children. Missions at St. Joseph's, Bardstown; the Day School and Orphanage in Louisville; and Nazareth.

Robinson, Constantia: Vows March 25, 1834. Talented convert from Cincinnati; great friend of Sister Xavier (Ann) Ross, instrumental in her conversion and vocation; entered and made vows with her, but did not join her in separation of Nashville community. Missions in St. Vincent, Union County; Louisville; twice treasurer at Nazareth, superior in Owensboro, and in opening group of St. Columba, Bowling Green.

Ross, Xavier: Vows March 25, 1834. Daughter of Methodist minister of Cincinnati, convert and SCN against his fierce opposition. Superior in both Presentation and orphanage. Superior of St. Mary's, Nashville; leader of group withdrawing in 1851 to form separate community there. Led group to Leavenworth, Kansas, to form Sisters of Charity of Leavenworth.

Spalding, Ann: Vows January 21, 1818. Sister of Catharine Spalding. Most of mission life at St. Catherine's, Lexington, as teacher and as superior. Died of poisoning by a slave girl, May 15, 1848.

Spink, Angela: Vows August 24, 1820. Superior of first group to St. Vincent Academy, December 1820; known for labor that enabled survival. Nazareth, 1830: assistant to Mother Catherine and member of NLBI Board; elected Mother 1831, resigned 1832. White River, Indiana, 1832–1833; returned to St. Vincent, Union County. Died and is buried there.

Stuart, Mildred: Vows November 21, 1817. One of three SCN Sisters sent to prepare move to Nazareth; in first group with Mother Catherine to Scott County, 1823. Procuratrix at Nazareth, infirmarian at St. Joseph's, Bardstown, then at Nazareth, 1831 till death in 1841, age fifty-five.

Suttle, Elizabeth: Vows December 31, 1816. Pioneer of school at Long Lick, Breckenridge County. At St. Vincent, Union County, during crisis of 1830s; received letters about it from Bishop David. Superior of Presentation, treasurer at Nazareth, Superior at St.

Vincent, Union County, 1845–1851 and 1854–1863. First Golden Jubilarian.

Taft, Sebastia: Vows October 18, 1830. From Vermont; moved to Cincinnati; convert at eighteen despite opposition of wealthy family. Was on one-year harsh mission at White River, Indiana; also at Vincennes mission, 1835–1838, as superior who had to close it. Several times at Nazareth as teacher and treasurer.

Vallee, Pelagia: Vows March 25, 1825. Canadian, entered from Vincennes. In Lexington and Nazareth Academy; Mother Catherine's assistant, Superior of Louisville Orphanage, and member of NLBI Board. Died of tuberculosis at Nazareth in 1846, age forty-two. Devoted to Catherine, who visited her before her death.

Villaneuve, Dorothy: Vows March 25, 1825. At St. Vincent, Union County, in 1890s; brief series of missions at Nazareth, Bardstown, St. John Hospital in Nashville, St. Thomas Orphanage, and school in Bardstown. In 1853 joined Sister Xavier in Nashville community but did not go with them to Kansas. Her later life is unknown.

Sources and Bibliography

Primary

Primary sources are located mainly in the Nazareth Archives at the motherhouse in Nazareth, Kentucky. Some still exist in handwritten form, but all are either in later typescript or in the original newsprint. Other sources, such as lists, newspaper abstracts, and census records, were found mainly in the public libraries of Nelson County or Louisville, Kentucky, or on internet websites.

The following abbreviations are used in the text:

CLMCC	Collected Letters of Mother Columba Carroll
CLMCS	Collected Letters of Mother Catherine Spalding
CLMFG	Collected Letters of Mother Frances Gardiner
DLB	Duplicate Letter Book
FDL	Flaget David Letters
FL	Flaget Letters
OLB	Original (Old) Letter Book

Annals of LaSalette Academy and St. Mary's Cathedral School, Covington, KY.

Annals of St. Thomas and St. Vincent Orphanages, 1833–1934. Folder with list of orphans for 1851–1853.

Biographical sketches of SCN, 4 vols.

Card file of early members' data.

Clippings, Vols. A, B, E, 2, 4, 5.

Council Minutes. SCN History Binder, Vol. 2. (These are summaries of decisions of the founding era. Full minutes are maintained in the vault at the SCN Center.)

Duplicate Letter Books 1, 2, 3, 4, 7, 8, 11, 14, 15, 19, 21, 22, 24.

Early Annals by Marie Menard, SCN.

FamilySearch.org. Records of St. Paul's Episcopal Church, Jefferson County, KY.

Federal Census for Louisville, KY, 1860. http://persiHeritage Quest online.com.

Federal Census for Nelson County, KY, 1840 and 1850. Distributed by Nelson County Genealogical Society, Bardstown, KY.

Flaget David Letters. 1 vol. Trans. S. Edward Barnes, SCN.

Flaget Letters. 3 vols. Trans. S. Edward Barnes, SCN, from originals photocopied in the archives of the St. Louis Archdiocese, St. Louis Priory, and the University of Notre Dame, Indiana.

Letters of Francis P. Clark to Sister Mary Ramona Mattingly, historian and archivist, 1960s and 1970s. Nazareth Archives. (Clark has two titles in the letters: "Collector of Material Pertaining to Catholicity in Kentucky" and "Director of Microfilming, University of Notre Dame." At Notre Dame, in the St. Louis archdiocesan archives in Chicago and Louisville, he microfilmed thousands of bound volumes or loose sheets of nineteenth-century documents. Among his finds were some of Catherine Spalding's correspondence, Bishop John Baptist David's, and Bishop Benedict Joseph Flaget's. These he photocopied and sent to Nazareth for translation by Sister Edward Barnes and deposit in the Archives. Thus Francis Clark saved vital parts of SCN history.)

List of Nelson County, KY, Marriages 1785–1859. Compiled and published by Ellen Tatum Smith, 2011.

Louisville Directory, 1832. Louisville: Richard W. Otis, pub., James Virden, Printer, 1832.

Metropolitan Catholic Almanac. Baltimore: Fielding Lucas, Jr. Vols. 1833–1834, 1840–1856. (This is the forerunner of the modern Catholic Directory and offers information on numerous persons of the early years of Kentucky Catholicism.)

Nazareth Academy Ledger, 1837–1854. (Old record of financial accounts of students. Kept in provincial finance office.)

Nelson County, KY, Marriage Index, 1860–1950. Compiled by Ellen Smith.

Nelson County, KY, Newspaper abstracts, September 1807–September 1890. Compiled by Carolyn Wimp. Vine Grove, KY: Ancestral Trails Historical Society.

Original record book of Nazareth Academy. Handwritten ledger. (Same records are in card file. Names and data for students of early era, also of parents, as far as known and preserved. A binder also was put together later, entitled "Nazareth Academy Enrollment: 1814–1891." It has some discrepancies from the card file, including some names not in the card file.)

SCN Permanent Records File.

SCN Photo Index of Clergy and Laity.

Secondary

Agee, Gary B. *A Cry for Justice.* Fayetteville: University of Arkansas Press, 2011.

Bevins, Ann Bolton, and James R. O'Rourke. "'That Troublesome Parish': St. Francis/St. Pius Church of White Sulphur, Kentucky." Georgetown, KY: St. Francis and St. John Parishes, 1985.

"Brief Sketch of St. Mary Academy, Nashville, Tenn. And other Institutions opened there 1842–1851 by SCNs—1851–1858 by the group which separated from Nazareth and later became SCLs of Kansas." Author unnamed. Ts. Sketch dated 12/15/1896 kept in Nashville Diocesan Archives. Copy given to Nazareth Archives.

Butler, Rev. Alban. *Lives of the Saints.* New York: Benziger Brothers, 1955.

Catholic Encyclopedia. New York: Robert Appleton Co., 1907. Vol. 2.

Creamer, Mary Michael, SCN. "Mother Catherine Spalding—St. Catherine Street, Louisville, Kentucky." *Filson Club History Quarterly* 63 (1989): 191–223.

Crews, Clyde F. *An American Holy Land: A History of the Archdiocese of Louisville.* Wilmington, DE: Michael Glazier, 1987.

"Deaths prior to 1911: Nelson County, KY." Ellen Tatum Smith, comp. Bardstown, KY: Nelson County Genealogical Roundtable, Publisher and distributor, 2007.

Dictionary of American Biography. Ed. Dumas Malone. New York: Charles Scribner's Sons, 1943.

Donnelly, Sister Mary Louise. *Maryland Elder Family and Kin.* Burke, VA: Nativity Parish, 1975.

Doyle, Mary Ellen, SCN. *Pioneer Spirit: Catherine Spalding, Sister of Charity of Nazareth.* Lexington: University Press of Kentucky, 2006.

Encyclopedia of Louisville. John E. Kleeber, Editor in Chief. Lexington: University Press of Kentucky, 2001.

Fox, Columba, SCN. *The Life of the Right Reverend John Baptist Mary David.* New York: U.S. Catholic Historical Society, 1925.

Gollar, C. Walker. "Early Protestant–Catholic Relations in Southern Indiana and the 1842 Case of Roman Weinzaepfel." *Indiana Magazine of History* 95 (3) 1999: 232–254.

Greater Louisville Illustrated. Louisville: National Publishing Co., 1908.

Harrison, Lowell H., and James C. Klotter. *A New History of Kentucky.* Lexington: University Press of Kentucky, 1997.

Krusling, Rev. Lawrence R., and Sister Peter Marie Murphy. *Mother Catherine Spalding: A Personality Study Based on Analyses of Her Handwriting.* Louisville, KY: SCN Health Corp., 1987. (Study by two certified graphoanalysts presented to the SCN for the 175th anniversary of the congregation.)

Lemarié, Charles, CSC. *A Biography of Msgr. Benedict Joseph Flaget.* 3 vols. Trans. Mary Wedding, SCN. Bardstown, KY: Sponsored by the Flaget-Lemarié Group and St. Joseph Proto-Cathedral Archives, 1992. Ts.

Lyons, John A. *Bishops and Priests of the Diocese of Bardstown.* Louisville: Privately printed by diocese, 1976. (Biographical sketches of all diocesan priests ordained up to 1841.)

McCutchan, Kenneth P. "The Religious Persecution of Father Weinzaepfel." http://web.usi.edu/boneyard/mccut65.htm.

McNeil, Betty A., DC. "The Role of Women in the Vincentian Culturescope." *Vincentian Heritage Journal* 26, no. 1: 143–177.

———. "The Sulpicians and the Sisters of Charity: Concentric Circles of Mission." *Vincentian Heritage Journal* 20, no. 1: 13–38.

Metropolitan Catholic Almanac and Laity's Directory. Baltimore: Felding Lucas, Jr. , 1850.

Metz, Judith, SC. "Who Was Margaret Cecilia George?" http:srcharitycinti.org/about/who_is_margaret.htm.

Rybolt, John E., CM. "Joseph Rosati, C.M.: Pioneer American Bishop." http://works.bepress.com/John-rybolt/42.

Schauinger, J. Herman. *Cathedrals in the Wilderness.* Milwaukee: Bruce Publishing Co., 1952.

———. *Stephen T. Badin: Priest in the Wilderness.* Milwaukee: Bruce Publishing Co., 1956.

Sisters of Charity of Nazareth photo index file.

Smith, Ellen Tatum. A List of Nelson Co., KY, Marriages 1785–1859. Pub. Ellen Tatum Smith, 2011.

Smith, Ellen, comp. Nelson County Marriage Index, 1860–1950.

Smith, Sarah B. *Historic Nelson County: Its Towns and Its People.* Bardstown, KY: GBA/Delmar, 1983.

Spillane, James Maria, SCN. *Kentucky Spring.* St. Meinrad, IN: Abbey Press, 1968.

"This Is Josh Silsbee." http:rjbuffalo.com/silsbee. Account of Joshua Silsbee (author unknown).

Webb, Benedict. *The Centenary of Catholicity in Kentucky.* Louisville: Chas. Rogers, 1884.

Wimp, Carolyn, comp. Nelson County Newspaper Abstracts, September 1807–September 1890. Vine Grove, KY: Ancestral Trails Society.

Index

www.ingramcontent.com/pod-product-compliance
Lightning Source LLC
LaVergne TN
LVHW050147080826
844660LV00002B/109

* 9 7 8 0 8 1 3 1 6 8 8 4 5 *